VIOLENCE IN CHINA

SUNY Series in Chinese Local Studies

Harry J. Lamley, EDITOR

VIOLENCE IN CHINA

Essays in Culture and Counterculture

edited by

Jonathan N. Lipman
and
Stevan Harrell

State University of New York Press

Published by
State University of New York Press, Albany

Printed in the United States of America

For information, address State University of New York
Press, State University Plaza, Albany, NY 12246

Library of Congress Cataloging-in-Publication Data

Violence in China : essays in culture and counterculture / edited by
    Jonathan N. Lipman and Stevan Harrell.
        p.   cm. — (SUNY series in Chinese local studies)
    Bibliography: p.
    Includes index.
    ISBN 0-7914-0113-8. — ISBN 0-7914-0115-4 (pbk.)
        1. Violence—China—History. 2. Social conflict—China—History.
    3. Subculture—History. I. Lipman, Jonathan Neaman. II. Harrell,
    Stevan. III. Series.
    HN740.Z9V58   1990
    303.6'2—dc19   88-32411
                                                                       CIP

10 9 8 7 6 5 4 3 2 1

*This book is dedicated,
with respect and gratitude,
to all of our teachers.*

CONTENTS

PREFACE

This volume began when Jonathan Lipman organized a panel on the topic of "Violence in Chinese Culture," held at the Annual Meeting of the Association for Asian Studies in Philadelphia in 1985. Christina Gilmartin, Harry Lamley, Jonathan Lipman, and Elizabeth J. Perry read papers; Fu-mei Chang Chen and Stevan Harrell acted as discussants. Michele Martin, then with SUNY Press, approached us after the session, asking if we were interested in expanding the group of papers into a volume. We were.

Elizabeth Perry's paper was already committed to *China Quarterly*, where it has since appeared, but we retained the other papers and in addition solicited contributions from Frederick P. Brandauer, Richard Madsen, Richard Shek, and Anne F. Thurston. Harrell's introduction is derived from comments he made at the original session.

We are indebted to Elizabeth Perry and Fu-mei Chang Chen, original participants, for helping us frame the issues treated in this volume; to Harry Lamley, who nobly separated his function as Editor of the SUNY series in Chinese Local Studies from his self-interest as author of one of the papers presented here; to Michele Martin, Rosalie Robertson, and Christine Lynch, our able editors at SUNY Press; and to three anonymous referees whose comments on the first draft of the volume helped us considerably to sharpen our arguments.

The original intent of the panel—to view violence in China as it occurs across a number of different social divisions, such as gender, class, religious affiliation, and ethnicity—has been expanded in the volume to include literary and philosophical treatments of violence, the large theme of revenge, and the widespread violence of the Cultural Revolution. Violence in China has also persisted. It struck in particularly stark form in the cruel massacre of students and other citizens in Beijing and Chengdu in June, 1989. By then our publication was already too far along for our authors to take this most recent violence into account in their analyses, and in any case none of us focuses specifically on the downward vertical violence of state repression. But it is nonetheless our hope that this modest volume might contribute in some small way to the understanding of such events, and to further study of the problem. Such comprehension might discourage their future recurrence.

S.H. and J.N.L.
January 1990

Chapter 1

Introduction

Stevan Harrell

Why does a culture that condemns violence, that plays down the glory of military exploits, awards its highest prestige to literary, rather than martial, figures, and seeks harmony over all other values, in fact display such frequency and variety of violent behavior, that is, of the use of physical force against persons? (Whether Chinese culture is more violent than other cultures is difficult to judge, but it is visibly not less violent than many.) And given that violence exists in spite of the norms deploring it, in what particular kinds of situations does violent behavior occur, and how can we explain its occurrence in these particular situations? Each essay in this volume treats violence across a different division in Chinese society—between sectarians and the orthodox order, among characters in literature, among ethnic-religious groups, between lineages, among urban Red-Guard factions, among similar factions in rural political movements, and among individuals in the home. In every case, the question asked is, why does violence occur in this situation; what are the motivations, perceived rewards, and consequences of violent behavior? And despite the wide variety of types and contexts of violence treated in the various chapters, despite the time range from the Northern and Southern dynasties to the Cultural Revolution and beyond, I believe there is a common framework in which all these kinds of violence can be understood. The task of this introduction is to set out that framework.

Violence requires two conditions: there must be a conflict, and there must be a motivation to settle that conflict by force. In order to understand when and where violence occurs, then, we must understand both where conflicts occur and why people are motivated to solve these conflicts by force. It is not enough, particularly in a culture that normatively abhors violence, to describe the social cleavages that give rise to conflict and rivalry; there are other ways of approaching conflict than by resort to force, and indeed most conflicts in Chinese society involve the repression, rather than the use, of force. It is only in the combination of a conflictual situation and a motivation to force that we can seek the roots of violent behavior.

This means, in turn, that we have to analyze the occurrence of violence on two levels: The level of social structure, where we find the sources of conflict, and the level of the forces that motivate individuals in situations of conflict to participate in violent solutions. Neither level is sufficient by itself.

Social structure and the roots of conflict

Conflict is, of course, endemic in the nature of social relations, and, in fact, the analysis of social structure is in many ways simply the analysis of social conflict: the units that comprise society are the units that come into conflict with one another or, to look at it from the other direction, those units that are solidary in the face of conflict with the outside. These units can range in size from a part of a family to the nation-state, and each individual belongs to at least a few of them. The only kind of personal violence that lies outside the web of social relations is that of the sociopath, who is not treated in this book, probably because he (and it almost always is a he) is unanalyzable in social structural terms, something that makes him especially fearsome. All other participants in violent behavior do so partly because they are in conflict-ridden social structural situations.

Conceptually, it is useful to classify the social divisions that underlie violent conflict into two kinds. Vertical violence involves dominance by one group over another, and the use of violence either from above, to suppress or prevent attempts by the subordinates to change the situation, or from below, to try to change a perceived unjust situation by force. Horizontal violence, on the other hand, involves disputes between equals over economic resources or political power. Both these types of divisions exist in a wide variety of situations in traditional and modern Chinese society. Here is a partial list.

Family conflicts

As the locus of the most constant and most intimate social relations in China, the family is potentially the locus of some of the most intensive conflicts. Some of these, such as those described in Christina Gilmartin's chapter herein, involve conflict between the male-dominance prescribed by ideology and custom and the attempts of women to confront or escape aspects of that dominance. In service of the *status quo*, women are beaten by those who stand to lose from any change: husbands, fathers-in-law, or, perhaps most commonly, mothers-in-law. Other family conflicts involve the attempt to socialize children by demonstrating the power of parents: Margery Wolf (1972) has shown that parents consider it legitimate, even necessary, to use corporal punishment to teach proper values to children and to keep the children in line.

Both these kinds of family violence are vertical: they involve the use of force to preserve the power of a dominant group (males or the elder generation) over a subordinate one (females or the younger generation). Other family conflicts are horizontal: they occur between equals who are rivals for power, money, or some other resource. The violence of brother against brother so graphically described in Margery Wolf's *The House of Lim* (1968) illustrates this well. Despite the strong ethical condemnation of disharmony within this most basic of social units, family violence seems quite prevalent in Chinese society.

Conflicts in local society

Within the neighborhood, the village, the urban quarter, many social cleavages can give rise to conflict, usually of a horizontal nature and taking the form of disputes over rival claims to resources or to social status. At the very lowest level, individual families may compete for space along narrow village lanes—violence was narrowly averted in the Taiwanese village where I lived when one man enlarged his house to the point where a neighbor feared that the lane that passed both their houses was too narrow to accommodate a coffin during a funeral procession—for irrigation rights, or over disputed pieces of land. Lineages may come to blows over land or water resources (Ahern 1973; Lamley, this volume); villages, not necessarily organized along lineage or other kinship lines, may do the same.

Not only economic resources, but political power may also be the basis for rivalry leading to violence. The anthropological literature on Chinese rural communities is full of examples of this kind of violence: such was certainly behind the maiming of the household head's elder brother in *The House of Lim* (Wolf 1968), as well as the beating senseless of the head of Ploughshare village by his rivals in 1972 (Harrell 1982: 144-47). And there is evidence that this kind of dispute continues to occur: a recent article by Perry (1986) discusses the continuing outbreaks of fighting between rival lineages and communities in the Chinese countryside after the decollectivization of agriculture in the late 1970s.

Ethnic group conflict

Within Chinese society, there have been and continue to be two kinds of cleavages that we would ordinarily classify under the "ethnic" heading. The first of these concerns divisions between the Han (the "ethnic Chinese" or, as we might better call them, the "Chinese by default" who have no self-perception of being "different" from the mainstream of Chinese culture) and other groups defined as separate by a combination of primordial sentiments and perception of advantage in certain situations (Gladney 1987). The protracted struggles between Han and Hui described by Lipman herein are one example of ethnic conflict: economic and political resources are at stake here, and the groups fighting over them define their group interest in terms of certain primordial characteristics, in this case, whether or not they are Muslims. At other times and places, Han clashed with other ethnic groups, as in the late Ming and early Qing, when Han encroachment on minority-held hill lands spurred several minority rebellions in China's southwest (Wiens 1967: 170-97).

Another similar axis of conflict tends to be labelled either "ethnic" (Gates 1981) or "subethnic" (Guldin 1984), where rivals over power or resources similarly define themselves in terms of primordial characteristics as they pursue perceived interests, but in this case all the parties to the conflict consider themselves Han (or Chinese), and the markers of differentiation in speech, dress, customs, and so on are at a lower level. Such subethnic rivalry was an important axis of conflict in some of the *xiedou* battles in Guangdong and Fujian, described by Lamley in this volume, as well as in the bloody altercations that took place in Taiwan during the mid-nineteenth century.

We generally perceive ethnic-group conflict as horizontal, according to our explicit or implicit segmentary model of ethnic organization and rivalry (Gates 1981). At the same time, it may be perceived by the participants as vertical, either in the case of a rebellion by an oppressed group, as in the case of the Hui under certain regimes, or as the suppression of a culturally inferior group with no claim to independent status, as in the case of Han relations with upland minorities in the Southwest.

Class conflict

Although the Maoist claim that class conflict is the sole driving force of Chinese history has been discredited both inside and outside China in recent years, class-based appeals and cleavages of class clearly were very important in certain types of violence throughout Chinese history. It is difficult, of course, to claim that any kind of violent conflict of any larger scale than a tenant revolt was *exclusively* class-based. Nevertheless, a large number of rebellions, including such sectarian revolts as promised a millennium with no more inequality, as well as such major uprisings as the Nian (Chiang 1954: 17-20) and Taiping in the nineteenth century, in fact appealed to many participants in terms of class struggle.

When we come to the twentieth century, we see the most explicitly class-based violence in Chinese history, with the Communist Party inciting great numbers of people to violence in the name of class struggle, particularly in the Land Reform campaign (two million dead) and in the Great Proletarian Cultural Revolution (several hundred thousand, probably). Here the political leadership has defined political violence as exclusively class-based, ruling out on theoretical grounds any other social divisions. At the same time, it has projected class as a basic division back onto much past violence whose motivation may have been more mixed and whose cleavages were more complex. Still, that class violence existed in traditional China is not really in question.

Sectarian exclusiveness

From at least the Northern and Southern dynasties period on, as Shek demonstrates herein, sectarian groups of Buddhist, Daoist, or eclectic imagery have perpetrated violence in the name of sectarian exclusiveness and its role in bringing on a millennium of justice and prosperity. This is in a sense vertical violence from below: people in a subordinate group use violence in an attempt to change the existing order. But as Shek points out, the cleavages that made the groups subordinate and drove them to sectarian violence were in a sense of the sectarians' own making. The act of joining a sect placed one in a group whose boundaries did not run parallel to those of ordinary social groups, and whose ideology defined its own members as the elect and outsiders as the condemned. Social cleavages defined in this way led to both sectarian uprising and government action to suppress actual or imagined sectarian violence.

There was also sectarian violence of a horizontal nature, although probably only within Muslim communities. The history of the Northwest in the Qing period is full of accounts of feuding between different Muslim sects, particularly the Khufiyya and Jahriyya Sufi orders (Lipman, this volume); they fought over resources as well as over doctrinal purity. This kind of sectarian violence, however, seems to have been peculiar to Muslims: within Han society, sectarianism was never the basis for local community organization the way it was among Hui. We do not find a social cleavage between a community that adheres to one sect and a neighboring community that adheres to another. Thus, community conflict in Han society was expressed in other than sectarian terms.

Large-scale political rivalry

This is horizontal violence on its widest and most destructive scale, and probably the type of violence that caused the most death and destruction in Chinese history: conflict between rival claimants to imperial or other large-scale political power. Chinese society has seen struggles for dynastic succession and/or regional overlordship at least since the second millennium B.C., and such battles have continued through the reciprocal shelling of Jinmen and Xiamen in the 1960s. But such violence has undergone a change in modern times. Until recently, parties to such conflict have based their rival claims on the same ideas of legitimacy: the Mandate of Heaven and the right to rule in Heaven's name. In recent times, warlords, Nationalists, and Communists have brought ideological rivalry into the definition of this kind of social cleavage. The Communists' right to rule is based on a different idea of legitimacy than that of the Nationalists. Nevertheless, when such rivals exist, they sweep great masses of the population into active participation as soldiers and militiamen, or passive participation as victims, in China's largest-scale violent behavior.

Government and its rivals

Finally, we come to what was, from the official standpoint, the most legitimate use of violence in the society: the enforcement of order and of rule by a particular regime, done by means of police action, military suppression of rebellion, and corporal or capital punishment of adjudged rebels and criminals. This kind of violence is of course the epitome of vertical violence: it is the ideologically legitimated use of force to preserve the claim of a power-holding group against those who would challenge it. The historical record clearly indicates that the Chinese state has rarely been reluctant to resort to force in its own defense. In the suppression of rebellion, indiscriminate slaughter was often the rule, and in the administration of justice, capital punishment has often been dealt out in great quantity. The 50,000 or more criminals executed in the early 1980s in a large-scale anticrime campaign (Amnesty International 1984) were the latest objects of this traditional vertical violence.

Motivation for violent behavior

Thus, a wide range of both vertical and horizontal conflict situations in Chinese society exist, but mere classification of such situations is not enough to understand the violence that occurred and occurs in China. After all, Chinese orthodox culture did not glorify violence; in fact, it actively abhorred it. At best, even military and police actions were necessary evils brought on by the imperfect development of structures of order and harmony in the society. The single kind of behavior most strictly forbidden and most strictly punished in Chinese children from early childhood was getting into disputes, particularly those that involved physical fighting. Children were ordinarily punished even for being hit by others: it indicated their inability to stay out of potentially dangerous scrapes (Wolf 1972: 66-73). As children grew older and could be educated at least partially by reason, they learned proverbs about the superiority of persuasion over force (*junzi dong kou, xiaoren dong shou*; The cultivated man uses his mouth, the inferior man uses his hands), as well as philosophical arguments for the superiority of moral example over force in bringing about prosperity and order. At levels from child training to political philosophy, the surface message was that violence was a bad thing, something to be avoided whenever possible and never to be sought or glorified.

Why, then, did so many of the situations described above lead to violent behavior? What motivated people in this cultural environment to flout some of the most basic tenets of morality and ethics, and to engage in forms of physical violence from wife-beating to millenarian rebellion? It seems to me there are three basic kinds of motivations that can override the general cultural abhorrence of violence.

First, there are situations where the conscious, internalized cultural value prohibiting violence is too weak to overcome emotions of anger and hatred, and violence breaks forth through the individual's culturally based inhibitions. The socialization in this case is incomplete; it has failed in its mission to create nonviolent, reasoning, enculturated individuals.

Second, there are countervailing claims abroad in the society. Despite the orthodoxy of nonviolence, a variety of countercultures has always existed that have given people very different messages about the desirability and use of violent behavior. For certain people and in certain situations, these countercultures were more compelling than the antiviolence of the orthodox culture.

Third, the culture itself is not entirely consistent. If Confucian philosophy and popular ethical notions both condemned violence, neither rejected it altogether, and both prescribed certain real situations in which resort to violence was the only moral alternative.

In examining the case studies of violence presented in the papers in this volume, we can see examples of all of these kinds of situations that motivate violent behavior. What all of them have in common is that they must necessarily be explained by individual motivation: except in certain situations where the third factor—exceptions within the culture itself—comes to the fore, probably the majority of conflict situations in all the categories described above either did not lead to violence at all or did so only sporadically. Daughters-in-law suffered quietly under the ideologically legitimated authority of their husbands' families; rival village leaders played politics peacefully; sectarian groups pursued the millennium through prayer and devotion rather than through taking up arms. Class oppression depended as much on ideological hegemony as on demonstrated force of arms. In short, the existence of conflict was only one factor in bringing about violence. To understand violence, we must examine in detail the three kinds of factors that led to the overriding of the cultural strictures against it.

The failure of norms: emotion and violence

Much of the violence that goes on in Chinese society, particularly on smaller scales, is only partly intentional. People's emotions get the better of them, and they do things that they knew all along were not only ethically wrong, but also would lead to bigger trouble and continued violence. This is, of course, why parents place such overwhelming value on inculcating nonviolence in their children: to hit back when one wants to is to start a round of troubles that might last for generations. For once a dispute has escalated to open violence, it is very difficult to settle without loss of face on one side or the other, and the continued thought of losing face causes the emotions to well up again. But children, who have not yet internalized the lessons of cooperation in the face of conflict, only gradually learn to contain their emotions and not strike out or strike back. When they do internalize this lesson, however, they internalize it on the level of personal values or ethics, not on the level of feelings. Whatever the inhibitions imposed by the culture, the feelings of anger and hostility are still there, and occasionally they break through. They do so most often in the presence of one or another of several factors: loss of face, protracted and escalating nonviolent conflict, desire for vengeance, or drunkenness.

Martin Yang (1945) has given us what is still probably the most satisfying definition of face as a feeling that one is getting the respect properly due to one's position. To preserve face for the other party is thus a requirement for anyone who wants to avoid escalation in a conflict that is already there. When face is lost, the danger of emotions getting out of hand increases, because face, as Yang points out, is a feeling, an emotion. There are many stories of families' ruining themselves with lawsuits, and sometimes resorting to violence when the lawsuit fails, because of the overwhelming anger and hopelessness that arises from the thought of not being able to restore the family's face once lost. Lamley's reference to "sensitive matters, such as pride and honor" as motivations for *xiedou* underlines this point. A vicious circle arises here, however: if one resorts to violence in what is perceived as an unjustified manner, one is risking a further loss of face. This kind of double bind is probably at the root of many of the suicides of literary and political figures in the Cultural Revolution, mentioned in Thurston's chapter. There was no way out for these people, once humiliated; consequently, they resorted to violence against themselves.

Loss of face often comes about as a result of a protracted and escalating, although originally not violent, conflict or confrontation. There are two stages of this in its propensity to incite violence: nonviolent conflict, when it reaches a certain stage, often sets off a further escalation to violent conflict, and once violence enters the picture, further violence becomes the only emotionally satisfying response. Both of these kinds of situations are graphically illustrated in many village political struggles. For example, in Ploughshare, north Taiwan, I witnessed part of a protracted struggle between two political leaders who maneuvered for power for years, undercutting and backstabbing each other in a variety of creative ways, but never resorting to violence until, one evening after a banquet, the leader of one family was assaulted by the drunken brother of the other leader—the struggle was escalating anyway, and the alcohol had helped to remove the cultural inhibition against such behavior. Everybody knew it was wrong; the assailant's own brothers condemned the act (while pointing out the purity of the motivation), but it was impossible to suppress the impulse. Several years earlier, two other families had quarreled and grown increasingly bitter toward one another. Finally, a threat of violence by one side led to an actual homicide by the other; the dispute was finally cooled only by the intervention of state violence by jailing the killer.

The cycle of recurring violence plays a part in many kinds of violent disputes described in this book. The Red Guard factions described by Thurston and others (Hinton 1972, 1983) originally resorted to violence because of escalation; once violence was a part of their repertoire, only increased levels of violence would fill their needs. In Long Bow village, as analyzed here by Madsen, violent action by one side opened the door for violent action by the other, and the cycle continued. It was thus in both the Han-Hui disputes of the northwest, described by Lipman here, and the lineage and subethnic feuding in the southeast, related by Lamley. The cycle of vengeance and the emotional break through the cultural inhibitions played a large part in motivating participants in all these struggles to violent behavior. Lamley's characterization of the feuding lineages as harboring "bitter and lasting mutual hostility" sums up the situation well—with such feelings dominant, the threshold of violent behavior falls.

We can thus see that several kinds of situations exist in which the emotions of anger and hatred for the adversary become so strong as to suspend the cultural curbs on violent behavior. In each case, the motivating factors, the conflicts that cause one to lose face or to dwell on slights, are clear enough. But I suggest that a further psychological aspect must be considered: the imperfect nature of the socialization process. If children are socialized to contain even their extreme anger in the service of social harmony, they are socialized by punitive means, most often by physical violence directed against them in the form of beatings. This method of socialization conveys a kind of double message to the children: one must internalize the values of nonviolence and the suppression of emotions, but one gets one's way (at least according to the parental example) by the exercise of violence. The very models the child is supposed to emulate in fact use violence against the child. In addition, if the child observes domestic violence against adults (such as one's own mother), this further reinforces the subtle message that one can get one's way by hitting someone. When the double message of socialization confronts a situation of real or perceived conflict, then violence is never far from the surface. This is perhaps one reason why foreign residents in Chinese villages (including me) have reported so many fistfights and other incidents of violent behavior between members of these communities.

Conflicting norms and countercultures

That the Chinese orthodox culture, with its norms of harmony and nonviolence, is not completely effective in socializing or containing the behavior of those people socialized into it is clear enough from the above, but this is not sufficient to explain the individual motivation for all acts of violence in Chinese society. Where emotion most certainly plays some part in most violent behavior, it is not always the only factor operating. In many social situations, in fact, the orthodox culture does not reign unchallenged even at the normative level. There are several kinds of countercultures, particular to localities, social classes, ethnic groups, or sectarian religions, that convey a different normative message about the desirability and appropriateness of violent behavior. People who participate in these countercultures are not only susceptible to emotional motivations for violence; they also often find in their countercultures justification or even positive encouragement to engage in violence.

The relationship between culture and counterculture in Chinese society is a complex one: a recent symposium on hegemony and folk ideology in Chinese society (Gates and Weller 1987) clearly showed that most Chinese, most of the time, participated to a varying extent in both the orthodox culture, which supported the hegemony of the *literati* class, and certain local or ethnic or religious countercultures that challenged that hegemony to varying degrees. We cannot classify anyone except perhaps a real *literatus* as completely influenced by the orthodox culture; even less can we find individuals entirely steeped in counterculture. But there is little doubt that the countercultures had influence on a wide spectrum of the population. Examining a series of countercultures demonstrates their importance for motivating and justifying violent behavior.

Local and ethnic countercultures flourished in various parts of the empire, and continue to have influence to this day. Local (as opposed to class-based or sectarian) countercultures were important primarily in places where community leadership was based on something other than the *literati* ideal of gentlemanly scholarship and leisure, usually on local military control exercised where there was no strong state authority. In such communities, participation in militias, in village guards (Watson 1975: 22-23), or in roving bands of marauders (Chiang 1954: 17-20) was the normal course of life for young men, particularly of the poorer classes. It was precisely in such communities that such phenomena as ethnic feuding and interlineage or intervillage *xiedou* took place. Several examples serve well to illustrate this point:

Jonathan Lipman, in his chapter herein, describes the militaristic culture of Hui communities that flourished during the period of Han-Hui conflict from the end of the eighteenth century to the beginning of the twentieth century. Here military participation was religiously sanctioned as sectarian struggle against heterodox Hui, as self-defense against antagonistic local officials, or, in a few cases, as ethnic warfare against the Han-dominated state itself. Military activity also led to possibilities of career advancement, culminating in the large number of Hui generals in the Guomindang army in the twentieth century, not to mention the thrill of battle and plunder graphically portrayed in local folk songs.

Another example comes from Taiwan in the nineteenth century, an area where government control was lax, at best, during this period. Landowning families, such as the Lins of Wufeng described by Meskill (1977), or the pioneer patent-holding families of the Taibei basin (Harrell 1989), originally based their control over local society not in the legitimacy of scholarship and upperclass leisure, but in a combination of landholding and control over local military forces. Again, young men of these communities were expected to engage in violent behavior, and they were rewarded for it, both immediately in the form of loot or at least wages, and in the longer term in the form of potential social mobility.

Finally, we have the feuding lineage communities of the Minnan region, so graphically portrayed by Lamley in this volume. Southern Fujian, it has been argued by a variety of scholars (Wang n.d.; Gates n.d.) was already partially free of the hegemony of Confucian orthodoxy because of its longstanding culture of maritime commerce and trade, and the consequent greater importance of merchants in the local leadership structure. Coupled with the inability of the weakened state to exert much control in this area throughout much of the Qing period (see Lamley, this volume), along with the strong feelings of lineage solidarity and rivalry with other lineages over diminishing resources, this formed the basis of what the officials in the region themselves saw as a deviant local counterculture. It is significant, I think, that the counterculture as an explanation of violence was explicitly used by the officials who looked at, disdained, and felt helpless before this local culture from the vantage point of the orthodoxy.

Another kind of counterculture was based in sectarianism, particularly in the beliefs of the explicitly millenarian sects. (For a typology of sectarian religions, see Harrell and Perry 1982.) The counterculture of millenarian sects is, in a way, more radical than that based in local traditions: to take the millenarian ideologies seriously was to expect a complete transformation of the current world order and its replacement by something totally different. Coupled with the belief that the transformation would come in a great cosmic cataclysm, and that the sectarians would survive while everyone else would be destroyed, this removed most of the inhibitions on violence present in the orthodox culture. As Shek points out, being a member of such an elect group allows one to ignore the social ties that bind one to the ordinary, nonsectarian community, and believing that the millennium is imminent gives one the incentive to burn bridges, literally and figuratively.

At the same time, especially in a volume on violence, I want to emphasize that most sectarians, like most members of minority ethnic groups, were peaceful most of the time, even among those sects that held millenarian beliefs and occasionally rebelled (Overmyer 1976, 1981). Even the most radical of sectarians did not always and irrevocably sever their ties with family, village, lineage, or other social group; they could not afford to because the millennium was usually not here quite yet. And members of many sectarian groups did not translate their millenarian ideas into antistate action, but rather remained in peace, waiting for the transformation to happen to them (Shek 1982).

A third kind of counterculture was based on social class. In a sense, this is the most amorphous type of counterculture to define, because class boundaries are fuzzier than either local or sectarian ones, and members of lower classes had very few ways in which to identify themselves in opposition to the elite in traditional China. (The *literati* were, of course, a strongly self-identified group, but they subscribed to the orthodox culture without question.) But insofar as there was something called *popular culture* (see the essays in Johnson, Nathan, and Rawski 1985), this popular culture was in some ways and in some forms a counterculture, portraying in theater, literature, storytelling, folktales, and other media a set of values that was ambivalent with respect to the orthodox culture. One of the areas in which considerable variance was found between this popular culture and the orthodoxy was in the glorification of violent deeds.

Consider, for example, theater—popular operas and puppet shows. They are very often full of military exploits, and indeed some of the most beloved and exciting sequences in various genres contain battles, particularly the acrobatic sword and spear fights so appealing to the eye. The plots of operas are usually not overtly countercultural: violence is usually depicted as necessary, given the villain's prior resort to it, but the message it conveyed was most likely far from a pacifistic one. It is most likely the military heroes who are most remembered by audiences. And Tanaka Issei's recent work clearly demonstrates that plays sponsored by nonelite people in market towns contained more violence, more supernatural intervention, and less conventional orthodox moralizing than plays sponsored by gentry or by lineages, and presented in villages. This also seems to indicate that insofar as there were class-based countercultures, they concentrated less in the peasantry than in small merchants and others without close ties to the land (Tanaka 1985).

The same is true for popular literature. Much research remains to be done, but the popularity of *wuxia xiaoshuo* (novels of roving knights) in the twentieth century is probably built on a traditional base. And we know of the popularity among all classes of the "mainstream" vernacular novels such as *Sanguo Zhi Yanyi, Shuihu Zhuan,* and, as described by Brandauer in this volume, *Xiyou Ji.* All these novels have long and sometimes descriptively gory fight scenes in them, scenes that are not only famous but also the basis for operas, plays, puppet shows, and other popular entertainments.

Of course, all these novels were also read by members of the *literati,* and Brandauer's tour-de-force explanation of violence in the Buddhist *xiyou* novels as rooted in Mahayanist idealism is convincing at the Mahayanist philosophical level of sophistication. But people who simply read the novel as entertainment, or who read the comic books derived from it, or who watch the operas, puppet shows, and now television serials, are probably taking the violence much more literally, thereby missing the subtle philosophical message intended by the author. Certainly Red Guards who used magic monkey Sun Wukong as a metaphor for their own rampages during the Cultural Revolution (Wagner n.d.) missed the point about Buddhist idealism entirely.

Another aspect of popular culture that needs to be explored more fully is the martial-arts tradition. We know that sectarian religious practice, especially in those sects that were known for their rebelliousness and among northwestern Muslims, included instruction and training in boxing, fencing, and other martial techniques (Naquin 1985: 278-79). At the same time, the more secular secret societies formed on principles of loyalty to the Ming or some other idealized *ancien regime* also emphasized martial-arts training. Joseph Esherick has suggested that, at least in western Shandong, there was a continuum of relationships between martial-arts groups and sectarians. Some boxing associations and boxing teachers were closely tied to sectarian groups and teachings, but more commonly boxers were independent of, or only loosely allied with, sectarians. Clearly, in Esherick's words, boxers "represented traditions of organization by ordinary peasants with no significant guidance or interference from the orthodox gentry elite" (1987: 54). In other words, boxing traditions were another violent aspect of the counterculture.

From all these examples, we can see that the elite, orthodox abhorrence of violence definitely did not operate in China, even on the cultural level, in the absence of competition. Certainly it was part of nearly every child's upbringing and every adult's internalized system of values, but for many, perhaps most Chinese, it competed with one or more countercultures that tended either to glorify or at least to tolerate violent behavior in many situations.

Violence in the orthodox culture

We have already seen how the orthodox culture's abhorrence of violence can be challenged on the cultural level by certain kinds of countercultures and on the individual level by the emotions of an incompletely enculturated individual. But there is a further explanation for much of the violent behavior in traditional and modern China. The orthodox culture itself, while idealizing non-violence, has never been pacifistic, and has always found situations in which violent behavior was justified as preferable to any alternative. This was particularly true when the ordering principles of the orthodoxy were themselves threatened. Such threats came in the form of military challenge to the dynasty; rebellion, particularly on the part of millenarians or others whose social values were at variance to the orthodoxy; crime; and even occasionally behavior inappropriate to one's position in society, such as the rebellion of the young or of women against family norms. In any of these situations, violence was justified, even in the eyes of the orthodox; let us examine briefly the justification for each one.

The opposition to military threats to dynastic rule needs little justification or explanation in a Chinese context: a government has always been thought to have the right to defend itself, according to all schools of political philosophy. Even the Mo-ists, who denied the legitimacy of offensive military action, still considered defense to be proper. And defending the dynasty against a millenarian or other clearly heterodox threat was even more acceptable. The Taiping Tianguo, for example, threatened not just the Qing dynasty but the whole dynastic tradition, and this was one reason why, in the end, the local elite of central China organized military action in support of the Manchus.

The use of violence against criminals was hardly more am-
biguous. Criminal acts were a threat to the social order, and had to
be stopped by any means possible. It is significant in this regard that
in Qing times officials, who were assumed to have internalized the
ethics of the orthodoxy, had to be stripped of their degrees before
being subjected to corporal punishment (van der Sprenkel 1962:53);
those who understood orthodox ethics ought to be dealt with in
nonviolent terms, while those who clearly did not understand—
most criminals and perhaps the masses in general—had to be dealt
with by violence because that was the only way.

I think the reluctance of Chinese governments to prosecute
cases of violence perpetrated against lower-ranking family members, including the present-day lax enforcement of laws and official
norms prohibiting violence against women, as described in Gilmartin's paper in this volume, may be explained in the same way as
the justification for violence against those who threaten the political
or the class order. In all these cases, vertical violence is justified by
the threats to the orthodox order posed by its opponents. Men are
allowed to beat their wives, or mothers-in-law their daughters-in-
law, or parents their children, because the husbands or mothers-in-
law or parents are representatives of the orthodox order, in the same
way as dynasties conceived of themselves as having the Mandate of
Heaven or the nineteenth-century local gentry considered themselves as representing China and civilization against the long-haired
semibarbarians of the Taiping Tianguo.

Looked at in this way, the antiviolence of the orthodox culture
seems to be directed not at violence in general, but at two particular
kinds of violence: horizontal violence, which represents, in its
embodiment of rivalry, a less-than-ideal harmony between the units
that comprise the social order; and vertical violence from below,
which, of course, threatens the order that the orthodoxy represents.
Toward vertical violence from above, the orthodoxy is much more
tolerant, and to understand this kind of violence, we can look
straight in the heart of the orthodoxy, rather than having to resort
to imperfect enculturation or the presence of countercultures to find
an explanation. The orthodoxy, imperial, republican (insofar as
there was an orthodoxy in republican times), and communist, has,

of course, always been a hegemonic ideology, and as such has never been able to renounce violence as the ultimate sanction behind its own power.

But with the coming of Communism, and particularly Maoism, to the position of state orthodoxy, the relationship between culture and violence in China became more complex than ever before. In being explicitly revolutionary and at the same time claiming orthodox status, Maoism forced a kind of ideological contradiction: it was an orthodoxy that sanctioned various kinds of violence that it defined for its own purposes as vertical violence from below. Class struggle was the motivating factor not only for the civil war and the land reform, when the Communist Party was in fact trying to overthrow a ruling class, but also during the Cultural Revolution, when class struggle came to be defined in terms of thinking and political behavior, rather than in terms of relationship to the means of production (Kraus 1981). Two orthodoxies were, thus, competing for people's allegiance, the covert one left over from the traditional hegemonic ideology, stressing harmony even in those days, and the much more powerful overt one that urged youth and workers to further violence in the name of completing the revolution.

Furthermore, Maoism, unlike the old orthodoxy, had few curbs on violence, no countervailing views of the desirability of harmony and accommodation, except with those comrades that one would accommodate anyway. Maoism demanded universal participation, as Thurston points out, giving people little choice but to engage in the struggle. It was antagonistic, seeing class struggle as a higher form of activity. It was absolutist as well, as Madsen points out here and elsewhere (1985), admitting of no compromise. As such, it ended up, perhaps in defiance of the Maoists' own wishes, sanctioning far more than just vertical violence from below, but also vertical violence from above, when the powerholders claimed class-based legitimacy, and even horizontal violence, as long as factional leaders and participants could justify to themselves that in shelling the next dormitory they were in fact engaging in class struggle. What was culture and what was counterculture between 1966 and 1969 is, in fact, difficult to say, but it is clear that the Maoist claim to orthodox status raised the level of violence in society appreciably, as it united the emotional, countercultural, and cultural motivations for violent activity.

Maoism achieved this unfortunate unification because it touched on the weakest point in Chinese culture's opposition to violence: the situation of revenge. In this situation, both counterculture and emotions traditionally urged violence; only the weak urgings of morality stood between the insulted child and the hit back, or between the lineage that had lost its irrigation rights and the nighttime attack on its rival. The very antagonistic structure of these situations combined with the emotions of face and personal pride to urge revenge, and the counterculture, in manifestations from sectarianism to class antagonism, already allowed violent vengeance. The traditional orthodoxy, as we have seen, was only partly successful in preventing violence in such situations, and indeed, as Madsen points out in his essay, was itself less than completely opposed to violent retaliation. But when Maoism, with the force of orthodoxy and the prestige of the beloved and supreme leader, urged Red Guards and others to "attack with reason and defend with force," it explicitly legitimated violent revenge, a response that had always smoldered under the orthodox surface of harmony and reason. Maoism not only gave orthodox legitimation to violence, it also conferred its legitimacy on the type of violence—revenge—that the traditional orthodoxy was least successful in containing.

In addition, as is evident from Madsen's analysis in this volume, it was when loyalty—to family members, kin, or others to whom one owned a debt of gratitude—entered the equation, that the traditional orthodox morality was least convincing in its strictures against violent revenge. And the cult of the Great Helmsman promoted during the Cultural Revolution explicitly replaced, for Maoist revolutionaries, traditional family and friendship loyalties with loyalty to the Chairman. It is no wonder, then, that all those who could have been conceived of as having attacked Chairman Mao—the Great Red Sun who was dearer to the Red Guards than their own family members—became targets for vengeful violence.

Maoism is gone now; class struggle has again given way to building socialism, and the official morality of contemporary Chinese society once again condemns horizontal violence and vertical violence from below. But as Perry (1986) has shown, the social cleavages and the countercultures still exist, and Gilmartin's paper in this volume suggests that the context of socialization, despite communist efforts at reeducation, is incompletely changed at best. Violence continues to be a part of life in post-Mao China.

References

Ahern, Emily M.
1973 *The Cult of the Dead in a Chinese Village*. Stanford: Stanford University Press.

Amnesty International
1984 *Human Rights Violations in the People's Republic of China*. London: Amnesty International Publications.

Chiang Siang-tseh
1954 *The Nien Rebellion*. Seattle: University of Washington Press.

Esherick, Joseph
1987 *The Origins of the Boxer Uprising*. Berkeley and Los Angeles: University of California Press.

Gates, Hill
1981 "Ethnicity and Social Class," in Emily Martin Ahern and Hill Gates, eds., *The Anthropology of Taiwanese Society*. Stanford: Stanford University Press.

n.d. "The Petty Capitalist Mode of Production in Chinese Society," unpublished paper.

Gates, Hill, and Robert P. Weller
1987 "Symposium on Hegemony and Chinese Folk Ideologies," *Modern China* 13, 1 and 3.

Gladney, Dru Curtis
1987 *Qingzhen: A Study of Ethnoreligious Identity among Hui Muslim Communities in China*. Ph.D. Dissertation, University of Washington.

Guldin, Gregory E.
1984 "Seven Veiled Ethnicity: A Hong Kong Chinese Folk Model," *Journal of Chinese Studies*, 1:139-58.

Harrell, Stevan
1982 *Ploughshare Village: Culture and Context in Taiwan*. Seattle: University of Washington Press.

1989 "From *Xiedou* to *Yijun*: The Decline of Ethnicity and the Transformation of the North Taiwan Local Elite, 1860-1895." *Late Imperial China*, forthcoming.

23

Harrell, Stevan, and Elizabeth J. Perry
    1982 "Syncretic Sects in Chinese Society: An Introduction," *Modern China* 8:283-303.

Hinton, William
    1972 *Hundred Day War: The Cultural Revolution in Tsinghra University*. New York: Monthly Review Press.

    1983 *Shenfan*. New York: Random House.

Johnson, David, Andrew J. Nathan, and Evelyn S. Rawski
    1985 *Popular Culture in Late Imperial China*. Berkeley and Los Angeles: University of California Press.

Kraus, Richard Curt
    1981 *Class Conflict in Chinese Socialism*. New York: Columbia University Press.

Madsen, Richard
    1985 *Morality and Power in a Chinese Village*. Berkeley and Los Angeles: University of California Press.

Meskill, Johanna M.
    1975 *A Chinese Gentry Family: the Lins of Wufeng*. Princeton, N.J.: Princeton University Press.

Naquin, Susan
    1985 "The Transmission of White Lotus Sectarianism in Late Imperial China," in Johnson, Nathan, and Rawski, eds., *Popular Culture in Late Imperial China*, pp. 255-91. Berkeley and Los Angeles: University of California Press.

Overmyer, Daniel L.
    1976 *Folk Buddhist Religion*. Cambridge, Mass.: Harvard University Press.

    1981 "Alternatives: Popular Religious Sects in Chinese Society," *Modern China* 7:153-90.

Perry, Elizabeth
    1986 "Rural Violence in Socialist China," *China Quarterly* 103:414-440.

Shek, Richard
    1982 "Millenarianism Without Rebellion: The Huangtian Dao in North China," *Modern China* 7:305-35.

Tanaka, Issei
1985 "The Social and Historical Context of Ming-Ch'ing Local Drama," in Johnson, Nathan, and Rawski, eds., *Popular Culture in Late Imperial China*, pp. 143-59. Berkeley and Los Angeles: University of California Press.

van der Sprenkel, Sybille
1962 *Legal Institutions in Manchu China*. London: Athlone Press.

Wagner, Rudolf
n.d. "Monkey Subdues the White-Boned Demon," unpublished paper.

Wang, Lianmao
1987 "Mingqing Shiqi Minnan Liangge Jiazu de Renkou Yidong" (Migration in Two Southern Fujian Lineages in the Ming and Qing Periods), paper prepared for the Conference on Chinese Lineage Demography.

Watson, James L.
1975 *Emigration and the Chinese Lineage: The Mans in Hong Kong and Britain*. Berkeley and Los Angeles: University of California Press.

Wiens, Herold J.
1967 (originally 1954) *Han Chinese Expansion in South China*. Hamden, Conn.: The Shoe String Press.

Wolf, Margery
1968 *The House of Lim*. New York: Appleton, Century, Crofts.

1972 *Women and the Family in Rural Taiwan*. Stanford: Stanford University Press.

Yang, Martin C.
1945 *A Chinese Village: Taitou, Shantung Province*. New York: Columbia University Press.

Chapter 2

Lineage Feuding in Southern Fujian and Eastern Guangdong Under Qing Rule

Harry J. Lamley

Feuding in one form or another has existed in societies throughout the world. Given the universal nature of the feud, however, we have relatively few detailed historical studies of the feud process and its many ramifications. This is certainly the case in respect to China, where traditional concepts of legitimate revenge and justifiable homicide have spurred on blood and communal feuding since classical antiquity. The paucity of scholarly research on the widespread communal feuding that prevailed under Qing rule (1644-1912) is particularly regrettable. No other major type of violence so well reflects the social tension and dissidence which plagued many Chinese localities, even during the High Qing period in the eighteenth century.

In this essay, I treat lineage feuding in southern Fujian and eastern Guangdong (Lamley 1977, 1986). This form of communal feud, carried on between rival lineages or surname groups, became endemic in the coastal prefectures of the region during the eighteenth century and gave rise to serious armed affrays. In the Yongzheng reign (1723-1735) such lineage and surname feud strife began to be labeled as *xiedou* (armed affrays) by concerned Qing officials. Gradually, the *xiedou* designation was also applied to interlineage conflicts elsewhere, as well as to communal feud strife between other types of rival groups throughout China and among Chinese settlements overseas (Lamley 1977:8-16). Nevertheless, this term was used most consistently in reference to the lineage feuding in Fujian and Guangdong, especially in those coastal prefectures where *xiedou* outbreaks were first reported and persisted through-

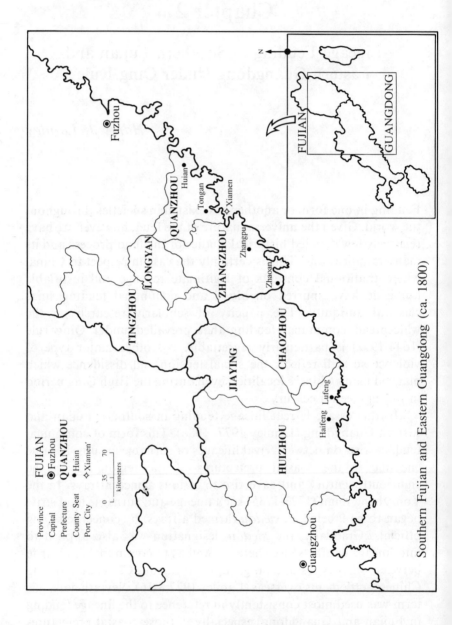

Southern Fujian and Eastern Guangdong (ca. 1800)

out the nineteenth century and much of the twentieth century.

Southern Fujian and eastern Guangdong had long been a turbulent region, well-suited to feuding. Scarce resources and a dense and unruly population nurtured fierce rivalries and violence. Under these unstable conditions, deviant customs and behavior were prevalent, and the regional milieu, as depicted in official accounts, harbored a subculture in conflict with norms and practices upheld by the state and the Confucian order. This tension indicated keen competition and general insecurity, as well as deep-rooted conflicts of interest between the traditional state and the commercialized local society. Under Qing rule, intense rivalry among powerful lineages and surname groups brought about widespread feuding that eventually involved entire local populations. In these coastal settings, extensive feud violence, expressed in frequent *xiedou* engagements, led to further alienation among the local inhabitants and fostered even more deviant ingroup counter-cultures.

Research on feuding in this region relies heavily on Qing documentary and literary references to *xiedou*. In the first section of this essay, I address Qing usages of the *xiedou* designation and modern approaches to the feud. In the next section, I address, historically, the regional background and local setting that gave rise to lineage feuding, especially the years during the Yongzheng reign, when *xiedou* outbreaks were first reported in Quanzhou prefecture, southern Fujian, and to violence in all four coastal prefectures during the remainder of the Qing period.

The third section deals with major traits peculiar to lineage and surname feuding in southern Fujian and eastern Guangdong, describing the feud alignments and networks that developed there. The open-ended nature of such feuds is stressed. Through systems of alliances, large confederations of lineage and surname aggregates, or entire multivillage and district populations, were often drawn into local feuds. Often, outside mercenaries were also hired to battle in armed affrays. The state, too, became party to the feud. This open-ended quality helps to account for the magnitude of the feuding and the fact that such Chinese communal feuds did not conform to precise restraints and customary rules commonly associated with the blood feud.[1]

The concluding section identifies causes and motives for this sustained feuding. Within a region characterized by scarce resources, a dense population, and a competitive, commercialized economy, lineage feuds certainly seem to have stemmed from general ecological and socioeconomic conditions. However, we must investigate more specific incentives and impulses relevant to "feud motivation" if the sources of communal feud hostility are to be identified in the context of a deviant subculture. The feud, after all, is a type of organized violence that can be perpetuated indefinitely by vindictive grievances and hate-filled disputes, even though they may seem petty or irrational to an outsider.

Xiedou usages and perspectives on the feud

The feud is a most difficult phenomenon to research, due to the inevitable lack of complete and accurate records. Feuds may lapse, then reappear. Moreover, observers external to any given feud are apt to know little about the vengeful strategies that serve to perpetuate the feuding (Black-Michaud 1975:33). On the other hand, strong ingroup feelings, including fear, shame, guilt, and pride, tend to make feuding a secretive venture for parties directly involved in the violence. The feud, after all, is by nature a private and sinister affair: basically, a state of bitter and lasting hostility between rival ingroups, characterized by murderous assaults in revenge for previous homicides, insults, and other alleged wrongdoing.

In Qing China, feuds were considered to be private conflicts *(sidou)* by the authorities, for neither local officials nor the government were objects of attack. Official records of communal feuding were commonly limited to specific homicide *(renming)* and affray *(douou)* cases resulting from *xiedou* outbreaks or other vengeful acts of violence. The amount of detailed information varied in such case records, but rarely did the authorities attempt to piece together a complete account of a continuous feud.

Endemic feuding, abetted by balance-of-power alliances between lineage and surname alignments, made the communal feud a perplexing phenomenon to Qing officials. Communal feuding was a type of disorder that they described by set phrases, then identified by the *xiedou* designation, and eventually classified under a separate category of violence called *xiedou*.

The xiedou *designation and category*

The *xiedou* designation began to be used consistently by Fujian officials in 1728, when pitched battles between local surname alignments were initially reported to the throne. This strife was deemed more serious than ordinary affrays due to the multitude of combatants and their array of weapons. So menacing were these armed affrays that the acting magistrate of Tongan county in Quanzhou, where the violence occurred, dared not approach the scene of battle. A local military official also failed to report or respond to this disorder (YZCZZ 1728:IX, 571-73).

The term *xiedou* was derived from commonly used phrases depicting armed strife, such as *liexie gedou* ("arrayal of weapons and pitched battles"), that appeared in official reports (YZCZZ 1728:IX, 465). The expression *jiuzhong xiedou* (literally, "gathering crowds and fighting with weapons"), which was used in a 1728 memorial submitted by the Fujian (Min-Zhe) Governor-General, suggests the relatively large scale of the pitched battles as well as something of the combined size of the lineage communities involved (YZCZZ 1728:IX, 571). Also clearly indicated in his 1727-1728 memorials is the element of revenge: in this case, smaller lineages retaliating against the aggressions of larger lineages over an apparently long period of time.

Thereafter, for almost a century, Qing officials attempted to devise a separate *xiedou* category suitable for major crimes committed during large-scale armed affrays. In their efforts to formulate a separate classification, they differentiated between *xiedou* violence and ordinary "collective and planned affrays" (*gongou* and *mouou*). Eventually, a more standard classification evolved that included three outstanding traits characteristic of preparations for *xiedou* engagements: namely "assembling crowds" (*jiuzhong*), "amassing funds" (*lianqian*), and "setting dates" (*yueqi*) for battle (Xue 1970:841). Thus, from the standpoint of the government, *xiedou* were battles carefully planned by communities at feud. In 1825, a separate substatute, which enumerated these three distinctions and applied specifically to *xiedou* vengeful homicide *(chousha)* cases, was incorporated into the Qing Penal Code. This particular substatute was restricted in its application to six southern provinces: Guangdong, Fujian (excepting Taiwan), Guangxi, Jiangxi, Hunan, and Zhejiang (Xue 1970:841).

Meanwhile, the *xiedou* designation was extended to feud strife between other types of rival groups in both official reports and the private writings of apprehensive literati.[2] In all, these *xiedou* accounts indicate that the most severe communal feuding took two major forms. One stemmed from lineage and surname rivalries and prevailed among groups based on demonstrated or putative descent and kinship such as the lineages and surname aggregates at feud in Fujian and Guangdong. The other developed from competition and hostilities between discrete communities with pronounced ethnic and/or native-place differences.

The various sets of rival groups involved in these two major feud forms functioned ordinarily as corporate communities. That is, they were communities in which at least some part of the communal wealth was owned or shared collectively on a continuous basis by corporate groups. These communities included lineages in Fujian, and Chaozhou and Huizhou to the southwest in Guangdong, be they lineages or lineage branches, villages or neighborhood groups, or discrete territorial groupings of a rural or urban cast. Such communities were enduring groups and tended to possess sufficient manpower and resources to engage in costly *xiedou* strife.

Feuds between corporate communities of this nature invariably involved the entire group membership at hand, including all social classes. Although the *xiedou* label occasionally may have been applied to intermittent affrays between landlord and tenant bands (Hsiao 1960:426-33), the designation was seldom indicative of direct class conflict among different social strata. This was also true in respect to *xiedou* outbreaks reported between rival sects, sworn brotherhood groups, and local associations—groups that may have represented a distinct class or definite class interests. Thus, the violence discussed in this essay appears to be almost entirely horizontal in orientation, taking place between rival, equivalent groups in society (Harrell, this volume). Class conflict crosscutting vertically structured communities, however, did sometimes influence the course of communal feuds, as when poor members of lineages at feud strove to perpetuate *xiedou* strife for their own benefit.

Approaches to the feud

Viewed in the context of organized violence, the *xiedou* may seem equivalent to the feud. Both terms refer to vengeful actions usually capped by retaliatory homicides. Western descriptions of the feud, similar to Chinese *xiedou* accounts, have tended to dwell on these violent aspects and on the means to regulate or pacify this deadly strife. Anthropologists, however, have adopted broader approaches to the study of feuding. More recently, some have come to recognize the feud, under conditions of scarcity, "as a type of generalized struggle extending into all spheres of social life at once" (Black-Michaud 1975:121). Others, such as E.L. Peters (1975:xxvii), have treated more with the competitive nature of the feud relationship while playing down the violent, homicidal aspects: "... feud is not necessarily manifested as a number of serially linked homicides. Feud is also advanced without a gun being fired or the loss of a single life."

Peters's general description of the "interminable" feud in Bedouin society, as "essentially a specific mode of competition" between discrete corporate groups, can readily be applied to Chinese communal feuds. His insightful approach enables one to perceive continuous feud competition as a series of transactions that serve to perpetuate the contest. From this perspective, the communal feud assumes the guise of a game of enterprise (Black-Michaud 1975:25). Armed affrays, on the other hand, represent a strategy frequently resorted to by the contestants. The *xiedou* thus appears distinct from the entire feud.

Such broad-gauged approaches to the feud reveal shortcomings inherent in Qing-period *xiedou* accounts. A major deficiency is that Chinese sources treat with short-term episodes of feud violence and seldom relate *xiedou* outbreaks to the course of a feud. Neither do Qing references usually disclose sufficient information concerning the many tangible and intangible factors (such as pride and honor) involved in feud competition. Certainly, the motives for retaliatory violence varied during the course of an enduring or interminable feud.

Furthermore, Qing accounts present a traditional participant's perspective rather than a more detached view of society. In accordance with the Confucian moral order, social harmony was deemed a natural attribute consistent with universal principles and primary ethical relationships. Therefore, biases pervade Chinese documentary and literary references to *xiedou* violence and people prone to feud. Standard accounts, for example, depict feuding (as manifested by *xiedou* outbreaks) as an abhorrent anomaly in Chinese society rather than as a customary practice that played a dominant role in tension-ridden localities of southern Fujian and eastern Guangdong. Meanwhile, Qing authorities assigned to that region disparagingly described the inhabitants as rapacious and vindictive.

Subcultural dissidence and violence

Qing officials, of course, tended to disparage the inhabitants for other bad tendencies besides their proclivity to feud. Provincial and local authorities, in fact, listed many different "customary evils" practiced throughout much of the region. These evils included gambling and smuggling, brigandage and piracy, resistance to taxation and arrest, a strong predilection for litigation and the martial arts, excessive idol worship, and "immoral" adoption practices (see, for example, Bian ca. 1894:132-47). Such illicit and heterodox behavior, when viewed from the standpoint of the state, marked the inhabitants in general as disorderly and their customs and practices as degenerate. The critical observations registered by Qing authorities clearly indicate a regional subculture of dissidence and violence.

A deviant subculture, however, must be defined against a more normal or orthodox cultural milieu. In this respect, Qing authorities, as with those of the previous Ming dynasty (1368-1644), looked upon this coastal portion of southeastern China as a decadent region, but one with a golden past. Following Ming accounts, Qing officials alleged that ideal conditions had prevailed there after outstanding Confucian scholar-officials—Han Yu in eastern Guangdong and Zhu Xi in southern Fujian—had introduced civilized ways during the Tang and Southern Song dynasties, respectively. According to local Ming gazetteers, these secluded coastal areas had then become virtual replicas of the ancient states of Zou and Lu where Confucius and Mencius had lived and taught (Guo 1547:176).

Qing officials holding such lofty conceptions of an idealized past became disturbed by the worldly antics and overbearing ways of the coastal populations. These inhabitants appeared overly proud and sensitive as to their reputations and self-esteem. Hence, they set great store by family and lineage honor and made a grand display of their filial and ancestral devotion (Zhao ca. 1788:78). They also seemed ostentatious in their dress and eating habits (Lan 1723:49-51). The coastal Hokkien people were highly competitive as well, not only in business matters but also with regard to their customary practices and community spectacles, such as their pretentious religious festivals and intervillage rock-fight rivalries (Chen 1826:81).

Local Qing authorities expressed concern about the vengeful temperament of such proud and aggressive inhabitants. These people were known to harbor old grudges and even to retaliate by kidnappings and feuds in revenge for hereditary grievances *(suyuan)* allegedly inherited from a previous life (Chen 1826:90). Officials also worried about the arms of these coastal inhabitants and their reputed propensity for violence when aroused by "obtrusive ruffians" *(chuanggun)*, "loafers" *(youshou haoxian)*, and other "bad sorts" who shared a "fondness for valor and fighting" *(haoyong doulang)*.

Qing authorities maintained that the disorder and moral retrogression evident throughout southern Fujian and eastern Guangdong had set in during the mid-sixteenth century. At this time, local inhabitants began to form militia groups for defense of their communities (Wang ca. 1800:618). Heterodox fashions and decadent customs emerged at about the same period, according to some accounts. Merchants competed for petty profits, and artisans made useless products, while peasants grew indolent and abandoned their holdings (Guo 1547:176). That is to say, from the official point of view, harmful commercial influences had impinged upon the Confucian order and a once austere society, introducing unorthodox practices, unwarranted competition, and frivolous lifestyles.

Viewed from this orthodox perspective, moral degeneration had begun in this region nearly two centuries before serious *xiedou* disturbances were reported there. Subsequently, over the remainder of the Qing period, officials included armed feud strife among their lists of degenerate "customary evils." *Xiedou* disorder eventually became the worst of these evils in their reckoning, as they beheld the divisive tendencies of the communal feud spreading to increasingly larger areas.

In localities long afflicted by *xiedou* disorder, the results of enduring feuds seemed especially abhorrent and degrading. Not only were lives lost and property destroyed, but also the enmity perpetuated by extensive feuding had a stultifying effect on the minds of the inhabitants. Officials claimed that entire local populations grew sullen and accustomed to brutality. Moreover, the people who participated in feud affrays appeared barbarized. They even slew friends and, on occasion, affinal relatives and committed other inhuman acts, behaving more shamefully than bandits (Xie 1867:102; Zhao ca. 1788:78-79; Lang 1933:96).

Excessive violence of this sort, committed by distraught inhabitants under abnormal social conditions, provides evidence of local communities turned inward against themselves and the norms of their society. In the context of deviant subcultural influences depicted by Qing officials, enduring feuds and widespread *xiedou* strife tended to create a completely alienated population in the coastal prefectures and to breed further crime and dissidence among hostile ingroups. In feud-afflicted areas, these ingroups may be said to have formed countercultures, or *contracultures* as defined by J. Milton Yinger (1960), for the normative systems of their feuding communities operated in open conflict with the traditional values of Chinese society.

Alienated communities at feud, turned inward against themselves and against the prescribed cultural norms, posed a serious challenge to the Qing authorities. The inhabitants became disaffected from government to the point that even harsh measures or reprisal did not assure lasting success in restoring order (Xu 1882:5.1a-2a, 10b). Enclosed within their communities and receptive to starkly deviant countercultural influences, they were perhaps more out of reach of state controls, both coercive and spiritual, than even outlaw bands. At least one official who complained of such totally alienated inhabitants, afraid of neither government and law in this world nor ghosts and spirits in the next, believed this to be so (Cheng ca. 1830:623).

The southern Fujian and eastern Guangdong Region

Geographically, southern Fujian and eastern Guangdong were well-situated for feuding. The region formed part of the troubled "southern sea frontier" and was distant from the imperial court in Beijing. It was also remote from Fuzhou and Guangzhou, the provincial capitals of Fujian and Guangdong, both in physical setting and regional culture. The region is set off from surrounding areas by mountains and the sea, and its Hokkien and Hakka populations spoke dialects unintelligible to most provincial authorities and residents of either provincial capital. For centuries, weak and negligent government had prevailed in this secluded region.

Meanwhile, scarce resources and an expanding population exacerbated tensions between the local authorities and the inhabitants, causing competition within the commercialized coastal areas to grow particularly keen. By the Qing period, a shortage of arable land existed, not only in the interior mountainous areas settled by the Hakkas but also to the east in the valleys and scattered alluvial plains inhabited by Hokkien speakers. Deficiencies of rice developed throughout the densely populated lowland areas situated in the four coastal prefectures of Quanzhou and Zhangzhou in Fujian, and Chaozhou and Huizhou to the southwest in Guangdong.

The background for lineage rivalry

As official accounts indicate, troubled conditions of a serious nature had existed in southern Fujian and eastern Guangdong from at least the Jiajing reign (1522-1566) of the Ming dynasty. During that period, *wokou* pirate-adventurers laid waste to many coastal ports and walled cities further inland, while large forces of mountain brigands *(shankou)* pillaged the interior. By the latter part of the sixteenth century, only a small percentage of the lowland population was engaged in agrarian pursuits. More of the inhabitants depended on fishing, handicraft industries, and trade (Ng 1971, 1972).

Large corporate lineages *(zongzu)* began to form and multiply in the coastal prefectures during that century. Lineage growth was related to the spread of extensive local trading networks and the development of a more highly commercialized economy (Atwell 1982:79, 81-82; Rawski 1972:64-94). The subsequent spread of corporate lineages, boasting ancestral halls and estates with households numbering in the hundreds and thousands, helped to foster an uneven division of power and wealth within local society. Strong lineage communities tended to become rich at the expense of their weaker neighbors, as did their constituent families and overbearing kinsmen.

Dominant lineages in the same vicinity also became bitter rivals. In Quanzhou during the chaotic Wanli reign (1573-1619), rival lineages readily "took up arms and battled one another" *(chixie xiangge)*, a form of communal violence portending the *xiedou* outbreaks staged during the Qing period (Hu 1968:I, 27). On occasion, lineage rivals also banded to defend their home areas against outside predatory forces.

Continuous turbulence in the region was symptomatic of weak local government. After the worst *wokou* raids between 1555 and 1564, the state was rarely able to adjust to the needs of the region's commercialized economy and expanding maritime trade. Restrictions initiated by Ming and Qing rulers in the interest of the state often imposed great hardships on the inhabitants.

The gap between state interests and the welfare of the coastal inhabitants was most evident from 1662 to 1681. In those years, the Qing court ordered that entire coastal populations, from Shandong in the north to Guangdong far in the south, be evacuated inland to defend against incursions by the Ming loyalist Zheng Chenggong (Koxinga) and his seafaring compatriots. Harsh evacuation measures were most stringently carried out in the four coastal prefectures of southern Fujian and eastern Guangdong (Hsieh 1930-31:589-91). There a battlefront existed between Qing forces and the Zheng regime operating from Xiamen (Amoy), Jinmen, and Taiwan. Within these coastal prefectures, untold suffering was experienced by millions of displaced inhabitants during this grim twenty-year period (Zhu 1986:399-412).

After the evacuation ended, intense competition ensued in the coastal districts of these prefectures. A multitude of survivors swarmed back to resettle arable lands, stake out claims to trading and fishing territories, and gain control of the salt producing and military-colonist fields that had been turned over to private hands. Lineages and surname aggregates undoubtedly played a role in this competition, which also took place elsewhere in southern China (Watson 1982:80). Thereafter, lineage competition remained exceptionally keen in Quanzhou and Zhangzhou, where access to coastal and overseas maritime trade, by way of the newly opened (1684) port of Xiamen, brought considerable wealth to the area. There the stakes of long-term rivalry became appreciably higher than elsewhere in the region (Ng 1983:55-57, 61). The advent of lineage feuds and surname alliances in Quanzhou and Zhangzhou, as eventually reported by the 1720s, indicates that under Qing rule powerful lineages had again become dominant in the lowland areas of southern Fujian, including the districts along the seacoast.

The Yongzheng setting

Under Qing rule, Quanzhou and Zhangzhou were deemed the most disorderly prefectures (excepting Taiwan) in a province already considered difficult to govern. Official reports of conditions there, dating roughly from 1726 to 1730 (during the Yongzheng reign), clearly reveal dissidence and tension when *xiedou* outbreaks were first identified. In 1726, acute shortages of rice brought about protests and local disturbances in these two most rice-deficient prefectures of Fujian (YZCZZ 1729:IX, 305-07). Soon thereafter, feud strife between rival surname alignments added to the tension in the coastal areas.

Friction between the local authorities and inhabitants appeared in other ways as well. Fights between soldiers and commoners were frequent, especially at the prefectural center of Quanzhou (YZCZZ 1730:XVI, 248-49). Resistance to taxes and arrest also prevailed among influential households and powerful groups ranging from gentry families close to the seats of government to members of belligerent lineages situated in remote areas (YZCZZ 1726:V, 503-04; 1728:XII, 160-62; 1729:XIV, 717).

More conducive to feuding was the tension evidenced by blatant forms of intimidation throughout local society. In a memorial, a military official native to Fujian described the discord in Quanzhou and Zhangzhou:

> The noble maltreat the base; the rich take advantage of the poor; great surnames inflict sorrow and harm on small surnames. Great surnames [also] contend with great surnames and do not yield until there is a resort to arms. Against their opponents they press litigation that lasts for years without regard for the law (YZCZZ 1728:XI, 714).

Other officials pointed out more specific unruly elements that promoted such discord. In 1726, the Fujian governor identified two such types: able-bodied males of the large surnames who, in bodies numbering in the thousands, resided together in lineages; and "loafers" who were often kinsmen of local military officials (YZCZZ 1726:V, 583-84). In the first instance, the governor was referring to the males of belligerent lineages who engaged in feud affrays and had joined in the manacing surname alignments then under official investigation. The other type with influential kinship connections engaged in illicit manipulations of all sorts. Eventually, their networks would help to manage *xiedou* buildups through the recruitment of mercenaries and the arrangement of feuding alignments.

In their memorials, Qing officials also alluded to two sensitive issues relevant to lineage feuding in Fujian. One concerned pettifoggers *(songshi)* who formed networks between Fuzhou and the various prefectural and county seats (YZCZZ 1729:XIV, 76). Their illicit networks maintained close connections with officials and yamen underlings on the provincial and local levels, as well as with so-called bad sorts outside of government who involved themselves in disputes and litigation as a livelihood (YZCZZ

1729:XII, 677; XIV, 83-84). Due to these networks and their widespread operations, lawsuits had become unusually complex and costly and the provincial legal system exceptionally cumbersome and corrupt.

Gross malfunctions within the legal system led parties engaged in disputes to take matters into their own hands, according to official reports. Hence, the inhabitants were prone to quarrel and fight, and eventually feud, without recourse to the law and without waiting for delayed court decisions (YZCZZ 1729:XII, 677). Then, too, vindictive parties readily took advantage of the pettifogger networks as a means to implicate and prevail over their opponents. Lineage feuding provided many occasions for vicious use of the law. Resort to litigation became a common strategy employed throughout the course of a feud.

The other issue involved the practice of assigning military officials who were natives of Fujian to posts in their home province, a practice prevalent in Fujian under the Qing. As a consequence, military posts at all levels, even the highest in the province, were often held by Fujianese (YZCZZ 1726:V, 583-84). These provincials had many kin whom they were obliged to protect (YZCZZ 1726:VI, 354). Unscrupulous blood-relatives, such as the "loafers" described above, took undue advantage of their status. Lineages at feud with access to such kinship connections also maintained direct or indirect links with the military in their areas. This helped them to prevail over their rivals and gave them leverage in their dealings with the government beyond the usual fees, bribes, and personal contacts. In their clandestine dealings, these lineages may also have played off the civil officials against the military. Ranking civil officials from outside the province reportedly were disdainful of the military officials and suspicious of their inbred military activities (YZCZZ 1728:IX, 464-65).

During these years, officials identified other social types who, in their estimation, promoted discord in southern Fujian. Boxing and fencing masters *(quanbang jiaoshi)* were described as ruffians with a "fondness for valor and fighting." Their followers included not only vagrants and loafers but also the sons and younger brothers of the local gentry (YZCZZ 1726:VI, 839-40). Unscrupulous members of old and honorable families *(shijia)* were also depicted as a baneful influence, for they relied on their family connections to intimidate others (YZCZZ 1730:XVI, 427).

Members of prominent gentry families, in particular, were cited for their illicit actions and bullying tactics. Some operated mines in prohibited areas; others established local periodic markets without licenses, seized the produce of peddlars, and pocketed the tax revenues. Gentry families were reportedly involved in organized crime as well, fencing for robbers or engaging in smuggling (YZCZZ 1729:XIV, 717; XV, 258-61). Even these prominent families depended on lineage protection for success or survival in their bold ventures. The local discord they generated, in turn, provoked interlineage feuding in the tension-ridden society of Quanzhou and Zhangzhou.

Subsequent conditions

Conditions favorable to lineage and surname feuding continued to exist in southern Fujian for the remainder of the Qing dynasty. The same was true in eastern Guangdong, where *xiedou* outbreaks were reported in Chaozhou by the mid-eighteenth century and in Huizhou a few decades later (Cheng ca. 1830:623). Tensions and discord remained a common feature throughout the region, and the communal feud became a dominant form of strife in the coastal areas.

Evidence of weak government was still readily apparent as well. Qing systems of local control, such as the *baojia* and lineage headship *(zuzheng)* systems established during the Yongzheng and Qianlong (1736-1795) reigns, respectively, soon became inoperative. Meanwhile, the Qing legal system continued to malfunction, proving especially inadequate in areas where feuds spawned large numbers of criminal cases. Moreover, friction between the inhabitants and local authorities still prevailed. Throughout Chaozhou prefecture, Qing officials and their underlings hesitated to enter localities where *xiedou* disturbances were rife, while the inhabitants of feud-afflicted areas dared not enter walled county centers even for trade (Cheng ca. 1830:623). Also, eastern Guangdong military officials were often Chaozhou and Huizhou natives, similar to the situation in southern Fujian. Hence, kinship connections with the local military made lineage feuding and government responses a sensitive issue (see, for example, Zhou 1884:462).

By the latter part of the eighteenth century, more rampant disorder developed in the area, as happened throughout most of China. In the four coastal prefectures ominous signs, reported earlier during the Yongzheng reign, became grave realities. Sworn brotherhood groups grew into more extensive secret societies, and organized crime developed broader networks. The use and distribution of opium, previously noted in Zhangzhou and Xiamen, also became widespread (SCSX Qianlong 1755:19.8b-9a). Besides the more extensive crime and dissidence, lineage and surname feuding continued to prevail as a dominant form of strife, except for periods when large rebel or government forces intruded on the local scene (Lamley 1981b:27-28).

Lineage and surname feuding

In the four coastal prefectures, the principal parties at feud were lineages, or lineage branches (sublineages), usually of neighboring villages. Single-lineage villages, or villages dominated by one particular lineage or sublineage, were common in the lowland areas. Interlineage conflicts escalated when other parties were drawn into the feud. The most substantial groupings among these auxiliary parties tended to be either surname groups, consisting of nearby lineages and branches, or else communities of local inhabitants identified territorially by their villages, neighborhoods, or districts. Feud alliances led to the formation of alignments of a temporary nature, or to the establishment of surname confederations of a more permanent character. The *bao* and *qi* alignments reported in Tongan county in 1728, for example, developed into confederations that lasted for more than 100 years (Huang ca. 1850:116).

These communal feuds have sometimes been referred to as village or surname conflicts. Invariably, however, the original sets of rival lineages remained the chief contenders and, initially at least, the feuding was financed by the corporate wealth of their lineage communities. This corporate funding was mainly derived from ancestral estate (*jitian* or *zhengchangtian*) proceeds (Liu 1936:357-59). *Xiedou* engagements were costly affairs, however, and proved to be a severe drain on corporate wealth. As the feuding continued, the constituent families of the lineage were forced to make "private" *(si)* contributions. Among rural communities in Zhaoan county (in Zhangzhou), lineage feud funds were said to have been calculated on the basis of field acreage and the number of able-bodied adult males claimed by each household (Chen 1826:93).

Rival lineages at feud may seem at times to have merged in much larger surname or territorial alignments, or even to have been drawn into other interlineage feuds on an auxiliary basis through participation in feud alliances.[3] Nevertheless, these rival lineages continued to be the principal parties in *their* feud, and the course of that feud reflected their enduring hostile relationship. Moreover, they normally continued to provide the major share of feud funds. Alignments or confederations formed through feuding alliances apparently did not corporately finance *xiedou* buildups; surname or territorial allies *per se* were reluctant, as a rule, to contribute money to someone else's feud.

Often, hardships caused by sustained feuding fostered division within the lineage community. Hence, during the course of a long-term feud, Chinese lineages did not always maintain the cohesion and solidarity that have generally been regarded as major attributes of groups at feud (Beattie 1964:267; Black-Michaud 1975). In general, however, the *zongzu* type of lineage, formed upon the principle of common patrilineal descent from distant ancestors and bound by agnatic kinship ties, was a durable institution in a highly patriarchal society. This kind of lineage generally proved to be hardy and flexible enough in its operations to engage in enduring feuds lasting many generations.

Lineage feud traits

Befitting a commercialized region with scarce resources, the area's interlineage rivalries centered around profitable enterprises, on things in short supply or those of intrinsic commercial value. Quite often, such rivalries were already deeply rooted, or else tended to become so, when disputes failed to be resolved or when the parties involved directly resorted to violent retaliatory actions. At this stage, even minor incidents unrelated to the major issues at hand could lead to further misunderstandings and vicious acts of vengeful strife: kidnappings, assassinations, and false accusations causing punishment or death, for example, and eventually extensive *xiedou* engagements.

Xiedou engagements amounted to mutual reprisals on the part of entire lineages (or sublineages). Hence, they often marked the outset of communal feuds. Early in the Qing period, these armed contests may have been staged more in order to overawe and intimidate the opponent than to bring about death and destruction (YZCZZ 1729:XII, 677). Certainly, the ceremonial "beating of gongs and arrayal of weapons" *(mingluo liexie)* heralding the outbreak of such engagements constituted an ostentatious form of competition for locals fond of valor and sensitive as to lineage honor. By the Qianlong reign, officials began to report in detail the procedures involved in staging deadly *xiedou* conflicts. These accounts indicate common practices of lineages at feud in Fujian and Guangdong (see, for example, HQZY 1766:4697-702).

The basic preparations for *xiedou* engagements, as summarized in the 1825 substatute, included the mobilization of manpower, gathering adequate funds, and setting the dates of battles. Manpower was needed mainly for the armed bands of braves *(yong)* who engaged in the fighting. The numerous able-bodied kinsmen of belligerent lineages were on hand for these engagements, although wealthy lineages sometimes preferred to hire mercenaries rather than risk the loss of their own men. Moreover, destitute men were contracted to serve as "substitutes" *(dingxiong)* for those who committed homicides in battle. Poor kinsmen are said to have competed for the chance to join feud bands as fighting braves, or to serve as "substitutes" when arrests were made, in return for benefits promised to their families (Wang ca. 1800:619). Nonkin destitutes were also exploited; during the nineteenth century, for example, lineages reportedly purchased young boys for adoption from impoverished families outside the lineage. When armed affrays occurred, these "adopted sons" were ordered to fight in the forefront of feud battles or to become "substitutes." During lulls in *xiedou* outbreaks, they were sent overseas to earn money for the lineage (Huang ca. 1850:121-22).

Xiedou engagements were expensive affairs. Hired mercenaries had to be paid, and pensions and other benefits were allotted to the families of "substitutes" executed for confessing to crimes of homicide. The purchase of arms and ammunition became another substantial cost during the nineteenth century, when modern firearms were used by lineages at feud. Even larger sums had to be set aside for expenses subsequent to armed affrays. Then the civil and military officials, along with their retinues of soldiers and yamen underlings, had to be bribed and paid fees as well as "travelling costs." Sometimes funds were also required to pay off the rival side when peace settlements or truces were arranged. Finally, money had to be raised for the costly litigation that ensued as an outcome of the crimes and destruction inherent in feuds (Liu 1936:361). The costs of bribes and litigation normally proved to be the heaviest expenses over the course of a feud. These costs required continuous payments that depleted the corporate and private wealth of lineages at feud and caused divisive tendencies within the lineage community (Chen 1826:93-94).

The timing of *xiedou* engagements was a serious matter of feud strategy, for incidents sufficient to incite armed affray could occur at almost any time. *Xiedou* outbreaks were reported throughout much of the year in southern Fujian and eastern Guangdong. They do not appear to have conflicted with the seasonal manpower needs of agricultural communities, for only a fraction of the dense population in the coastal areas was engaged in full-time farming. Moreover, *xiedou* were not confined to rural villages; territorial alignments encompassed market and port towns and the suburbs of walled cities as well. From general accounts, *xiedou* outbreaks appeared to be more frequent during the early course of a feud (an impression also conveyed by Liu 1936:362). However, the timing and frequency of feud affrays depended on conditions within the rival lineage communities involved, as well as on the general situation. Officials reported lull periods of lineage feuding in their areas, corresponding to low points of violence in local feud cycles (Huang ca. 1850:121-22).

What may be termed the "classic" version of the interlineage *xiedou* involved careful planning. The managers of such contests announced the dates of battle in advance, so that the communities could prepare and neighbors be forewarned of the impending outbreak of these grim but stirring spectacles of violence. However, Qing officials perhaps overemphasized date-setting as a consistent trait in armed feud strife in order to classify *xiedou* as a type of "planned affray." Sources indicate, especially during the nineteenth century, that *xiedou* often amounted to surprise attacks by one village on another (Dai ca. 1870:26b). Neither were *xiedou* arrangements always so carefully planned when leadership gravitated to less cautious elements within lineages at feud, or when parties from without, including powerful local chieftains and venal officials and underlings, sought to foment *xiedou* outbreaks for their own profit.

Qing accounts deal primarily with *xiedou* actions and provide relatively little information on the less violent aspects of the communal feud. They do reveal that lineages kept score of the dead and wounded so that they might retaliate in kind or use such figures in peace negotiations. Unlike parties at feud elsewhere in the world (Black-Michaud 1975:240), however, the respective sides also took pains to conceal or dismember corpses following *xiedou* battles, instead of publicly disclosing the numbers slain. By reducing or eliminating homicide counts in this manner, lineages attempted to avoid the trouble and expense involved in official investigations and criminal proceedings. Following active armed affrays, truces or settlements were sometimes arranged. In areas of Guangdong, "tittering elders" representing both sides of the conflict reportedly met to joke, exchange betel nut, and create an atmosphere conducive to peace negotiations (Niida 1952:360). Overall, though, few if any customary rules and binding obligations developed for the pacification of interlineage feuding. Truces and peace settlements appear to have been drawn up and then broken primarily on the basis of feud strategies.

The lack of customary restraints regulating interlineage feuds can be attributed in part to the crucial role played by the Qing government in the feud process. When crowds gathered and homicides occurred, local officials were obliged to intercede and make arrests. No matter how corrupt the authorities proved to be, or how tardy they were in their responses, the government eventually took action during sustained communal feuds that gave rise to *xiedou* violence and major crimes. The homicide and affray cases that resulted were tried and reviewed in yamen courts at various levels. Feud-related lawsuits over "minor" disputes and grievances, initiated on behalf of rival lineage clients, were similarly judged in the local government courts. Hence, litigation formed an important element in the course of interlineage feuds; and the Qing legal process, involving arrests, trials, and punishment, served as a principal form of control in lieu of any well-developed customary restraints. In this respect, the state became a third party to the communal feud.

Furthermore, dedicated officials at times attempted to arbitrate between rival lineages or to sponsor mediation that could lead to truces and pacification. Prominent gentry and other influential local parties, who served as mediators, acted on behalf or in support of the government. Local officials, through their runners and agents, may have influenced or kept track of mediatory efforts as well.[4] Such positive efforts by the Qing government to foster constraints to local feuding, however, were offset by the antics of venal officials and underlings who sought to incite and profit from *xiedou* strife. Due to their malicious influence, the state became more often a predatory party to feuds than a pacificatory third party. The efforts by lineages at feud to gain advantages by way of officials and underlings through bribes and connections served to reinforce this predacious role of the government in the feud process.

Nineteenth-century feuding

During the nineteenth century, the importation of modern firearms had a profound effect on lineage feuding in southern Fujian and eastern Guangdong. Previously, a variety of old-style weapons had been employed in *xiedou* engagements, varying from sharp-edged farm implements to an assortment of knives, clubs, spears, and musketry—mainly gingals *(zhuchong)* and fowling pieces *(niao-qiang)*. Such weapons were plentiful and had been in common use among the inhabitants throughout the coastal areas since the mid-Ming period (Chen 1826:85; YZCZZ 1728:IX, 573). Because these weapons generally had only a short range, armed feud affrays had consisted of closely drawn pitched battles on appointed fields of combat. During the nineteenth century, the increasingly widespread use of Western-type rifles, along with both old-style and modern cannons, led to modifications in the style of warfare. Armed feud bands fought more frequently from protected positions instead of engaging in open combat as before. This new style of engagement also brought on armed assaults against villages, including surprise attacks.

Vicious armed reprisals against rival settlements adversely affected entire local populations. Homes and villages were burned down; crops and fields were trampled upon or dug up; orchards were destroyed. Pillaging also took place, and inhabitants not engaged in combat were molested (Zhang ca. 1886:XIV, 14.9a-b). As a result, villages became more heavily fortified, with stout walls, cannon emplacements, and watch towers (Niida 1952:386).

The widespread use of modern firearms and a new style of combat created a need for skilled marksmen in feud affrays. So-called gunmen (*qiangshou* or *chongshou*), trained in the use of Western-type rifles as well as old-style muskets, were contracted as mercenaries by lineages at feud in the more prosperous coastal areas. These hired killers added to the terror spawned by feud strife. When not employed in *xiedou* violence, they were contracted for other vengeful acts of violence, such as assassinations, or they robbed and pillaged on their own. An idea of the prevalence of such gunmen and their menacing nature may be gained from the feud-afflicted conditions in Tongan where, in 1837, some 248 gun towers spread over 168 rural districts of that county were torn down. Constructed from rock slabs taken from nearby ruined dwellings, these towers had enabled marksmen to lie in wait for adversaries and to rob passersby (Huang ca. 1850:117). The actions of professional mercenaries undoubtedly increased the number of feud-related incidents elsewhere as well (Scarth 1860).

Feud alignments and networks

The prevalence of skilled mercenaries engaged for local feuds indicates greater outside participation and the escalation of large-scale feuding. Interlineage feuds had already assumed extensive proportions by way of surname and territorial alignments. By the early nineteenth century, the development of professional mercenary bands, detached from local lineage and surname groups, further escalated feud warfare in some coastal areas. Local chieftains and "strongmen" *(tuhao)*, along with the ruffian and loafer types described above, organized networks among these professional bands and other armed gangs to foster feud buildups. These networks sometimes superseded feud alignments formed through intergroup alliances.

Surname alignments were the first mode of extended feud buildup reported in conjunction with *xiedou* outbreaks. In 1729, a year after the existence of *bao* and *qi* alignments was officially reported, other different-surname *(yixing)* alliances bearing similar descriptive group titles (*tong, hai,* and *wan*) were identified in Quanzhou (YZCZZ 1729:XIV, 717). This so-called *huizu* ("assembled lineages") form typical of feud buildups in Zhangzhou as well, gave rise to "surname affrays" *(xingdou)*. Rival alignments, based on alliances among local descent groups bearing the same or different surnames, were generally rural in nature, spanning a number of villages in a given locality or district. Some surname confederations lasted for many generations, as noted above, and probably maintained roughly the same local alignments.

Territorial alignments, in contrast, tended to be more extensive but less enduring in nature. Termed *huixiang* ("associated districts"), these alignments sometimes encompassed several districts, including towns and suburban areas. In order to survive, virtually all households had to support the feud alignment that "protected" their particular locality whenever far-reaching "district affrays" *(xiangdou)* occurred (Xie 1867:103-04). The feuding networks, organized and controlled by local chieftains and "strongmen," also brought about territorial buildups of a paramilitary character. Such networks appear to have drawn primarily criminal and vagrant elements into *xiedou* engagements.

These feuding networks developed after gangs of professional mercenaries had become organized into "banner societies" *(qihui)* in a number of counties. For example, Red and White Banners operated in Zhangpu county in Zhangzhou, as did banner societies displaying the same colors in Huian county in Quanzhou. Elsewhere, the Red and Black Banners active in Haifeng and Lufeng counties in Huizhou remained in operation well into the twentieth century (Xie 1867:104; Lang 1935:117-21). In areas of these counties local banner societies functioned as competing bands under different banners. When *xiedou* outbreaks were staged, each hired out to a rival side. The Red and Black Banners of Lufeng were perhaps the most notorious of these mercenary societies. They came into existence after the territorial or *huixiang* form of feud alignment had developed there during the 1820s. By approximately 1860, these two societies had expanded their operations to ten or more counties in Huizhou and Chaozhou (Xu 1882:5.53b).

The intrusion of criminal elements into communal feud operations is evident in Lufeng, where Red and Black chieftains readily recruited banner gunmen for feud buildups, along with bandits and indigents. Whenever they learned of impending *xiedou* outbreaks, these chieftains negotiated contracts for their recruits, then assumed control of the fighting (Xu 1882:5.53a-54b). Similarly, local strongmen are said to have become the chief instigators of *xiedou* strife in areas of Chaozhou. These ruffians had close contacts with bandits and the "fences" *(wozang)* and pawnshops that served their gangs. When feud violence flared up, they mustered bandits by the hundreds and collected crowds of vagrants from many districts (Lin ca. 1890:144-45).

Lineages suffered from this unbridled feuding. Lineage leaders who had originally instigated armed feuds tended to lose control as power gravitated into the hands of professional criminals, often from outside the lineage. Tension also mounted within feud-ridden lineages when corporate funds were depleted and each household was forced to contribute money or able-bodied males. Under these circumstances, lineage members reportedly turned against one another, and poor kinsmen extorted money from wealthy ones (Huang ca. 1850:119). Such intralineage friction between rich and poor households appears to have been common under the impact of continuous *xiedou* strife. Changes in lineage leadership and the impoverishment of wealthy kinsmen were frequent (Cheng 1826:93). In large-scale feud buildups, when the management of *xiedou* engagements was taken over by desperadoes who may have been virtual strangers to the principal lineages at feud, the tension and anxiety was undoubtedly even more acute.

In order to support more costly and devastating feud affrays, lineages had to turn elsewhere for financial support beyond corporate estates and private contributions. Nineteenth-century sources indicate that belligerent Fujian and Guangdong lineages oftentimes depended heavily on remittances (and arms) received from kinsmen overseas. From at least the Opium War period (1839-1842), it also appears that powerful households, along with other lineage elements, more frequently resorted to organized crime to augment their income. In Quanzhou and Zhangzhou lineages, members were reported to be active in opium rings and salt smuggling. They also engaged in protection rackets, jailbreaks and robberies, and figured in syndicates dealing with stolen property (Huang ca. 1850:103-04, 125-26, 132). Through these criminal activities and their connections with mercenary gangs, lineages at feud may also have established links with secret societies in the region, or at least so local officials thought (*Canton Archive* 1853).

Causation and motivation

Having described the background and nature of lineage feuding in southern Fujian and eastern Guangdong, we may conclude by identifying causes and motives for this enduring type of violence. From a broad perspective such feuding seems to have been a response to unstable ecological and socioeconomic conditions and a product of the keen competition and rivalry that prevailed in the commercialized coastal prefectures. These general factors of historical causation, however, do not serve to explain fully the more specific incentives and impulses which motivated lineage feuding under Qing rule. Such motivation is also vital to the understanding of the feud process considered in the context of a deviant regional subculture and local countercultures. Endemic communal feuding was both a product and a catalyst of the dissidence and violence that had long prevailed in the region.

Historical causation

Lineage feuding amounted to an extreme form of competition for scarce resources in a relatively overpopulated area. However, the model of "total scarcity" applied by anthropologists to impoverished regions of the Mediterranean is not suitable for this region. For overseas maritime trade, interregional commerce, and remittances from Hokkien communities abroad brought wealth to the region. Local industries—commercial agriculture, handicrafts, fishing, and salt production—also helped to enrich the coastal lowland economy.

Issues of local contention included land and boundary disputes and controversies over water rights. Attempts to monopolize local markets, transportation systems, and mineral resources also created rivalries between lineage communities, as did competition over grave sites and even marriage, in localities where there were shortages of marriageable females (Niida 1952:378; Xie 1869:102; Chen 1826:83). Furthermore, intangible matters that were felt to be vital to communities at large served as pretexts for feud conflicts in the local competition for control of scarce resources. The redemption of debts, misunderstandings involving reputation and pride, and disputes hinging on ancestral and lineage honor were common examples of such sensitive issues.[5]

The rival lineages of the coastal prefectures figure in reckonings of historical causation as well. They were the aggressors in the feud: communal feuding was initiated and financed for both predatory and defensive purposes. The momentum and possibly the outcome of the contest depended on the fortitude of the principal lineages involved. Large and powerful lineages were apt to experience division among their branches and family units, and even the richest lineages stood to become impoverished over time. Meanwhile, small and weak lineages, lacking adequate wealth and manpower or powerful allies, were in danger of utter extinction in feud-afflicted localities (for example, see Fielde 1894:128-31).

Yet, the *zongzu* lineage proved to be an effective instrument for the communal feud. Obligations based on agnatic kinship and common descent formed enduring bonds for the lineage community. Extensive kinship and descent ties also figured in feud alliances and were important in forming connections with kin who served as local military officials or yamen underlings. Clearly, the principal lineages at feud functioned as discrete corporate groups. Their discreteness, as Peters (1975:xxvi) illustrates in the case of Bedouin feud competition, enabled them to operate decisively without being hampered by a multiplicity of crosscutting ties of the kind that tended to induce compromise. Marriage links between lineages at feud, for instance, did not prevent mutual acts of violence. In fact, affinal relationships reportedly were severed during *xiedou* engagements (Zhao ca. 1788:78; Freedman 1966:112-13).

Corporate lineages at feud also operated as wealthy economic units in their respective localities. Befitting the commercialized setting, such lineages relied in part on contractual agreements and cash payments to carry on their feud hostilities. "Substitutes" were contracted within the lineage, and mercenaries were hired on a monetary basis. Later on, the services of professional mercenaries required a more extensive use of contracts until, ultimately, local chieftains and strongmen served as outside contractors in negotiations involving feud buildups in some areas. Although such buildups were based on contractual agreements rather than on obligations of agnation and descent, corporate and private lineage wealth still financed these paramilitary ventures. In addition, wealthy lineages could afford the services of pettifogger networks vital to their feud strategies. Such litigation contracts, as well as other illicit connections with criminal or yamen networks, were established at great cost, usually through patron-client relationships.

Moreover, belligerent lineages functioned as powerful political entities in a region where weak government prevailed. Anthropologist Maurice Freedman (1966:115-17) argues that lineages in Fujian and Guangdong grew so powerful that they were able not only to oppose rivals in their area but also to fend off and make use of the state as well. Nevertheless, local government played crucial roles as a party in the feud process. We must also note that even powerful lineages did not challenge the legitimacy of the dynasty. Neither did they disavow orthodox beliefs and practices, based on ancestor worship and patriarchy, that were intrinsic to the Chinese lineage. Hence, in its pacification efforts, the Qing state was inclined to be tolerant of unruly lineages in southern Fujian and eastern Guangdong even though they exercised a pernicious influence through their bitter and destructive feuds (Lamley 1981b:29-30).

Feud motivation

Because the feud is such a private and secretive sort of operation, the motives and strategies that serve to perpetuate feuding are usually difficult to detect. In the case of the lineage feuds discussed here there is little direct evidence as to which particular incentives and impulses gave rise to feud violence at any given time. Even the various sorts of feud leaders—the managers who masterminded and "screened" the violence and the "fierce and stupid" kinsmen who more openly took command during armed affrays—are hard to trace, as Fujian officials acknowledge in their initial reports of *xiedou* outbreaks (YZCZZ 1728:IX, 571-72). However, it seems clear that motives and strategies tended to change during the course of a feud, as did the leadership. Judging from Qing documentary accounts, the parties who sought to instigate or capitalize on lineage feud strife, whether bellicose kinsmen or enterprising outsiders, came from virtually all social levels. Lineage and surname feuding in Fujian and Guangdong cannot simply be attributed to the selfish designs of the gentry-landlord class nor to the interests of an alleged "feudal aristocracy."[6]

Furthermore, one may infer that feud motives were intelligible, at least in their intent and probably consequences, to the lineage members involved. For such motivation, to be effective, must derive from attitudes, behavior, and values familiar to the group as a whole. In southern Fujian and eastern Guangdong, where bitter rivalries and vindictive practices had long persisted, the inhabitants were well-attuned to the cultural and psychological influences that stimulated lineage feud violence.

Official accounts depicting a deviant regional subculture, although biased, are helpful in identifying sources of this mode of communal violence. Villagers and townspeople tended to cluster in discrete surname communities that nurtured distant and unfriendly relationships with neighboring and other outside groups. Prolonged rivalry among these estranged groups bred hostility and violent practices. Intense competition over scarce resources and disputes touching on sensitive matters, such as pride and honor, further served to make violent behavior acceptable and commonplace among competing groups. Moreover, deeply ingrained traditions relating to organized violence, such as those perpetuated by militia organizations and martial arts associations, were cherished by the inhabitants as essential to their survival. Hence, Qing authorities found it as difficult to confiscate household weapons and disband boxing and fencing societies as to inculcate norms of harmony among the inhabitants (YZCZZ 1728:IX, 573; 1726:VI, 839-40).

In this hostile environment, human life was treated lightly by disgruntled multitudes who shared but little of the region's slender resources. Throughout most of the coastal areas, where there existed great disparities of wealth, belligerent lineages drew heavily from this indigent manpower to stage armed feud affrays. As feud patterns became more extensive through alliances and networks, larger segments of the population were caught up in communal feud violence. These villagers and townspeople also became subject to reprisals on the part of vengeful adversaries and targets of abuse by corrupt officials and their soldiers and underlings. Closed off and under great tension, they, too, became susceptible to more deviant norms and practices characteristic of ingroup countercultures.

At this stage of open-ended feuding, the motivation behind outbreaks of communal strife was undoubtedly diverse and even contradictory in nature, given the sizable populations involved and the variety of lineage leaders and outsiders who manipulated feud strategies. Even under these extreme conditions, though, two elements still appear to have been dominant in lineage feud motivation. One was the impulse of fear; the other was profit.

Fear has always been a companion to the feud. Recurrent acts of homicidal revenge naturally tend to foster dread and anxiety among bitter rivals. Open-ended communal feuding induced fear and tension of an even greater scope. Costly *xiedou* engagements threatened not only to bring death and destruction to lineage communities and neighboring localities but also to incur state intervention and deplete the resources of the lineages involved. The possibility of ultimate defeat at the hand of stronger adversaries was also a terrifying prospect. Under such threatening conditions fear became a powerful impulse that helped to maintain cohesion within lineages and to counter divisive tendencies among their branches and household units. Fear also served to alienate feud-ridden communities and localities from most outside contacts and to strengthen ingroup inclinations. Although the alienated inhabitants may have seemed unafraid of government and law, as Qing officials claimed, lineage members at feud were reportedly fearful of the overbearing types they encountered, including soldiers, runners, and unscrupulous "bad sorts," as well as branch leaders and family heads within the lineage who collected feud funds by intimidation (Chen 1826:93).

Fear, however, seems to have been offset by the prospect of profit, for the feud was regarded as a potentially profitable venture by all concerned. Rival lineages and alignments expected to profit at the expense of their opponents. Even though armed affrays were expensive and constituted an economic risk, lineages nonetheless calculated their corporate funds and private resources, then invested in *xiedou* contests to gain both tangible rewards and intangible benefits. A variety of predatory individuals also sought to profit from enduring feud strife. These included government authorities, banner-society chieftains, local strongmen, professional mercenaries, pettifoggers and their networks, and other sorts who gained a livelihood from litigation and violence. Meanwhile, destitute elements, both within and outside of feuding communities, fed off the feud during violent intervals as "substitutes" and mercenaries.

The profit motive was so keen that one may liken lineage feuding to a business venture or enterprise. Indeed, in feud-afflicted areas of the four coastal prefectures, feuding amounted to a native industry, akin to organized gambling, smuggling, and other illicit operations. This "feud industry" offered rather steady employment to indigent inhabitants and encouraged some to assume careers as professional mercenaries. It also had some positive impact on the local economy. Concentrations of corporate lineage wealth were redistributed, and remittances were attracted from kinsmen overseas for investment in feud affrays. Characteristic of a native industry, feud enterprise appealed to the popular temperament, for the coastal Hokkien people were venturesome and prone to gamble and take risks in their business pursuits.

Unlike most illicit businesses, however, the general operation of this localized "feud industry" was neither tightly controlled nor systematically managed. Rival lineages, the principal directors and investors, failed to develop binding rules and restraints for their feud ventures. Moreover, their open-ended communal feuding allowed outside participants and manipulators to engage in this enterprise and at times exert control over local feud operations. On the other hand, neither were there many outside restraints or deterrents to feud enterprise. The state, functioning as both a predatory and a pacificatory party to the communal feud, provided only partial constraints to the feud process through the working of weak local government. Limitations of funds and resources available for feuding, coupled with the fear of retaliatory actions and their consequences, served as ad hoc checks to the growth of the industry.

The lack of effective restraints, either of a formal or informal variety, to this lineage feuding is a feature that makes the Chinese communal feud seem strikingly different from the blood-feud that anthropologists have studied in tribal societies (Black-Michaud 1975; Boehm 1984). Within most tribal societies the blood-feud operated in accordance with clearly set customary restraints and functioned as an effective jural mechanism by which conflicts could be warded off and disputes solved. In contrast, belligerent lineages in southern Fujian and eastern Guangdong flourished in a deviant subculture and turbulent society only loosely controlled by the state. Violent customs and practices had long prevailed there in defiance of orthodox norms prescribing harmony. In the coastal prefectures rival lineages and their open-ended feuds operated within this subcultural tradition of hostility with few constraints and tended to breed further dissidence and violence. Obviously, the "peace in the feud" concept that Max Gluckman (1956) has related to blood-feud conditions in Africa does not apply to the violent local climate engendered by belligerent lineages and the communal feud in Fujian and Guangdong under Qing rule.

Notes

1. In this essay, the term *communal feud* denotes relatively un-restrained feuding between rival groups within a given society. The *blood-feud*, on the other hand, has been described as a conflict more subject to control by customary rules and restraints. Maurice Freedman, who dealt with lineage feuds in southeastern China in his major work on the Chinese lineage, came to prefer the term *vendetta* rather than *feud* or *blood-feud* on the basis of this distinction (1966:107-08). For useful definitions of the terms *feud, vendetta,* and *war,* see J. Beattie (1964:267-68). Recent anthropological research on the blood-feud is discussed in Black-Michaud (1975). Also useful is the excellent study of blood revenge by Boehm (1984).

2. The term was frequently used in reference to the subethnic feuding between groups of Chinese settlers in Taiwan during the eighteenth and nineteenth centuries. These settler groups hailed from various parts of southern Fujian and eastern Guangdong and formed rival enclaves based on distinctions of speech, religious observances, and native-place origins (Lamley 1981a:291-309). Distinctions of ethnicity and provenance also tended to set overseas Chinese communities apart. The *xiedou* designation, however, was only applied occasionally to feud affrays in Southeast Asia and North America. The term was used more often with regard to interethnic feuding throughout mainland China: rather frequently in reports of Hakka-Punti strife in Guangdong and Guangxi; and less often in accounts of Han vs. Muslim and Commoner vs. Christian affrays. Also, feud conflicts between sects or sworn-brotherhood groups were sometimes labeled *xiedou*. During the nineteenth century, armed affrays between villages in various parts of China were also referred to as *xiedou* at times (Lamley 1977:10-16).

3. See the model for interlineage conflicting alliances in Baker (1979:144-46). I have not been able to ascertain whether such feuding alliances stemmed from earlier intervillage alliances of the type that David Faure discusses in respect to the New Territories of Hong Kong (1986:28-29).

4. A more careful watch seems to have been kept on belligerent lineages during the Yongzheng reign as reflected in the awards and honors that were bestowed on lineage communities that remained at peace (SCSX Yongzheng 1726:26.14b).

5. Baker's (1979:219-25) appendix on *fengshui* fighting in Zhejiang is indicative of local conflicts related to both tangible (grave sites) and intangible (pride and ancestral honor) matters. Bitter rivalry over geomantic sitings nurtured feuding throughout southeastern China.

6. A recent study of *xiedou* strife in Guangdong stresses the role of the landlord-gentry class in lineage feuding by the mid-Qing period (Tan 1985:8-11). Liu (1936:365-66) relates feud strife between large and small lineages in Fujian to the tradition of aristocratic Chinese lineages of the distant past when noble ranks and hereditary privileges prevailed among upperclass lines of descent.

References

Atwell, William S.
1982 "International Bullion Flows and the Chinese Economy Circa 1530-1650," *Past and Present* 95:68-90.

Baker, Hugh D.R.
1979 *Chinese Family and Kinship*. New York: Columbia University Press.

Beattie, J.
1964 "Feud." In J. Gould and W.L. Kolb, eds., *A Dictionary of the Social Sciences*. New York: Free Press of Glencoe.

Bian, Baodi
ca. 1894 *Bian Zhijun (Songchen) Zhengshu*. Taibei. 1968 reprint.

Black-Michaud, Jacob
1975 *Cohesive Force: Feud in the Mediterranean and the Middle East*. Oxford: Blackwell.

Boehm, Christopher
1984 *Blood Revenge: The Anthropology of Feuding in Montenegro and Other Tribal Societies*. Lawrence, Kan.: University Press of Kansas.

Canton Archive
1853 *Canton Archive*. Public Record Office. London: F.O. 682 137/6 (7:F-L).

Chen Shengshao
1826 *Wensu Lu*. Beijing. 1983 reprint.

Cheng Hanzhang
ca. 1830 "Lun Xi Dou Shu." In JSWB 1887.

Dai Chaochen
ca. 1870 *Conggong Sanlu*. n.p.

Faure, David
1986 *The Structure of Chinese Rural Society: Lineage and Village in the Eastern New Territories*. Hong Kong: Oxford University Press.

Fielde, Adele M.
1894 *A Corner of Cathay: Studies from Life Among the Chinese*. New York and London: Macmillan and Co.

Freedman, Maurice
    1966 *Chinese Lineage and Society: Fukien and Kwangtung.* London: Athlone.

Gluckman, Max
    1956 "The Peace in the Feud." In Max Gluckman, *Custom and Conflict in Africa.* Oxford: Blackwell.

Guo Zhunzhen
    1547 *Chaozhoufu Zhi.* Reprinted in Rao Zongyi (comp.), *Chaozhou Zhi Huibian.* Hong Kong, 1965.

HQZY
    various *Huang Qing Zouyi.* Taibei. 1967 reprint. (Qing memorials are cited by separate dates.)

Hsiao Kung-chuan
    1960 *Rural China: Imperial Control in the Nineteenth Century.* Seattle: University of Washington Press.

Hsieh Kuo-ching
    1930-31 "Removal of Coastal Population in the Early Tsing Period." *Chinese Social and Political Science Review* 15:559-96.

Hu Puan
    1968 *Zhonghua Quanguo Fengsu Zhi.* 2 vols. Taibei reprint.

Huang Juezi
    ca. 1850 *Huang Juezi Zousu Xu Naiji Zouyi Hekan*, compiled by Qi Sihe. Beijing. 1959 reprint.

JSWB
    1887 *Huangchao Jingshi Wenbian*, compiled by He Changling. Taibei. 1963 reprint.

Lamley, Harry J.
    1977 "Hsieh-tou: The Pathology of Violence in Southeastern China." *Ch'ing-shih Wen-t'i* 3 (7):1-39.

    1981a "Subethnic Rivalry in the Ch'ing Period," in Emily M. Ahern and Hill Gates, eds., *The Anthropology of Taiwanese Society.* Stanford, Calif.: Stanford University Press.

    1981b "Belligerent Lineages at Feud Under the Ch'ing." Paper presented at the Conference on Orthodoxy and Heterodoxy in Late Imperial China: Cultural Beliefs and Social Divisions. Montecito, Calif., August 20-26.

1986 "Hsieh-tou Violence: Manifestations of the Chinese Communal Feud During the Ch'ing Dynasty." Paper presented at the Second International Conference on Sinology. Taibei, December 29-31.

Lan Dingyuan
1723 *Ping Tai Jilue*. Taibei. 1958 reprint.

Lang Qingxiao
1933 "Zhongguo nanfang xiedou zhi yuanyin ji qi zizhi." *Dongfang Zazhi* 30 (19):81-96.

1935 "Qingdai Yuedong Xiedou Shishi." *Lingnan Xuebao* 4 (2):103-51.

Lin Daquan
ca. 1890 "Lin Taiye Wenchao," in Wen Tingjing, comp., *Chayang Sanjia Wenchao*. Taibei. n.d. reprint.

Liu Xingtang
1936 "Fujian di Xuezu Zushi." *Shihuo Banyue Kan*, 4 (8):356-68.

Ng Chin-keong
1971 "The Fukien Maritime Trade in the Second Half of the Ming Period—Government Policy and Elite Groups' Attitudes." *Nanyang University Journal* 5:81-100.

1972 "A Study of the Peasant Society of South Fukien, 1506-1644." *Nanyang University Journal* 6:189-212.

1983 *Trade and Society: The Amoy Network on the China Coast, 1683-1735*. Singapore: Singapore University Press.

Niida Noboru
1952 *Chūgoku no Nōson Kazoku*. Tokyo.

Peters, E.L.
1975 "Foreword." In Jacob Black-Michaud, *Cohesive Forces: Feud in the Mediterranean and the Middle East*. Oxford: Blackwell.

Rawski, Evelyn S.
1972 *Agricultural Change and the Peasant Economy of South China*. Cambridge, Mass.: Harvard University Press.

Scarth, John
1860 *Twelve Years in China: The People, the Rebels, and the Mandarins, by a British Resident*. Edinburgh: T. Constable and Co.

SCSX
various *Da Qing Shichao Shengxun*. Beijing. ca. 1879. (Imperial
instructions are cited by separate reigns, dates, and juan numbers.)

Tan Dihua
1985 "Luelun Qingdai Guangdong Zongzu Xiedou." Reprinted in
Qingshi Yanjiu Tongxun 3:6-11.

Wang Zhiyi
ca. 1800 "Jing Chen Zhihua Zhang Quan Fengsu Shu." In JSWB 1887.

Watson, Rubie S.
1982 "The Creation of a Chinese Lineage: The Teng of Ha Tsuen,
1669-1751." *Modern Asian Studies* 16:69-100.

Xie Jinluan
1867 "Gezinan Jilue," in Ding Yuejian, comp., *Zhi Tai Bigao Lu*.
Taibei. 1959 reprint.

Xu Gengbi
1882 *Buziqiezhai Mancun*. n.p.

Xue Yunsheng
1970 *Duli Cunyi Zhongkan Ben*, Huang Jingjia, ed. Taibei.

Yinger, J. Milton
1960 "Contraculture and Subculture." *American Sociological Review*
25 (5):625-35.

YZCZZ
various *Gongzhongdang Yongzheng Chao Zouzhe*. 32 vols. National
Palace Museum, ed. Taipei. 1978 reprint. (Memorials are cited by separate
dates and volume numbers.)

Zhang Zhidong
ca. 1886 *Zhang Wenxiang Gong Quanji*. Beijing. 1937 reprint.

Zhao Yi
ca. 1788 *Yanpu Zaji*. Beijing. 1982 reprint.

Zhou Hengzhong
1884 *Chaoyangxian Zhi*. Taibei. 1966 reprint.

Zhu Weigang
n.d. *Fujian Shi Gao*. Vol. 2. Fujian.

Chapter 3

Ethnic Violence in Modern China:
Hans and Huis in Gansu, 1781-1929

Jonathan N. Lipman

Let us begin with a question common to ethnic conflicts all over the world: Why do people who have lived in proximity for decades, generations, even centuries, whose towns and villages resemble each other very closely in many ways, and who share significant cultural traits and perhaps even a common language but who define one another as different—why do such people sometimes take up weapons and kill one another in large numbers? Answering this question, whether for northern Ireland or Palestine, Afghanistan or California, requires a subtle comprehension of specific places and times as well as some general rubric for understanding motivation toward violence. In this chapter, I address only the former objective, the description and interpretation of particular instances of ethnic violence in China. For an exploration of the latter, see Harrell's introduction herein.

China, as with the United States or the Soviet Union, is a polyethnic nation-state with a single dominant ethnic group and a host of minorities. Unlike many other societies, however, China's largest ethnic group, who call themselves Hans and who are usually called *the Chinese* by us, represent 94 percent of the population, an unassailably vast majority. But living among and around the Hans are people of diverse languages and cultures, ranging from the millions of Turkic speaking people lumped together by the Chinese state as Uigurs to the few thousand Mongolian-speaking Muslims of the Bonan group, whose culture and language have been tucked away in an isolated northwestern Chinese valley since the time of Chinggis Khan. Thus, to speak of "ethnic violence" in China, we

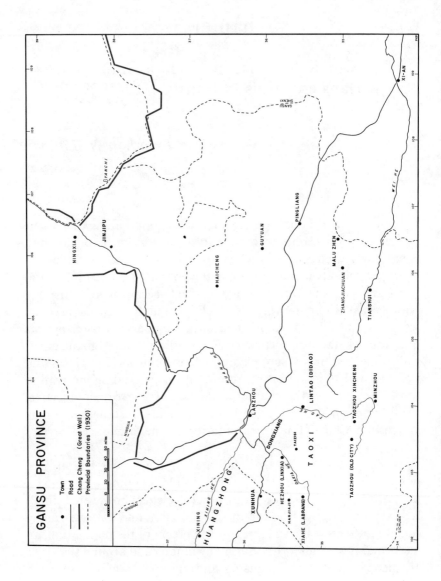

may mean either violence between minority ethnic group(s) and members of the Han majority or violence among ethnic minorities, as when the Tibetans and the Huis, Chinese-speaking Muslims, massacred one another in the 1920s.

The violence in our present cases took place between Muslims, most of them Huis, and Hans in Gansu province between 1781 and 1929. Although ethnic violence in China certainly cannot be explained by reference to these cases alone, they will serve as an introduction to more general points. These points will take us beyond the narrow interests of Sinological minutiae toward comprehension of China's society as a complex, evolving one, and toward understanding of Muslims in societies they do not dominate. This "Islamic studies" aspect of the present work has important implications for our Western vision of Muslims as well as for Han perceptions of their own domestic Muslim minority.

Two stereotypical explanations have been offered for violent conflict between Muslims and others throughout modern Chinese history, including the Manchu Qing dynasty (1644-1912) and the Republican period (1912-1949). The first states that Muslims simply are violent people, that by virtue of their doctrine and their history they are more likely than other folks to behave violently. This explanation, familiar to most Westerners in our image of the Muslim fanatic, has also generally been accepted in China, by local Hans in areas where Muslims live in sizable numbers; by officials charged with keeping Chinese society orderly, harmonious, and balanced; and by Christian missionaries, for whom Muslims were a familiar enemy, closer in doctrine to Christians than most citizens of China but inevitably antagonistic to the teachings of Christian truth.

The other explanation for Han-Muslim violence, offered by post-1949 scholars in the People's Republic and nationalistic Muslim citizens of China on both sides of the Taiwan Strait, maintains that Han-Muslim violence was caused by oppressive, discriminatory, ethnocentric Manchu Qing policy, which set ethnic group against ethnic group in order to stabilize the dynasty's exploitative rule. This divisive policy, in their view, caused an unnatural antagonism amongst people who should live together in harmony, united by an all-encompassing Chinese culture, expressed proverbially as *"Sihai zhi nei, jie xiongdi ye."* (Within the four seas, all are brothers.)

Neither of these "explanations" holds up under scrutiny. For the first, we often find calm and peace between Muslims and their Han or other ethnic neighbors, even alliances among them for economic or other gain. Chinese-speaking Muslims often acted as mediators between other ethnic groups, and when conflict broke out between Hans and Muslims, uninvolved Muslims often rushed in to repair the breach, or even to side with the Hans.

As for the second explanation, that which blames Qing policy for the antagonism among ethnicities in modern China, it clearly stems from the anachronistic imperatives of the late nineteenth and early twentieth centuries, from the Chinese nationalist movement. That movement, associated most closely in Western eyes with the name of Sun Yat-sen, contained a powerful dose of anti-Manchu ethnoracial identification. All of its adherents claimed unity among the various ethnicities of China, excluding the Manchu dominators of course, though of necessity including the "Manchu people" as a legitimate Chinese ethnic group. But Han-Muslim violence was neither unique to the Qing nor consistent throughout the dynasty's centuries. So even if Qing policy was inherently anti-Muslim, racist, ethnocentric, or oppressive, we cannot find constant violence in areas where Huis and Hans lived in proximity. This should prompt us to seek better and more complex explanations.

Some violent incidents

My specific narrative of ethnic violence begins with some local accounts in order to capture the flavor of the events. The following story occurs in an Arabic chronicle, collected by a twentieth-century Hui scholar and previously held inside the Jahriyya order of Naqshbandi Sufis. The Sufis of China, devotees of a mystical doctrine of meditational, individual unity with the divine, built exclusive communities distinguished from other Muslims by ritual, by loyalty to saints (called *shaykhs* in Arabic and Hui Chinese), and by their secret initiation rites.

As Sufis did elsewhere in the Muslim world, Chinese Sufis declared that their particular version of Muslim ritual represented a revival, a cleansing of Islam from the corruptions of secularization and, in China, from the impurities of acculturation to Han ways. Despite its fundamentalist message, Sufism, unlike some earlier forms of Islamic organization, found coexistence with a non-Muslim state relatively easy. Although holy wars were sometimes sponsored by Sufis, they could live Muslim lives, by their own doctrine, in a China inevitably ruled by non-Muslims without engaging in constant strife with the Hans.

Sufis arrived in China during the seventeenth and eighteenth centuries, during the expansion and height of the Qing dynasty, when Manchu-Han power had proved itself against all enemies, including Central Asian Muslims. In fact, the Sufis who came to China made one another the immediate objects of violence, rather than the state or the Hans. Competing Sufi orders fought over mosque-building rights, over territory, over loyalty to different *shaykhs*, over matters of ritual.

The violence in this particular account took place around 1780 between members of two competing Sufi suborders, the Khufiyya led by Ma Laichi, which had a longer history in the region, and the Jahriyya of Ma Mingxin. The latter had recently returned from Yemen bearing the charisma of the pilgrim to Makkah, the initiation ritual of a new Sufi group, and the authority of authentic Arabic texts from the Muslim heartlands. The narrator belongs to the Jahriyya, and his antagonists to the Khufiyya:

> After the morning prayers, as I passed Ma Laichi's street, oh God! A crowd gathered against me. Taking long poles and short sticks and whips they beat me, and the women stood in the doors and threw garbage! With God's help, not knowing how I found the courage and strength, I beat them one by one, broke their weapons, and defeated them. Thus the vengefulness grew deeper, for Ma Laichi's fourth son took a crowd with him to the magistrate and said we had set up a new religion to deceive the people. The court decided against us, and I was dragged in and beaten forty strokes, while Ma Mingxin received three. As they beat him, the bludgeon split in two! . . . The next day after dawn prayers, I again went by Ma Laichi's street and cursed the people from one end to the other. The revengers said, "How can he be so bold?" and again went to court. The magistrate decided, "All should return to their native places" (Ma Xuezhi 1980).

Here we have an apparent anomaly—two groups of Muslims, competing over matters internal to their community, appealing to a non-Muslim, a Qing magistrate in a secular court, for judgment of their case. We might find such an appeal antithetical to Muslim autonomy and to Muslim law, but the eighteenth-century Gansu Muslims clearly did not. The magistrate, however, could not satisfy their desire for decisive judgment, and the violence between the two groups escalated into full-scale street riots in 1781.

The Qing officials reacted as they would in any ordinary case of violence—they locked up the reputed leaders of the disruptive group, in this case the more recently arrived Jahriyya. Part of the Khufiyya argument in the case rested on their more settled, longer existence in Gansu. The Jahriyya received the pejorative appellation of "New Teaching," with its taint of heterodoxy and innovation, both anathema to the conventional, conservative Qing officials. The state and its delegated authorities further distinguished between these groups in terms of behavior: The Jahriyya Sufis appeared to the Qing to be more militant, more intransigent, more *Muslim*, than the apparently more acculturated Khufiyya adherents. This perception, more illusory than real, damaged Qing policy many times in the following century.

Ma Mingxin was arrested and locked up, not in the local jail at Xunhua but in the provincial capital of Lanzhou. His followers did not accept this state intervention calmly, although they had earlier taken recourse to Qing justice, but rather armed themselves to free their *shaykh*. The hopelessness of 3,000 armed Muslims opposing the might of the Qing state at its height, so obvious to us, was also clear to at least some Muslims, as witness a ballad collected in the 1930s. The leader of the rescue force, Su Sishisan (Su Forty-Three), and his assistant Han Er (Han Two) are being lectured by Han's wife, a woman with a clear grasp of reality. All three were Salars, Turkic-speaking Muslims from the upper Yellow River valley:

> Husband you hear, and Su hear, too,
> You bug the Emperor, and he'll get you!
> You trouble the man, that's a heavy crime,
> The moment he's mad, that's the end of your time!
> The Emperor's men are as hot as the sun,
> And your Salars are a cloud on the run.

As soon as the sun shines, the cloud is dead,
Can't you get that into your head? (Wang Shumin 1948)

But despite his wife's warning, Han, Su and their Salars attacked the prefectural capital, killed two officials there, then moved rapidly and secretly and besieged Lanzhou, the provincial capital, where they knew their *shaykh* to be a prisoner. The provincial officials, thoroughly alarmed, brought Ma Mingxin in chains onto the city wall, hoping to awe his followers by this display of their power over the *shaykh*. Rather than bowing to the inevitable success of Qing law and order, Su and his men fell on their knees before their leader and said their prayers beneath the city wall. Convinced of the intransigence and fanaticism of the Jahriyya Sufis, and frightened of what Ma might do if he were freed, the Lanzhou officials had him executed forthwith.

Warfare ensued between aroused Muslims seeking vengeance on the one side and the combined forces of social order on the other, forces that probably included Khufiyya Muslims. It lasted that entire summer of 1781, ending only when an imperial commissioner, Agui, organized Manchu, Han, Tibetan, and Mongolian troops (indicating the area's ethnic diversity) against the Jahriyya Muslims and massacred them in their mountain forts south of Lanzhou. The Qing proscribed the Jahriyya suborder and set limitations on all Muslim religious proselytizing. They also rewarded Khufiyya adherents who had served with Qing forces against their coreligious antagonists (Yang Huaizhong 1981).

The next 100 years brought sporadic outbreaks of violence in all the major Muslim centers of the northwest, heightened tensions among ethnic groups, and an increasingly common conviction on the part of both civil officials and local populations that Muslims are inherently violent and warlike people. This sanguinary period, coinciding with the degeneration of order all over China, culminated in the "Great Rebellion" of the northwestern Muslims, which began almost inadvertently in 1862 and was suppressed by the Qing, with great slaughter, in a series of campaigns led by Zuo Zongtang (Liu and Smith 1980).

The "Great Rebellion" was not a single coordinated antistate movement by organized Muslims but rather a series of reactions and actions taken by some Muslim communities to defend themselves against what they perceived to be state pogroms. It began as a market brawl in southern Shaanxi and rapidly spread westward as communities retreated to hilltop forts or attacked their neighbors rather than be passive victims of violence they knew was coming. The unanimity of the Muslims, the ferocity of Han attacks, and the final outcome varied widely from area to area, even from county to county.

Despite Han fears, the militant Jahriyya did not declare an open *jihad* but rather, through its *shaykh* Ma Hualong, pursued a twisting course of attempted accommodation and local resistance. The Hui of various parts of Shaanxi and Gansu provinces had no unified command, no overall strategy. In addition, significant groups of Muslims either allied with the state or lay low. Despite this inchoate opposition, the Qing took more than a decade to pacify the region, in the process reducing the once-thriving Shaanxi Hui communities to virtually nil and laying waste the fertile fields of central Ningxia.

Zuo Zongtang's sometimes genocidal pacification, which included forced migrations, wholesale slaughter, and a renewed proscription of the Jahriyya, left a permanent mark on Gansu. The Khufiyya commander at Hezhou, Ma Zhan'ao, obtained advantageous terms of surrender from Zuo and proceeded to use his armies against other Muslim communities in the name of the Qing. The nature of Hui secular leadership evolved in this new and potentially acculturating direction (Lipman 1984b).

In 1895, more than 100 years after the initial Jahriyya-Khufiyya clashes, internecine conflict again brought "rebellion" to parts of Gansu. This time the conflict was caused by the arrival of one Selim, a missionary from Arabia, who converted some members of the Khufiyya to a new ritual form, but not others (Guan Lianji and Wang Jing 1983). Their conflict, as with the earlier one, ended in a Qing magistrate's court and was similarly decided—the judge simply could not prove the merits of one side over the other and sent them home with a lame admonition to behave (Mu Shouqi 1971:24.40b-42b).

Followers of the two sides among the Salars at Xunhua began to fight matters out in the street, and the edgy officials in Lanzhou sent a military official to Xunhua with troops and orders to pacify. He tried to awe the Salars into submission in a way deemed effective by precedent—he executed eleven leaders of the faction opposed to Selim's teachings. At the same time, another Qing general, a local man familiar with the territory but resolutely anti-Muslim, proclaimed a general attack on Muslim communities and made proclamations in favor of a clean sweep, a washing away of the Huis. These actions, perfectly justifiable in light of Qing methods of social control, produced an unpredicted effect: Large numbers of Muslims of diverse groups united in the face of what they perceived to be Qing brutality and besieged Xunhua city with a sizable army.

Eighteen months of violence followed, tens of thousands died, and the Muslim communities of Hezhou and Xining, the largest in the area, were both torched by Qing armies and local militias. The Muslim insurgents, though members of diverse Sufi orders and non-Sufi groups of various Muslim ethnicities, united to protect themselves from Qing armies and, in some cases, to settle scores within their communities. Contrary to popular Han images of Muslims as invariably and ferociously loyal to one another, the attacking Qing armies, which actually broke the rebellion, were led by Muslims, some of them heads of Sufi suborders, even members of the same group within which the original violence had begun.

As a final case, let us consider 1928. In the midst of a devastating famine and drought and a series of small but brutal wars, the unsuccessful Muslim general Ma Tingxian attacked several towns in eastern Gansu. Calling upon one of them to surrender, he met unexpected resistance from the Han residents and their Han magistrate, who was loyal to another local warlord. The Muslim troops, eager for the loot and cash bonuses they would receive for success, surrounded the town and took it with great slaughter— more than one-half of the 15,000 inhabitants, all of them Hans, lost their lives in a twenty-four-hour bloodletting (Ma Peiqing 1980).

This same Ma Tingxian had been responsible for the massacre of thousands of Tibetans the previous year, when Tibetan robbers had taken several women from his entourage and refused to relinquish them. In a description by an American missionary, this man appeared to be eager for power and loot, exhausted by battle and ridden by blood-lust (Ekvall 1929). His men, most of them

Hezhou and Xunhua Muslims, looted and raped with abandon, behaving in the same way Qing troops had done when turned loose on Muslim neighborhoods.

Local causes for ethnic violence

With these stories in mind, I may outline some of the important causes for ethnic violence in China. None of them could stand alone, nor did their combined presence guarantee violence. But in the available cases, all were present, and in the most important cases, all were crucial.

First, consider the geographic and demographic environment. Although reputed to be a "Muslim province," in fact Gansu never had more than 25 to 30 percent Muslim population, and those Muslims were concentrated in widely separated areas. So, too, were the Hans scattered about the landscape, often separated from other Hans by wide belts of unsettled land or by areas occupied by antagonistic ethnic groups. Poor transportation and a violent climate—Gansu was and still is famous for thunderstorms, hail, torrential downpours out of season and drought, as well as extreme winter cold—made communications uncertain at best, impossible at worst, rendering communities profoundly insecure in the face of potential ethnic enemies.

No centralized plan for anti-Qing resistance existed in the 1860s; some communities joined together to fight, others belonged to Sufi networks which connected them to distant centers, but others held out alone or declared loyalty to the dynasty. In 1895, the Xunhua Muslims had to appeal to coreligionaries in Hezhou and Xining, both 100 kilometers distant over mountainous country in opposite directions, for aid against the Qing. Although elements within both Xezhou and Xining responded, no unified command or Muslim leadership ever emerged, and the insurgents of each region basically fought for themselves.

That is to say, Muslims were never a united minority (Lipman 1984a). The Han imagery, which calls the Muslims loyal to one another and fiercely protective of coreligionaries, correctly describes ethnic solidarity when faced with a local enemy. But Muslim solidarity has never prevented Muslims from killing one another if other considerations warranted it. And in Gansu, such considerations were legion. For example, numerous dialects of four languages (Chinese, Tibetan, Mongolian, Turkic) were used by sizable groups of Gansu Muslims, and Muslims tended toward cultural lives associated with their languages, separating them from coreligionaries in matters such as food, housing, productive life, and even religion. Muslims in regions dominated by Tibetans, for example, often intermarried with Tibetan women and produced families rich in religious diversity. One family numbered among its sons both a practicing Muslim and a Buddhist monk (d'Ollone 1911:234-35).

More significant for our purposes, Gansu Muslims divided themselves by membership in religious organizations. From the seventeenth century onward, these tended to be either Sufi orders or anti-Sufi groups. A vast wave of Sufism swept across the Muslim world in the seventeenth century, with its attendant revivalism and pan-Islamic sentiment, aiming to reunite Muslims both politically and theologically with the worldwide congregation of Islam. Its effects in China, however, tended not to be so much fundamentalist, that is unifying, as divisive. Charismatic leaders, such as Ma Mingxin and Ma Laichi, went "west" to Arabia to receive the True Doctrine and returned, filled with exclusivist zeal. Their orders and suborders, distinguished from one another both by religious minutiae and by loyalty to different leaders, became foci for deep and abiding hostility among Muslims.

Here we must clarify this issue by distinguishing two different types of Muslim community in China, for they differed not only in structure but also in their reaction to Han or state violence. Non-Sufi Muslims belonged to local mosques which hired religious professionals through a formal application procedure and supervised them through a council of elders. Their community structure, tightly-knit, had no institutional ties to the outside. Mosques rarely exceeded 2,000 souls. Their practice of Islam followed a somewhat sinified version of the Sunni, Hanafi tradition, and they called themselves *Gedimu*, or "the old way."

Sufi communities, on the other hand, were led by *shaykhs* who held their position as leader of an order or suborder for life and could pass it to a chosen successor. Because substantial property often accumulated in the hands of such a leader, hereditary succession became the rule, and powerful lineages, called *menhuans*, became associated with orders, suborders, or the tombs of earlier *shaykhs*. These Sufi orders and related *menhuans* were not limited to a single community but often stretched into large, diverse networks, united by loyalty to their *shaykh* and his version of Islamic ritual, but divided by distance and, often, by intervening settlements of Hans and other ethnic groups. The largest of these networks, the Jahriyya suborder of Naqshbandi Sufis, founded in Gansu in the 1760s and associated with Ma Mingxin, the imprisoned leader of 1781, at its height included mosques from Yunnan to Manchuria.

Another form of Muslim intercommunity network lay in the economic sphere. Muslims held a trade advantage over Hans in China proper by virtue of their ability to work outside their own local systems. By contacting coreligionaries, Muslim traders could obtain supplies, credit, and other necessities impossible for Hans except through the establishment of local place associations in major trading centers. In North China, at least, Muslims engaged widely in transportation, restaurant and inn-keeping, butchering and meat retailing, and other occupations demanding a wide geographical acquaintance. These connections did not, however, prevent rivalry among Muslims. In some cases, economic relations paralleled Sufi orders or other divisive entities within the Muslim communities, thereby exacerbating differences and giving rise to violent opposition between Muslims.

In the cases above, 1781, the 1860s, and 1895, Muslims fought on both sides in a local war. They divided by religious order, for in 1781 Jahriyya Muslims arrayed themselves against the state and Khufiyya Muslims for it. Having surrendered his Hezhou base to Zuo Zongtang in 1872, Ma Zhan'ao attacked other Muslims in the name of the Qing. In 1895, geographical area seems also to have played an important part. While some Muslims in Xining, Xunhua, and Hezhou responded to the clarion call, the Muslim gentry of Taozhou, a few dozen kilometers to the south, joined with Han and Tibetan notables to quell violent elements in their own communities and keep the peace (*Taozhou Ting Zhi* 1907:18.3b).

Although this evidence lay before the state authorities and the local Hans, they nonetheless continued to see Muslims as invariably and fiercely loyal to one another in time of crisis. The existence of numerous antagonistic groups and subgroups within the Muslim communities brought into play another crucial fact of northwestern violence, one we observed in all the stories above—the involvement of the state. In Qing law and local custom, any concerted violence against any representative of the state constituted rebellion, a tradition derived at least from Ming law and actually in force long before that. Thus, Muslims behaving violently, even if they were fighting one another, could be construed, charged, pursued, and punished as rebels by local officials.

Here we come to a crucial point in the argument on violence, for previous analyses have stressed discriminatory Qing policy in explaining antisocial behavior among Muslims. The Qing state held officially to the doctrine of *Han Hui yi shi tong ren* (equal benevolence toward Han and Hui), as it tended to do toward all ethnic groups under its sway. But local enforcement, often undertaken by local gentry or militias under the command of the magistrate or other imperial officials, partook of the local Han cultural ethos, one which was often actively and vociferously anti-Muslim.

Virulent anti-Hui sentiment may be found in the memorials of many local Qing officials, and they abound in the archives. Imperial responses, however, tended toward moderation and tolerance. Even after the 1781 rebellion, for example, the Qianlong Emperor refused to proscribe Islam or censor Muslim religious books, content with banning the "rebellious" Jahriyya (Leslie 1986:126-28). For local Hans, however, the Huis remained a terrifying and immediate danger. Selective memory of previous Muslim violence, especially after the 1781 uprising and its smaller sequel in 1784, gave Gansu Hans a convenient bogeyman, a familiar enemy. Mothers in east Gansu threatened their babies with the Muslims, who would come and kill bad Han children if they would not stop crying (Xu Wanli 1974).

This image intensified in the twentieth century. Ma Tingxian's depredations in 1929 were opposed by many Muslims in Gansu, but none had the resources or desire to go into the field against him. Nor did any centralized state power, for none existed. He chose a time of political chaos and economic disaster to act violently, succeeded in carrying off his campaign and accumulating a small fortune in loot, then fled to Tianjin with the spoils. Every important Muslim leader in the province deplored his actions, but he got away with it and lived comfortably in the east until the People's Republic executed him in 1959. Local Hans in Gansu obtained but small comfort from the negative judgment of provincial Hui gentry on Ma Tingxian; they knew that the predatory young general had acted "as Muslims always do"—in solidarity with fellow Muslims, unpredictably, violently.

Another little-known aspect of Muslim communities intensified this image of a terrifying other. In their mosques, which also served as community centers, Muslims in China often established schools for the study of the martial arts. An obvious need in the face of ethnic antagonists, these schools fostered the Han image of Muslims as warlike and aggressive. Their martial arts, predominantly Chinese in origin but somehow "a little different" in style, continue to characterize the Huis as violent; a recent individual men's *wushu* champion of China is a Muslim.

Moreover, in both elite and popular Han imagination, all non-Hans partake of an unsavory and barbaric character, demonstrated by their lack of a Confucian social life; their often "immoral" marriage customs; their association with horses, flocks, and nomadism; and their predilection for raiding Han agricultural settlements. Chinese Muslims constituted an especially threatening minority for they maintained separate, exclusive communities, calendars, and lives despite their strong physical and cultural resemblance to Hans.

In an atmosphere of such strong, local stereotypes, imperial officials from outside the northwest could easily be convinced, despite threats of Imperial displeasure, that some groups of Muslims, or all Muslims, represented a threat to social order, one which had to be countered by strong action whenever it erupted into overt violence and strictly controlled even when it did not. In the case of the Gansu Muslims, this intervention often had precisely the opposite of the desired effect. Rather than being awed into submission, the Muslims used Qing official violence as a goad to solidarity, however partial it may have been. This happened despite the Muslims' fairly regular use of Qing courts to settle internecine disputes, even those which had a strong religious component. This predilection for litigation invariably surprises scholars of Muslim societies elsewhere, who are accustomed to Muslims under non-Muslim rule settling their own problems internally. More research is needed on the social and political alignments within Muslim communities which led them to make such extensive use of non-Muslim justice.

We must include here one more vital component of the ethnic violence in Gansu, one which is difficult, unquantifiable, but nonetheless common in ethnic violence in many other cases as well. Violent behavior, especially for young men facing an obvious, local, familiar enemy and with the sanction of their own elders or community, appears to be exciting, challenging, and (dare one say it) enjoyable. When successful, it results in significant economic gains. The prospect of new and previously unattainable wealth, of women, of killing a feared, hated, and despised Other, seems to be a very enticing one, despite the danger. The enemy can be made less than human, deserving of violent death. From Gansu to *West Side Story*, from Belfast to Uganda, we find wildly diverse groups of young men engaging in ethnic violence, sometimes with the imprimatur of the state, at others in a self-conscious, antistate movement. It would be feckless to draw general conclusions about the nature of young males from this observation, but it certainly must be included in our analysis.

For Qing officials, designation as "rebels" or "weed people" sufficed to justify intervention by the armed force of the state. For ordinary folks, proximity and strangeness, revenge for past wrongs and fear of present attack, could well justify violence, especially if rumors flew of trouble within minority, in this case Muslim, communities. As the proverb says, "When Old Teaching Muslims and New Teaching Muslims fight, it's a matter for swords and troops before it's over!" We cannot discount this social perception, although it seldom appears in sober accounts of massacres or personal memoirs. We can certainly hear it in the songs of Ma Tingxian's troops as they celebrated the massacre at Li Xian:

> Our commander Ma Tingxian
> Brought us here to take Longnan,
> To wear brocade and live it up!

Our Holy Book is very clear,
Han and Hui are nowhere near,
Never mix them up!

Our mullah tells us what is true,
So follow him in all we do!
Or risk our very lives . . .

Join in, join in, all join in!
We'll find a girl after we win,
First take her goods then rape her some!

Kill them, kill them, come if you can,
Without your vengeance, you're no man!
Our time has come!
(Mu Shouqi 1971:*fubian* 5:38a-39a)

We may certainly infer a variety of motivations to violence from this text, for the young Huis who sang this song proceeded to kill more than 7,000 civilians in a single day! They wanted to "wear brocade"—to loot the goods of Han merchants, which were generally beyond their means. In short, they wanted to have a good time, and in their province at that time, "living it up" meant rapine and predation on the ethnic enemy. Their commander approved, their *mullahs* approved, their immediate historical experience demanded that they strike first.

They certainly wanted to follow the ideological and political tenets of their community, to obey the *mullah* and the *Qur'an* as he interpreted it, which raises for us the question of religious leadership in ethnic violence. The Chinese *mullahs* and *shaykhs* may have desired ethnic warfare as an expression of separation from Han society, a violent determinant of identity for Huis. Many Chinese sources note the unswerving loyalty of Muslims to their religious leaders, especially within Sufi orders. The Huis, of course, could enhance Han fears of their martial virtue with slogans of religious fervor, while the Hans could distance themselves from "those violent Muslims" by characterizing Islam itself as violent. But this does not demonstrate the inherent violence of Islam any more than the Irish Republican Army's predations, whatever the political justice of their cause, prove the inherently violent nature of Roman Catholicism.

The young men, wanting to please their leaders and elders, also wanted to rape some women, an activity common to marauding armies everywhere in the world and considered especially degrading to the men of the vanquished foe. They wanted to use the *wushu* they had studied in the mosque and, in the twentieth century, the Western-style weapons bought for them by local warlords such as Ma Tingxian. Those weapons, however, were not unqualifiedly Muslim. Indeed, Ma Tingxian's rifles came via his older brother, who had received them from Zhang Zuolin, the Han warlord of Manchuria (*North China Herald* 1928; Mu Shouqi 1971:31.41b).

This did not, however, cause their battalions of young men to become politicized in the Chinese fashion, to join parties or chant modernist slogans. For in all this, those young Muslims wanted revenge. Vengeance does not play a very positive role in our list of appropriate motivations for human action, but it haunts us in our literature, from Hamlet to Hemingway, in our daily lives and our politics at every level (Jacoby 1983). In China, as elsewhere, men must repay wrongs done to them, to earlier generations, to comembers of solidarity groups. Min Fuying, a well-known Gansu Muslim, joined with a rebellious army in order to pay a debt of blood incurred through the murder of his grandfather by the grandfather of a contemporary antagonist who had joined a Qing army operating against local Muslims (Guan Lianji and Liu Cihan 1982; Mu Shouqi 1971:24.40b-42b).

These are not arcane or obscure motivations, nor are they unique to Hans or Muslims or Tibetans. In China, the motive of revenge represents an intersection of high and popular cultures, the legitimate reason for violence at all levels of society (Harrell, this volume). As we think about ethnic violence in many parts of the world, we must consider collective memory, the legends and songs and stories and poems chronicling the tragic, undeserved deaths of forebears at the hands of evil Others whose descendants deserve death as much as the actual perpetrators themselves. If we are to be men, we must right these former wrongs.

Conclusion

I conclude by summarizing the causes adduced for ethnic violence in China:

1. First, I examined the interlocked nature of Gansu Muslim and Han societies, which made both vulnerable to ethnic enemies on the local level and thus subject to fear and rumors as well as actual violence. This appears true in any area of China where ethnic groups live in proximity and the Hans do not hold an invulnerably dominant position.

2. Paradoxically, another cause lay in the existence of networks, often antagonistic to one another, of Muslim (especially Sufi) institutions after the eighteenth century and in the conflicts among Muslims created by their rivalries. These conflicts, often violent, increased Han fear of the Muslims and made ethnic confrontation and escalation more likely.

3. Perhaps most obvious in these stories, by law and by precedent the Chinese state intervened in Muslim community quarrels if they turned violent, an intervention seen as unjustifiable by many Muslims. In all of the Qing period cases, trigger-happy officials killed Muslims, causing immediate and violent reaction rather than submission or humble loyalty. This type of state action, undertaken by local officials, seems very similar to the presence of armed majority police in a minority neighborhood. People will be hurt, and revenge will be taken. In 1929, in the absence of a strong state, Ma Tingxian escaped vengeance or punishment for his bloodthirsty campaigns for thirty years, living and trading in Tianjin, far from local politics and local hatreds.

4. Last is the profit and enjoyment to be reaped from ethnic violence, especially in an already rowdy border region and especially in otherwise hard times. Lacking other means to make a fortune, in the presence of an ethnic antagonist, some young men turn to violence. The state may call it crime, but within minority communities it often constitutes "doing well for ourselves," the heroic or at least legitimate activity of young men. Loot, rapine, revenge, the enjoyment of violence made virtuous by its role in protecting Us against Them—these justify violence in many economically and socially marginal groups as well as by the forces of the majority or the state.

What must surprise us most about northwest China is not that so much ethnic violence took place there but rather that it so rarely became widespread. In fact, many of the Muslims of Gansu, like

Muslims elsewhere in China, found their best interests served by an alliance with the state or with non-Muslim neighbors against some of their coreligionaries. As with black Americans, Irish Protestants, Israeli Jews or Palestinian Muslims, black South Africans or Indian Muslims, divisions within ethnic communities must always be part of our examination of violence. Such divisions can cause further violence, by bringing state power to bear against feuding minorities. They also cause widespread fear of minority groups which have a reputation for ferocity and violence. On the other hand, divisions within a minority community may make the state's job easier—it can use one faction of minority people against another.

We have considered here two themes often left out of our study of Chinese society—ethnic difference and violence. The former often strikes Hans as eccentric and unnecessary, given that only six percent of China's population is non-Han. In fact, my friends among the Chinese academics look upon my interest in the subject rather as American historians would view a German scholar who came to Harvard or Berkeley to study the Navajo. But vast areas of China are inhabited by non-Hans, including many who dwell on strategic international or provincial borders, so that their status, their interaction with Han society, their participation in or opposition to the Chinese state—all have played and will continue to play important parts in Chinese life.

The latter theme, violence, strikes a much more delicate nerve. China's elite has, for millenia, claimed a harmonious and peaceful character for Chinese society, a Confucian vision in contrast to the barbaric Others which surround it (Harrell, this volume). But the evidence presented here challenges that perception: Why is China's elite ideal so very different from social reality? Why has China's state and social structure been unsuccessful in fulfilling the promise of an orderly society proposed by Chinese philosophers? This chapter provides some answers, complex and local, with regard to violence between ethnic groups in China. This theme must be explored for ethnic conflict elsewhere in China, including the current upheavals in Tibet, to bring the vague niceties of China's "unity of many nationalities" *(minzu tuanjie)* into question. Such investigations can offer a more profound, accurate, and sympathetic understanding of Chinese history. For it will correctly make Chinese history look more like our own.

References

d'Ollone, H.M.G.
1911 *Recherches sur les musulmans chinois (Research on the Chinese Mulims)*. Paris: Leroux.

Ekvall, Robert
1929 "Revolt of the Crescent in Northwest China," *Asia and the Americas* 29:944-47, 1004-7.

Guan Lianji and Liu Cihan
1983 "Yibajiuwu Nian Hehuang Shibian Chutan" ("Preliminary Investigation of the 1895 Hehuang Incident"). *Xibei Shidi* 4:46-53.

Guan Lianji and Wang Jing
1982 "Huasi Menhuan di Xingshuai" ("The Rise and Fall of the Huasi Menhuan"), *Xibei Shidi* 1:56-62.

Jacoby, Susan
1983 *Wild Justice: The Evolution of Revenge*. New York: Harper and Row.

Leslie, Donald D.
1986 *Islam in Traditional China: A Short History to 1800*. Canberra, Australia: Canberra College of Advanced Education.

Lipman, Jonathan
1984a "Patchwork Society, Network Society: A Study of Sino-Muslim Communities," in R. Israeli and A. Johns, eds., *Islam in Asia* II. Denver: Westview Press.

1984b "Ethnicity and Politics in Republican China: The Ma Family Warlords of Gansu," *Modern China* 10(3):285-316.

Liu, K.C. and Smith, R.
1980 "The Military Challenge: The Northwest and the Coast," in J. Fairbank, ed., *The Cambridge History of China* XI(2):202-73. Cambridge: Cambridge University Press.

Ma Peiqing
1980 "Wo Suozhidao di Ma Tingxian" ("The Ma Tingxian I Knew"), *Gansu Wenshi Ziliao Xuanji* 9:150-68.

Ma Xuezhi (Muhammad Mansur)
1980 *Zhehelinye daotong shi xiaoji (Selections from the History of the*

Jahriyya Way). Yinchuan: Xibei Wusheng(qu) Yisilan Jiao Xueshu Taolun Hui.

Mu Shouqi
   1971 reprint *Gan Ning Qing shilue (History of Gansu, Ningxia, and Qinghai).* Taibei: Guangwen.

North China Herald
   1928 October 20, 1928.

Wang Shumin
   1948 "Qianlong Sishiliu Nian Hezhou Shibian Ge" ("Ballad of the 1781 Hezhou Incident"), *Xibei tongxun* 3:2.

Xu Wanli
   1974 "Cong Hezhou Shuoqi" ("Speaking of Hezhou"), *Gansu wenxian* 3:45-47.

Yang Huaizhong
   1981 "Lun Shiba Shiji Zhehelinye Musilin di Qiyi" ("The Eighteenth Century Uprisings of the Jahriyya Muslims"), in Ningxia Zhexue Shehui Kexue Yanjiusuo, *Qingdai Zhongguo Yisilan Jiao Lunji (Essays on Islam in China During the Qing).* Yinchuan: Ningxia Renmin Chuban She.

Chapter 4

Sectarian Eschatology and Violence

Richard Shek

A significant amount of violence in traditional China, particularly that which caused the greatest concern for the government, was perpetrated by religious sectarians who espoused beliefs and practiced rituals the authorities deemed heterodox. In recent years, Chinese sectarianism has become a subject of study by historians, thereby making it possible to explore the question of linkage between sectarian faith and violence.[1] Indeed, some historians have already paid special attention to this issue. In late 1959 and early 1960, for example, mainland Chinese historians conducted a heated debate on the relationship between religion and "peasant wars" in "feudal" China (Shi Shaopin 1962). Suzuki Chūsei wrote a popular book on the subject (1974), while Susan Naquin has focused her studies on two religion-inspired rebellions, the Eight Trigrams of 1812 (1976) and Wang Lun's rebellion in 1774 (1981).

In order to examine this relationship between sectarianism and violence further, I propose to analyze the central focus of sectarian religion itself in detail. Only in so doing can one determine if Chinese sectarianism possessed any inherent proclivity toward violence. First, however, a brief explanation of what I mean by *sectarianism* is necessary.

By *sectarianism* I mean a wide spectrum of dissenting religious groups that operated outside the mainstream of established clerical traditions. Informed by an acute sense of eschatology, these lay-oriented groups preoccupied themselves with messianic hopes, confident about their own salvation. They saw the present world as essentially corrupt and doomed. They developed a salvational scheme that did not rely on the temples and priests of either folk

87

religion or state-recognized Daoism and Buddhism. In addition, they created an alternative community, which provided identity, solidarity, and sustenance to its members, rendering unnecessary those constituted by family, lineage, and village. In late imperial times, this sectarianism was best represented by the White Lotus cults, but its origins can be traced to the Yellow Turbans of Eastern Han, as well as the Buddho-Daoist groups of the Six Dynasties and the Sui-Tang period. It thus has a history lasting nearly 2,000 years. Although the Taiping believers in the nineteenth century constituted the largest sectarian movement in Chinese history, the magnitude of the subject renders its inclusion here unfeasible.

As indicated above, the central content of sectarian belief is eschatological messianism, which has three major components: (1) the expectation of an imminent cosmic upheaval that precedes the arrival of a messianic figure, who will bring a violent end to the existing world; (2) the deliverance of the faithful (the *electi*) from oppression and misery; and (3) the horrors of the apocalyptic battle from which the savior and his chosen people will emerge triumphant. To be sure, not all the sectarian groups throughout history subscribed to the same set of eschatological beliefs, nor did they worship the same deities or expect the same messianic figures. The content of sectarian faith evolved and metamorphosed in response to times, places, and leadership. Yet, by the fifth century, a complete eschatology of messianic salvation did develop, and its broad outlines became the cornerstone of most sectarian faiths thereafter. The following examines each feature of this eschatology closely, citing relevant information from numerous sectarian groups, in order to show how each might have contributed to the not infrequent violent actions of sect members.

Cosmic crisis and messianic deliverance

One major tenet of sectarian belief is the notion of the impending demise of the present world, usually represented as violent, destructive upheaval, brought about by the actions of superhuman powers. Such a violent end to the existing age is the result of both natural and human causes, according to the sectarians. On the one hand, there is the belief in the inevitable cyclical dissolution of the physical world. On the other, there is the expectation that as the moral degeneration of the human race reaches its nadir, the cosmos responds with a cataclysmic self-destruction to purge all evil elements and make a clean start. This belief in the periodic decay of the existing world was espoused by both Daoism and Buddhism since the Later Han period.

Underlying the Daoist notion of cosmic crisis is "the idea that the physical universe passes through a number of longer and shorter cycles of different length that take place at the same time. Periodically this complicated process will reach a nodal point, when the beginning of several cycles coincide" (Zurcher 1981:36-37). It is at such nodal points that cosmic disasters will occur. Another Daoist explanation of this crisis, outlined in the Classic of Highest Peace *(Taiping Jing)* in Later Han times, focuses on the concept of *chengfu* ("transmit and bear the burden") (Kaltenmark 1979:24). This is the inheritance of sins through successive generations, an idea similar to, but not identical with, the Buddhist notion of *karma.* For the author(s) of the *Taiping Jing,* evil has been accumulating over innumerable generations, reaching perilously close to the point of ultimate reckoning, hence the urgent need for drastic measures to be taken to avert disaster.

The significance of such an expectation and, more important, acceptance of the demise of the present world should not be overlooked. As Wolfgang Bauer has so aptly pointed out, these "transitional periods" were the most important phases of human history for the Daoists. They were "the times when the wall separating this world and beyond became transparent, when heavenly emissaries peopled the world and where it was precisely from the most profound misfortune and the most destructive struggle that the 'Highest Peace' might be born" (1976:125). In other words, these cosmic destructions are perceived as opportunities for starting afresh and creating something far better than the existing order. They are to be welcomed, rather than feared.

In a similar fashion, although perhaps with less enthusiasm, classical Buddhism also espouses beliefs in the periodic dissolution of our universe. According to traditional Buddhist cosmology, as related in the Lokadhatu Sutra *(Da Loutan Jing),* world systems evolve and disintegrate through a series of cosmic periods known as *aeons*. At the end of each Great Aeon *(da jie)*, the physical universe is destroyed by the three "*kalpa*-disasters" of water, fire, and wind. After an intervening period of emptiness and darkness, a new "receptable-world" comes into being and a new cycle begins (Zurcher 1981:38).

Paralleling this idea of *kalpa*-disasters marking the end of a world is the equally potent notion of the gradual (but inexorable) decay and final disappearance of the Buddha's teaching. This pessimistic view, expressed in Buddhist canonical writings and reemphasized by numerous apocryphal texts compiled in the late Six Dynasties, envisions three stages *(san jie)* for the unfolding of Buddha's *dharma*, each to last several centuries. Starting with the Buddha's *parinirvana*, the first period is that of the "True Doctrine" *(zheng fa)*, during which the Buddha's precepts are faithfully followed. In the second period, known as the time of Counterfeit Doctrine *(xiang fa)*, the Buddha's teaching is adulterated and undermined by distortion and immorality of both the *sangha* and the laity. In the third period, that of the end of the Doctrine *(mo fa)*, even the semblance of religious devotion is abandoned, and the world is plunged into darkness and ignorance, lost in sin and injustice. In time, the next Buddha will appear, and the *dharma* will be restored (Zurcher 1981:39).

In addition to the Daoist and Buddhist eschatologies described above, Manichaean influences further enhanced the expectation of doom. Introduced from Persia in the seventh century (possibly earlier, as argued by Liu Cunyan and others) (Liu 1976:30-55; Shigematsu 1936:97-98; Chen 1981), Manichaeism subscribed to a dualistic view of the world, wherein the forces of Light, under the leadership of Mani, would engage in a fierce struggle with the forces of Darkness. For the Manichaeans, cosmic history also progresses in three stages: the first characterized by a clear division between the realms of Light and Darkness, the second by a blurring of this division that results in the struggle between the two, and the third by the ultimate triumph of Light over Darkness and the creation of a realm of everlasting peace. Central to Manichaean belief is the conviction that history is fast approaching the end of the second stage. Hence, followers of Mani must prepare themselves for the final battle and the fiery destruction of the present world.

It is thus quite clear that Daoism, Buddhism, and Manichaeism held eschatological views that anticipated cosmic disasters that would mark an end of the existing universe. Moreover, such a destruction was seen as a necessary step toward the creation of something better. In established Daoism and Buddhism—Manichaeism never gained official recognition or respectability—these eschatological visions had been dimmed, deemphasized, and relegated to the background. Only among peripheral groups holding these traditions was the eschatological hope preserved, earning for them the label of sectarianism. Let me examine some concrete manifestations of this acute sense of cosmic crisis and imminent destruction by several sectarian groups:

The Yellow Turbans

Apparently inspired by the *Taiping Jing*, the Yellow Turbans rebelled in 184 A.D. (Levy 1956, 1961; Michaud 1958). This Daoist text, one should recall, predicts disasters caused by the accumulation of sins over centuries. But it also promises salvation in the form of the arrival of the "Breath of Taiping" through the practice of ideal government and morality. Moreover, knowledge of this ideal government and morality has been revealed to humanity by Heaven through a divine man—the Celestial Master—and should be implemented by a ruler of virtue (Kaltenmark 1979:21). Relying on this salvational scheme of the *Taiping Jing*, the Yellow Turbans (who called themselves practitioners of the Way of Taiping) organized themselves, practiced faith-healing, and waited for the dawning of the new age. They saw their opportunity in 184 A.D., the *jiazi* year, the beginning year of the sexagenery cycle. Declaring the time to be auspicious, they proclaimed that "The azure heaven is dead; the yellow heaven is about to be established" (Li Guangbi 1958:65). Although totally crushed in the end, the Yellow Turbans set the precedent for eschatological movements in China. Admittedly, they were not yet fully messianic. Their leader Zhang Jue only conferred upon himself the title Heavenly Prince General, not clearly identifying himself as the savior. However, the next major eschatological movement would radically change the situation.

The Li Hong Cults

By the fifth century, a full-fledged messianic eschatology, principally inspired by Daoism, appeared on the scene. Propagated by adherents of the Li Hong Cult (Seidel 1969-1970; Sunayama 1971:1-21), an expectancy of messianic deliverance was expressed most unequivocally in the *Tai shang dongyuan shenzhou jing* (Sacred Chants from the Deep Vault of the Most Exalted One, *Daozang* 170): "The Dao says: 'Listen to me attentively! I will speak to you now about the era to come and the period of the end . . . . In the *jiawu* year . . . the doctrine of the Dao prospers and Muzi Gongkou (Li Hong) is destined to rise again!" (*Shenzhou Jing* 1:3-4; Seidel 1969-1970:238). In the same vein, the *Lao jun yin song jie jing* (Codes of Lao Jun Chanted to Music, *Daozang* 562), the extant version of a text compiled by Kou Qianzhi (365-448 A.D.), no friend of the Li Hong sectarians, confirmed that they repeatedly used the slogan: "The Venerable Lord *(Laozi)* should reign, and Li Hong should appear" (4a-b, cited in Yang 1956:41; and Seidel 1969-1970:241). This Li Hong centered eschatology gave rise to numerous uprisings from the fourth to the sixth centuries.

Maitreyan cults and their antecedents

While the Li Hong movement was primarily Daoist in orientation, a contemporary cult surrounding *Yueguang tongzi* (Prince Moonlight) was principally inspired by Buddhism. As related in the sixth century text *Shouluo biqiu jing* (Scripture of the Monk Shouluo, *Tripitaka* 2873), followers of this minor Boddhisattva figure (Candraprabhakumara in Indian hagiography) were convinced that "Prince Moonlight will soon appear; there will be terrible disasters" (Zurcher 1982:48). At least one movement had been motivated by this belief in the messiahship of Prince Moonlight. Between 516 and 517 A.D., during the reign of Emperor Xiaowen of Northern Wei, the monk Faquan attracted a large following by calling a nine-year-old boy, Liu Jinghui, the incarnation of Prince Moonlight and creating a cult around him (Zurcher 1982:45; Sunayama 1976; Tsukamoto 1974:175-79).

As it turned out, Prince Moonlight was only a forerunner of the much more powerful and attractive Maitreya Buddha, whose linkage to sectarian eschatology was intimate after the sixth century. As the Future Buddha, the one "who has yet to come," Maitreya was originally a highly respectable figure in orthodox Buddhism. His residence was believed to be in Tushita Heaven, and his eventual descent in the distant future was associated with an age of peace, prosperity, and the virtuous rule of a universal monarch (Cakravartin. *Zhuan lun sheng wang* in Chinese, Sacred King, Turner of the *Dharma* Wheel) (*Tripitaka* 452-54, 456-57). In fact, Maitreyan devotionalism was practiced among some elite circles of the Eastern Chin period, notably that headed by the eminent monk Daoan (312-385 A.D.) (Zurcher 1972:I, 194-95). Its popularization among the devout Buddhists in North China during the early sixth century was evidenced by the large number of stone statues and other images of the Maitreya Buddha in the cave-temples of Longmen (Kenneth Chen 1964:172; Tsukamoto 1974:241-461).

However, this orthodox Maitreyan worship was paralleled by a radically different form of devotionalism, one that was character-ized by a chronological shift in the expected descent of Maitreya himself. Instead of a future incarnation amidst prosperity and joy, aeons removed from the present, the Maitreya Buddha, as portrayed in some apocryphal texts compiled since the sixth century (*Tripitaka* 2153, 2146, 2154), would arrive imminently in the current period of misery and decay. More significantly, Maitreya would appear as a savior and a world-redeemer, delivering the faithful and damning the evil. He would rid the world of all injustices and create a millenium of unspeakable happiness. This transposition in the timing of Maitreya's descent had the most serious implications for Buddhist sectarians.

By assuming truly messianic qualities, Maitreya came to be associated with the oppressed and the downtrodden elements in society. He alone could deliver them from injustice and misery. Moreover, Maitreya's coming would also signal the end of *mo fa*, a degenerate and immoral period. Naturally, this type of Maitreyan messianism invited the suspicion and hostility of the government as well as the clerical establishment. As Zurcher succinctly stated:

> No political regime could accept the idea that the *mo fa* era was at hand, because that period is characterized, inter alia, by a cruel,

corrupt, and tyrannical government; and the established church could not approve it either, because in *mo fa* texts the traditional *sangha* is invariably described as degenerate, ignorant, and indulging in all kinds of forbidden practices (1982:14).

Yet because of the devastating anti-Buddhist campaigns of Emperor Wu of Northern Zhou, launched between 574 and 577 A.D., the fear of *mo fa* became real and widespread. This contributed to the Maitreya cults' involvement in a whole series of antidynastic and anticlerical uprisings since the sixth century, indeed all through Chinese history until modern times (Shigematsu 1931; Kasegawa 1980).

Some notable Maitreyan rebellions in the Northern Wei, Sui, Tang, and Song periods include the following:

515 A.D.   The monk Faqing rebelled, using the slogan, "The New Buddha has appeared; the Old Devil will be eliminated." The New Buddha was a clear reference to Maitreya. This rebellion was vehemently anticlerical, slaughtering monks and nuns and burning temples as it moved.

610 A.D.   On the first day of the lunar New Year, a band of white-robed Maitreyan believers, with incense and flowers, entered the palace through the Jianguo Gate. They "prepared for rebellion" by seizing the weapons of the palace guards.

613 A.D.   Two incidents occurred involving Maitreyan believers in this year. Song Zixian, who called himself the incarnation of Maitreya, planned a grand assembly for his followers, during which he plotted to attack the carriage in which Sui Yang Di was riding. A monk named Xiang Haiming, claiming to be the Maitreya Buddha, adopted imperial titles and began the reign *Baiwu* (White Crow).

710s A.D.   Wang Huaigu declared that "the Sakyamuni Buddha has declined; a New Buddha is about to appear. The house of Li (Tang Dynasty) is ending, and the house of Liu is about to rise."

1047 A.D.   Wang Ze, an army officer, used an almost identical slogan to that adopted by Wang Huaigu three centuries earlier, proclaiming that "the Sakyamuni Buddha has declined; the Maitreya Buddha should rule the world."

All the above Maitreyan uprisings ended in failure soon after they erupted. Yet they showed the persistence and resilience of the belief in Maitreya's messiahship. When this messianic faith was merged with other powerful eschatological traditions, as it apparently was during the early fourteenth century, the appeal was so overwhelming that it was instrumental in causing the downfall of the Mongol dynasty (Shigematsu 1931; Kasegawa 1980; Jiang Bochun 1978; Wang Ming 1984:250-59; Overmyer 1976:82-85).

The early White Lotus movement of Han Shantong

The Maitreya cult, although severely persecuted, survived all the dynastic transitions from Sui to Yuan. In the early fourteenth century, echoes of the same messianic call for the descent of Maitreya could be heard in the incidents involving Guo Pusa (Guo the Boddhisattva, 1325 A.D.) and Bang Hu (Hu the Cudgel, 1337 A.D.). In the meantime, Maitreyan eschatology also interacted with other sectarian traditions and gradually merged with them. The most spectacular example of this hybridization was undertaken by Han Shantong (d. 1351 A.D.), the grand patriarch of the White Lotus tradition.[2]

Before Han Shantong's appearance, two distinct White Lotus groups already existed in Yuan China. The first, known as the White Lotus School *(Bailian Zong)*, traced its origin back to Huiyuan's Amidist devotionalism. Its principal spokesman was Pudu, author of the *Lianzong Baojian* (Precious Mirror of the Lotus School, 1312 A.D.). Although by this time it was chiefly a lay-oriented devotional organization, the White Lotus School was considered orthodox and perfectly respectable.

The other, however, was vehemently denounced by Pudu. Referred to as the White Lotus Assembly *(Bailian Hui)*, it was portrayed by Pudu as a degenerate and distorted form of White Lotus teaching. He complained that this imposter tradition was "neglectful of productive undertakings," "transmitted heterodox doctrines," "mingled the sexes to disrupt proper human relationships," "used reckless words to delude the multitudes," and "irresponsibly discoursed on fortunes and misfortunes" (Noguchi 1986:131, n. 43). As it turned out, government officials had discovered in 1281 A.D. just such a White Lotus group. They reported that it used all sorts of prognostication devices, exorcism charms, and astrological charts to deceive people and foment trouble. Han Shantong's grandfather seems to have belonged to one of these White Lotus Assemblies and passed down his belief to his grandson.

Han Shantong proved to be an innovator. In addition to inheriting the unorthodox White Lotus faith, he also incorporated Maitreyan and Manichaean ideas into his teachings, which were embodied in the White Lotus Sect *(Bailian Jiao)*. Evidence of this merger of several eschatological traditions may be found in the slogan used by Han at the start of his rebellion: "The empire is in utter chaos. Maitreya Buddha has incarnated, and the Manichaean King of Light has appeared in this world" *(Gao Dai* 7, cited in Wu Han 1956:260). This was the ultimate eschatological declaration. The tremendous upheaval and disorder that plagued late Yuan society were seen as signals for the appearance of the messiah and the arrival of the millenium. Maitreya, in particular, became the terrifying God of Doom, his coming attended by cataclysmic destruction throughout the empire. One poem composed during the late Yuan by Li Fu illustrates the destructiveness of Maitreya vividly:

> What kind of god is this Maitreya, who has sown so
>   many seeds of misfortune?
> The flying squirrels shake the earth and stir up huge
>   dust storms.
> Smoldering smoke blankets the land, and people's live-
>   lihood has been made unbearable.
> Blood stains all the rivers, while the ghosts and spirits
>   wail bitterly.
> Only once in a hundred years will people encounter such
>   disasters.
> As of when have the punishing weapons of Heaven, which
>   stretch for thousands of miles, announced their arrival?
> Even in a barren field (wicked world) there may be hidden
>   precious jade (good people).
> But alas! They all perish into a heap of ashes!
> (Suzuki 1974:73-74).

Han Shantong never lived to realize his messianic dream. He was captured and executed soon after the rebellion began. His son Han Lin'er, later found by one of his lieutenants, was enthroned as the Lesser King of Light *(Xiao Mingwang)* and adopted the dynastic name *Song*. But it was Zhu Yuanzhang, one of the numerous ambitious soldiers of fortune in Han's service, who emerged triumphant as the next emperor. To eliminate all threats to his empire-building efforts, Zhu had Han Lin'er drowned in 1366 A.D., but adopted Ming as his dynastic name two years later, in an attempt to pacify his former religious associates. He was trying to convince them that their King of Light had indeed ascended the throne!

The later White Lotus beliefs of the Eternal Mother cult

After Zhu Yuanzhang founded his own dynasty, he turned against the very sectarian tradition from which he first built his power base (Dardess 1970). The White Lotus Sect was ruthlessly suppressed and driven underground. Still, it continued to haunt Zhu and his descendants. Throughout the Ming period, about 170 cases of White Lotus related incidents were recorded (Noguchi 1986:32). Meanwhile, White Lotus eschatology became more systematized, particularly after the turn of the sixteenth century. Aided by a new medium of religious expression, propagation, and transmission— *baojuan* (precious scrolls)—White Lotus sectarians developed a highly mature form of messianic salvationism.

Central to this latter-day White Lotus belief was the figure of the Eternal Mother *(Wusheng Laomu)*, the supreme matriarch of the pantheon of deities and Buddhas, and progenitor of the human race. Seeing that her offspring have become mired in lust and greed, totally forgetful of their true origins and therefore suffering endlessly in the samsaric world, the Eternal Mother weeps in compassion for them. She also vows to despatch gods and Buddhas to rescue them. The repentant ones will be delivered by Maitreya, the last Buddha in a three-stage cosmic time scheme. As chief of the Eternal Mother's envoys, Maitreya will ferry the chosen people back to the Native Land of True Emptiness *(zhenkong jiaxiang)*, where they will reenter the holy womb, never to be reborn. As with earlier eschatologies, this one also sees Maitreya's coming to be accompanied by cosmic catastrophes in the form of floods, epidemics, earthquakes, and all kinds of unspeakable disasters, during which the entire universe will be torn asunder and all the evil elements will be purged from the world (Overmyer 1976:130-61; Overmyer 1985; Naquin 1985, 1976: ch. 1).

The eschatological expectation of the imminent decay of existing order, in varying degrees of maturity and sophistication, has been a major tenet of sectarian thought from the Yellow Turbans to the Ming-Qing Eternal Mother cults. The preceding pages have shown that it offers a most threatening challenge to the existing temporal regime and clerical authority. The very anticipation of the advent of a new age implies a negation of the present one, thereby undermining the legitimacy of the current establishment.

It can also be argued, of course, that eschatological aspirations were not totally absent in elite and orthodox thought, either. In the Six Dynasties, both the Maoshan aristocratic Daoists in the South and the reformed Celestial Masters tradition of Kou Qianzhi (365-448 A.D.) in the North were informed by a strong sense of eschatology. What makes the sectarian version so menacing is its chiliastic militancy. Espoused primarily by people who do not enjoy the benefits of the existing order, this sectarian messianism provides a powerful incentive to put a violent end to the status quo. Often oppressed and wronged by the powerholders of the existing regime, they are little inclined to preserve it. As the image of the messiah is that of a vengeful savior, who will forcefully remove all injustices and punish the wicked, believers in this figure are more prone to expect the explosive destruction of this world and all its evil elements. Moreover, the obsession with survival and salvation after the kalpic change encouraged militant and violent actions to expedite this transition to the guaranteed redemption. It is understandable that sectarians have always been viewed with apprehension and hostility by the authorities.

The idea of closeness and election

A second major aspect of sectarian eschatology is the sense of closeness felt by members. As the *electi* destined to survive the apocalyptic destruction and to enjoy the millenium that follows, sectarians often see themselves as the designated helpers of the messiah figure in accomplishing his world-cleansing task. Inherent in their messianism is the exclusionist and "sectarian" distinction between "we" and "they." It is true that, as Daniel Overmyer has so tirelessly pointed out, the sectarians subscribe to the idea of universal salvation. Yet, it must be kept in mind that the sectarian understanding of universal salvation pertains to the universality of opportunity for salvation, and not necessarily the universal deliverance of the human race as a whole. A corollary of the eschatological vision is the expectation that only the faithful and the devout are to be admitted into the millenium, and that the nonbelievers (the wicked and evil ones) are to be destroyed without mercy. In fact, only through the total annihilation of the damned and the doomed can one's salvation, that is, one's election, be confirmed.

This notion of the "chosen people" was represented by the Daoist term *zhongmin* (literally, "seed people" or the right kind of people), popular in both orthodox and sectarian Six Dynasties texts (Yoshioka 1976). Among sectarian sources, the *Taishang dongyuan shenzhou jing* of the Li Hong cult adopted the term *zhongmin* to refer to the elect (*Shenzhou Jing* 1:2), who were understood to be the survivors of the kalpic disasters. Two passages from this text will illustrate the sense of election and the horror of the imminent holocaust:

> The Dao says: The great catastrophe is fast approaching. Floods will inundate the entire Central Kingdom. The empire will be totally destroyed, and the whole population will perish. Only followers of the Dao and the receivers of this text will be saved by nine dragons (coming to their rescue) (*Shenzhou Jing* 1:8).

> The Dao says: In the *renchen* year (392 A.D.?) there will certainly be a titanic calamity. Water will surge upward for thousands of feet. The practitioners of the Way will enter the mountains, and by so doing they will escape this calamity. From the third to the ninth month of that year, the entire population will perish. Thirty seven thousand demons of pestilence will appear; their main task is to kill people. The disbelieving are doomed to be destroyed. There are ninety diseases that kill. When the Perfect Lord manifests himself, the evil ones do not recognize him. They will be slaughtered by the killer demons sent from Heaven (*Shenzhou Jing* 9:2).

In similar fashion, the *jia*-section of the *Taiping jing chao* (Excerpts from the Classic of Highest Peace), a Six Dynasties interpolation of the famous Daoist canon, carries a clear notion of the elect:

> With the arrival of the great and small *jiashen* years, the evil will be exterminated and the good will be delivered to salvation. The good people are the *zhongmin*, while the evil people are the discarded chaff. As the designated time approaches, the demons and monsters emerge in droves. They wreak havoc with pestilences and wars. Floods will appear from all directions, and the evil will be drowned. From thirty to fifteen years before *jiashen*, calamities occur with increasing intensity and frequency. Those who follow the instructions of the Divine Man of the Great Way are the chosen ones, while those who refuse them will be washed away as discarded chaff (Yoshioka 1976:225, 237).

The sense of chosenness was equally pronounced among the Buddhist sects. The *Shouluo biqiu jing* and the *Puxian pusa shuo zhengming jing* (Scripture of the Realization of Understanding Preached by the Boddhisattva Samatabhadra), both apocryphal texts compiled in the sixth century and belonging to the Prince Moonlight cult, contained clear messages of election for the faithful. Small in number (only between 84,000 and 87,000 members), the elect were primarily lay people who, by virtue of their religious devotion, would enjoy salvation by being physically transported to the Magic City of great splendor in the Tushita Heaven or an island in the ocean (Zurcher 1982:39-41; 1981:53-54).

For later White Lotus sectarians, the idea of election for the devout was similarly prominent. Referred to as *youyuan ren* (the predestined ones) and *huangtai zi* (offspring of the imperial womb), the chosen people were promised salvation after the apocalyptic destruction. They would proceed to a "city in the clouds" *(yuncheng)*, where their identity would be checked individually before they were admitted. For this reason, the rituals of "registration" *(gua hao)*, "submitting names" *(biao ming)*, and "certifying contracts" *(dui hetong)* were instituted at the time of initiation for many Ming-Qing sectarians (*Longhua Jing* 3:21). These rituals were designed to have the election of the faithful visually and vicariously confirmed so that, after the kalpic disasters, they would rejoin the Eternal Mother with assurance.

Very often, membership in a sectarian group was proof of one's election and guarantee of one's salvation. Some sectarians in the

Qing dynasty asserted that "all nonbelievers are destined for hell. Only devout sect members will have direct access to the celestial palace, not having to descend into hell" (Sawada 1972:116, 152). At the time of the Eight Trigrams Uprising in 1813, captured sect members confessed to their investigators that they were led to the belief that "if you join the sect, you live; if you don't, you die" (Naquin 1976:13).

Membership, however, was the result of an individual and voluntary choice, at least ideally. Likewise, the sense of chosenness was also individualistic, so much so that some sectarians even regarded their nonbelieving relatives as belonging to the group of the doomed. At the time of reckoning, the *Shoule biqiu jing* ominously predicts, "The father will not know his son, nor will the mother know her daughter" (*Tripitaka* 2873; Zurcher 1982:39). Interestingly, during the Maitreyan uprising of the monk Faqing in 515 A.D., the sectarians were also described as being so fanatical that "fathers, sons, and brothers did not know one another" (*Wei Shu* 19; Kegasawa 1980:30 n. 11).

What becomes evident is that sectarian participation removes one from one's kinship ties, at least spiritually. The member assumes his new identity as a religious elect, which sets him apart from his closest relatives, if they are nonmembers. This new identity contributes to the breakdown of traditional family bonds and creates instead a sense of brotherhood with the community of the devout. The famous chant of the Ming-Qing White Lotus believers—*zhenkong jiaxiang, Wusheng Laomu* (Native Land of True Emptiness, Venerable Mother of Eternity)—best illustrates this sectarian mentality. Their native place is not the village where they were born, but is, in fact, in Heaven in the land of true emptiness, where they will eventually return as inheritors of the millenium. Their true mother is not their natural mother who gave them birth, but the Eternal Mother who tearfully waits for their return to the holy womb.

This view totally undermines the very foundation of traditional morality. One of the primary functions of morality is to preserve harmony and to prevent the use of violence, which may threaten the survival of the human community. In traditional China, the cornerstone of this morality lay in family and other social relationships. Together they exerted a potent constraint on the use of violence, which was always pictured as disruptive and destructive of human relationships. When these very familial and social ties are deprived of their primacy as a direct result of the sense of chosenness, one is liberated from a major constraint on violence.

The severance of emotional ties contained in traditional relationships enables one to do hitherto unthinkable things, including violent sacrifices for the newly formed community of the elect. This is precisely what the government finds worrisome. One late Ming memorialist expressed his concern:

> Where there is a sect, there will be a sect leader. Ignorant people delude and mislead one another. Though unwilling to contribute to the public coffer, they gladly support financially their own private assembly. They treat their own kin and relatives with indifference, but are most generous and liberal with their fellow sect members. They will risk decapitation rather than disobey the order of their sect leader. This phenomenon is widespread throughout the empire, but is most noticeable in the capital (Veritable Records of Emperor Wanli, Wanli 43/6).

The apocalyptic battle and the final judgment

The climax of sectarian eschatology is the final apocalyptic battle, when the elect will be separated from the doomed, and when the salvation of the faithful will be confirmed. Many sectarian texts describe in vivid detail and hair-raising horror the utter devastation that will occur. The *Taishang dongyuan shenzhou jing* of the Li Hong cult mentions ravaging floods, wars, and, with elaboration and exactitude, the diseases and pestilences that will occur at the time of cosmic crisis. A dazzling array of demons, goblins, and spirits are despatched as executioners to slaughter all the wicked and purge the world in preparation for the coming of the Perfect Lord.

The *Shouluo jing* and the *Zhenming jing* of the Prince Moonlight cult are equally descriptive of this cosmic calamity. The former describes three scourges *(san zai)* that will ravage the world: floods, epidemics, and murderous demons. Water, for instance, will stand forty li deep upon flat land and inundate the world with raging waves and thundering noise. Epidemics will afflict the survivors from the flood with innumerable forms of disease, causing widespread disability and death. And demon kings, riding on dragon horses and brandishing clubs and axes, will descend on earth and shout, "Kill!" The world will be plunged into darkness for seven days, during which the demons will devour more people (Zurcher 1982:65, 69).

The *Zhenming jing* provides an even more terrifying picture:

> After seven days and nights of darkness and cosmic convulsion, a demon king will appear, wearing a black garment with red cords and armed with a red club, at the head of a huge horde of demons who destroy the sinners. Then the cosmic conflagration takes place; the whole world is burnt down by an Asura-king holding seven suns in his hands. Even the mountains melt and disappear; the world has become a scorched plain (Zurcher 1982:38).

Later White Lotus *baojuan* lose none of the imagination in portraying the horrors of the final judgment. The *Longhua jing* (Dragon Flower Sutra) is illustrative:

> In the *xinsi* year there will be floods and famines in North China, with people in Shandong being the hardest hit. The populace will practice cannibalism upon one another, while millions will starve to death. Husbands and wives will be forced to leave one another, and parents and children will be separated. Even those who manage to flee to northern Zhili will be afflicted by another famine and perish. In the *renwu* year disasters will strike again with redoubled force. There will be avalanches and earthquakes; the Yellow River will overflow its banks and multitudes will be drowned. Then the locusts will come and cover the earth, devouring what little crop there remains. Rain will come down incessantly and houses will crumble.... In the *guiwei* year, widespread epidemics will occur . . . .

While sectarian scriptures portray the apocalyptic destruction as a cosmic happening principally carried out by spirits and demons, some sectarians felt compelled to take it upon themselves to participate in the violence in order to expedite the arrival of the millenium. Thus, the eschatology of the sectarians seemed to have provided a major motivation for their engagement in violence against the state, the established church, and all nonbelievers.

During the movement of the Daoist rebel Sun En (d. 402 A.D.), for example, cruel violence was perpetrated against the officials, who were slaughtered and cut into slices, to be offered as food to their wives and children. Those who refused to eat were in turn dismembered. At the same time, nonmembers were also massacred in large numbers, resulting in the decimation of entire populations in some areas. Conversely, Sun called his followers "the long-living" *(changsheng)*, assuring them that his magical power could protect them from real death (Eichhorn 1954).

The violent nature of the rebellion led by the Maitreyan monk Faqing in 515 A.D. was equally blood-curdling. It has already been pointed out that Faqing's followers acknowledged no kinship ties. But the following description is even more telling:

> They claim that killing one person makes a member a Boddhisattva of the First Stage *(yizhu pusa)*, killing ten therefore makes one a Boddhisattva of the Tenth Stage *(shizhu pusa)* . . . . Their principal preoccupation is to kill . . . . With the gathering of such a violent bunch, their power increased tremendously. Wherever they went, they levelled temples, massacred monks and nuns, and put Buddhist texts and statues to the torch (Kegasawa 1980:30 n. 31).

This uncompromising attitude, as well as the love of killing, were evident in the Manichaean movement of Fang La, who rebelled in 1120 A.D. In slightly more than one year, the rebellion ravaged the coastal area of Zhejiang and penetrated into Jiangsu and Jiangxi, bringing death to several million people (Kao 1962-63). One explanation for the heavy casualty figure was the belief held by Fang La and his followers that killing was a deliverance from suffering. As related in the *Qingqi kouguei* (Bandit Movements of Qingqi), Fang La's uprising struck terror into the hearts of the officials:

> [Fang La and his followers] declared that life is painful, and that to kill a man is to save him from pain. This they call "salvation." He who brings about the salvation of many others can become a Buddha . . . . Their greatest harm is that they take enormous pleasure in killing. They especially hate Buddhism because the Buddhist prohibition against killing is at variance with their principles (Kao 1966:225).

An interesting twist in the argument for mass killing arises here.

Instead of claiming justification for killing government officials, the Buddhist clergy and other nonbelievers because they represented evil elements that needed to be purged, Fang La and his associates said that such killings were intended to bring ultimate deliverance to the suffering masses. That is, they were acts of compassion. As will be pointed out, this view can be applied toward one's own death, thereby eliminating one's fear of it.

Two more instances of justification for killing can be cited to illustrate the point that sectarians were not averse to using violence in realizing their eschatology. When Zhong Xiang and Yang Yao rebelled in 1130 A.D., a mere ten years after Fang La's movement, they claimed that "the laws of the state are illegitimate laws, the killing of people is the carrying out of the *dharma*, and the plundering of properties is the act of equalization" (*Sanchao Beimeng Huibian* 37). And during the height of the late Yuan revolutionary period, a ballad was circulated among the Red Turban/White Lotus sectarians, part of which runs: "Heaven sends the demon armies to slaughter the unjust *(buping)* .... Only when the unjust are completely exterminated can the Highest Peace *(taiping)* be realized" (Yang Kuan 1962:326).

As alluded to earlier, if the death of others can be rationalized, then the death of oneself can equally be viewed with equanimity. For death is not extinction but the doorway to life everlasting. In fact, death is not irreversible demise, it is only an appearance intended to fool one's adversaries. Besides, death brings the ultimate reward—genuine salvation. With this mentality, sectarians show little fear of death, for it only brings them back to the paradise once lost. Thus, Sun En's female followers would, when under hot pursuit by government forces, dress up their babies in their best clothing and throw them into the river, bidding them farewell: "We congratulate you because you will enter heaven before us. But we will soon follow you" (*Wei Shu* 96; Eichhorn 1954:341). When Sun En's movement failed, he and more than 100 of his followers drowned themselves, leaving behind the legend that they had actually returned to the island of the blessed as water immortals.

This disregard for death persisted well into the Ming-Qing period. Huang Yubian, the zealous investigator of sectarians in the early nineteenth century, was exasperated by their casual attitude toward punishment and death. He observed: "All those who practice sectarian religion view death as entrance to paradise. They simply cannot be stopped from embracing their faith with punishment" (Sawada 1972:113). He repeated this remark later in a slightly different way: "Ignorant men and women are not fearful of violating the law or of committing seditious acts. As they are eager to return to Heaven, they are happy to face capital punishment. Thus penalties are totally useless in deterring them" (Sawada 1972:152). What disturbed Huang even more was the sectarian claim that the heavier the punishment one received at death, the more glorious one's ascent to Heaven would become:

> Noncapital punishment will enable one to avoid Hell, but is not enough to reach Heaven. Death by strangulation will ensure one ascent to Heaven, but there will be no red drapes to wear in celebration. Death by decapitation will guarantee one entrance to Heaven, wearing red drapes. Death by slow-slicing will ensure one's entry in a crimson gown. (Sawada 1972:3, 66, 113, 153)

With this frame of mind, death had indeed lost its sting for the sectarians. It seemed that the more heinous the crime committed in this life, the more exalted one's position would be in the next. There was absolutely no deterrence to engagement in violent acts against the state, the clergy, and all nonbelievers.

Conclusion

This essay explored the relationship between sectarian religion and violence in traditional China. I argued that the messianic eschatology of the sectarians has played a pivotal role in shaping their mentality and their behavior with regard to violent acts. Furthermore, I identified three components of this eschatology: the imminent demise of the existing order brought about by the coming of a savior, confidence in one's predestined survival of the cosmic disasters, and the vivid representation of the apocalyptic battle that will result in victory and salvation.

The expectation of cosmic upheaval produces a mentality that not only accepts the passing of the existing world but actually welcomes it. As Lü Kun (1536-1618 A.D.), one of the most prominent officials of the late Ming, observed:

People of heterodox faith organize White Lotus sects that spread throughout the empire. Wherever there are sect leaders and preachers, they manage to attract large followings . . . . Only wishing there are changes in the existing world, they are not happy to see peace in the realm (Ming Shi 226).

The notion of kalpic transition denies the existing order's claim to immutability and permanence. It allows sectarians to realize that this world is not the best of all possible worlds and that a new beginning will arrive in time to replace the current age, to sit in judgment over the entire past. The present world is relativized and doomed to oblivion.

At the same time, the cosmic crisis is seen by the sectarians as an opportunity leading to all the desirable things unattainable and unavailable to most of them in the present age. After his thorough investigation of sectarian religion, Huang Yubian concluded:

The source of rebellion and sedition lies in the gathering of people. Sect leaders deceive their followers with the notion of *kalpa,* lure them with seditious texts, and delude them with charms and chants . . . . Moreover, they equate rebellion with acting on the *kalpa.* They say, "Once you encounter this *kalpa* you will ascend to heaven; when you survive this *kalpa,* you will become exalted" (Sawada 1972:113).

The sense of predestination and chosenness contributes to the creation of a community of the elect bent on struggling with the outside world. Loosened from the traditional mooring of kinship and other social ties, the new religious brotherhood can undertake all sorts of antisocial actions in the name of group benefit. As there is no more obligation to the traditional relationships, one is liberated from the main orthodox constraint on violence, namely that it may disrupt such relationships. The heightened sense of "we" against "them" produces a combativeness which may result in violence.

Finally, the prospect of the apocalyptic battle in the spiritual and the natural worlds may provoke the sectarians into active participation in armed conflict. The horrors of the apocalypse undoubtedly help to dull the sensitivity toward violent acts in real life and make one more accepting of their occurrence. When killing is explained as deliverance, and death as liberation, there is little deterrence to violence.

When combined, these three aspects of messianic eschatology can produce a powerful inclination toward, and readiness for, violent action. It is small wonder that ruling governments in traditional China have always viewed sectarianism with utmost suspicion and hostility. To be sure, not all eschatological groups rebelled, and for those that did, factors other than their eschatology might have been involved. This essay does not intend to suggest that all sectarian organizations in traditional China were invariably seditious and violent. Nevertheless, it remains true that sectarianism, because of its eschatology, is always potentially subversive. Its messianic belief creates a sense of urgency and immediacy that differentiates it from orthodox religion. Moreover, its salvationism accepts and tolerates, if not encourages, the use of violence to achieve religious goals. It is therefore understandable that sectarians have been responsible for a substantial portion of the violence undertaken in traditional China.

Notes

1. Mention must be made of the contributions of the following scholars, who have greatly enhanced our understanding of Chinese sectarianism: Li Shiyu and Yu Songqing on the Chinese mainland; Dai Xuanzhi and Tao Xisheng outside of mainland China; Suzuki Chūsei and Noguchi Tetsurō of Japan; and of course Daniel Overmyer and Susan Naquin in North America. Their published works are too numerous to be listed here. Relevant citations are made throughout the chapter.

2. Studies on Han Shantong and his White Lotus group are too numerous to be listed here. See Noguchi 1986:107-27; Soda 1974; Overmyer 1976:98-100; Wu Han 1956.

References

Bauer, Wolfgang
1976 *China and the Search for Happiness: Recurring Themes in Four Thousand Years of Chinese Cultural History.* New York: Seabury Press.

Chen, Kenneth
1964 *Buddhism in China.* Princeton, N.J.: Princeton University Press.

Chen Yuan
1981 *Chen Yuan Shixue Lunzhu Xuan* (Selected Historical Studies by Chen Yuan). Shanghai.

Dardess, John W.
1970 "Transformation of Messianic Revolt and the Founding of the Ming Dynasty," *Journal of Asian Studies* 29:539-58.

Eichhorn, Werner
1954 "Descriptions of the Rebellion of Sun En and Earlier Taoist Rebellions," *Mitteilungen des Instituts für Orientforschung* 2:325-52.

Jiang Bochun
1978 "Suimo Nongmin Zhanzheng yu Fanfo Langchao" ("Peasant Wars and Anti-Buddhist Tides in the Late Sui"), *Lishi Yanjiu.*

Kaltenmark, Max
1979 "The Ideology of the T'ai-p'ing Ching," in H. Welch and A. Seidel, eds., *Facets of Taoism.* New Haven, Conn.: Yale University Press.

Kao Yu-kung
1962-1963 "A Study of the Fang La Rebellion," *Harvard Journal of Asiatic Studies* 24:17-63.

1966 "Source Materials on the Fang La Rebellion," *Harvard Journal of Asiatic Studies* 26:211-240.

Kegasawa Yasunori
1980 "Zuimatsu Mirokukyō no Ran o Meguru Ichi Kosatsu" ("An Investigation of the Maitreyan Uprisings of the Late Sui Period"), *Bukkyō Shigaku Kenkyū* 23:15-32.

Levy, Howard
1956 "Yellow Turban Religion and Rebellion at the End of the Han," *Journal of the American Oriental Society* 76:214-27.

1960-1961 "The Bifurcation of the Yellow Turbans in Later Han," *Oriens* 13-14:251-55.

Li Guangbi
"Handai Taipingdao yu Huangjin Da Qiyi" ("The Way of Highest Peace and the Great Yellow Turban Uprising in the Han Period"), in Li Guangbi, et al., eds., *Zhongguo Nongmin Qiyi Lunji (Collected Essays on Peasant Uprisings in China)*. Beijing.

Liu Cunyan
1976 "Traces of Zoroastrian and Manichaean Activities in Pre-T'ang China," in *Selected Papers from the Hall of Harmonious Wind*, 3-55. Leiden: Brill.

Michaud, Paul
1958 "The Yellow Turbans," *Monumenta Serica* 17:47-127.

Naquin, Susan
1976 *Millenarian Rebellion in China: The Eight Trigrams Uprising of 1813*. New Haven: Yale University Press.

1981 *Shantung Rebellion*. New Haven: Yale University Press.

1985 "The Transmission of White Lotus Sectarianism in Late Imperial China," in D. Johnson et al., eds., *Popular Culture in Late Imperial China*, 255-290. Berkeley and Los Angeles: University of California Press.

Noguchi Tetsurō
1986 *Mindai Byakurenkyōshi no Kenkyū (Studies of White Lotus History During the Ming)*. Tokyo.

Overmyer, Daniel L.
1976 *Folk Buddhist Religion*. Cambridge, Mass.: Harvard University Press.

1985 "Values in Sectarian Literature: Ming and Ch'ing Pao-chuan," in D. Johnson et al., eds., *Popular Culture in Late Imperial China*, 219-254. Berkeley and Los Angeles: University of California Press.

Sawada Mizuho
1972 *Kochu Haja Shōben (An Annotated Version of the Puoxie Xiangbian)*. Tokyo.

Seidel, Anna
1969-1970 "The Image of the Perfect Ruler in Early Taoist Messianism: Lao-tzu and Li Hung," *History of Religions* 9:216-47.

Shi Shaopin
1962 *Zhongguo Fengjian Shehui Nongmin Zhanzheng Wenti Taolun Ji (Collected Discussions on Peasant Wars in Chinese Feudal Society).* Beijing: Sanlian.

Shigematsu, Shunsho
1931 "Tō-Sō Jidai no Miroku Kyōhi" ("Maitreyan Sectarians in the Tang-Song Period"), *Shien* 3:68-103.

Soda Hiroshi
1974 "Byakurenkyō no Seiritsu to Sono Tenkai" ("The Founding and Development of the White Lotus Sect"), in *Chūgoku Minshū Hanran no Sekai (The World of Chinese Popular Rebellions).* Tokyo.

Sunayama Minoru
1971 "Ri Kō kara Ko Kenshi e: Seireki Shigo Seiki ni okeru Shūkyōteki Hanran to Kokka Shūkyō" ("From Li Hong to Kou Qianzhi: Religious Uprisings and State Religion in the Fourth and Fifth Centuries"), *Shūkan Tōyōgaku* 26:1-21.

1976 "Gekkō Dōshi Ryu Keihi no Hanran to Shura Biku Kyō" (The Uprising of Prince Moonlight Liu Jinghui and the Scripture of the Monk Shoule), *Tōhōgaku* 51:1-17.

Suzuki Chūsei
1974 *Chūgokushi ni okeru Kakumei to Shūkyō* (Rebellion and Religion in Chinese History). Tokyo.

Tsukamoto Zenryū
1974 "Hokugi no Bukkyōhi" ("Buddhist Sectarians of the Northern Wei"), in *Tsukamoto Zenryū Chosakusho (Collected Works of Tsukamoto Zenryu),* vol. II, ch. 5.

Wang Ming
1984 "Nongmin Qiyi Suocheng de Li Hong he Mile" ("Li Hong and Maitreya as Depicted in Peasant Rebellions"), in *Yanyuan Lunxue Ji (Festschrift for Prof. Tang Yongtang).* Beijing.

Yang Kuan
1962 "Lun Zhongguo Nongmin Zhanzheng zhong Geming Sixiang de Zuoyong ji qi yu Zongjiao di Guanxi" (Revolutionary Thought in Chinese Peasant Wars and Its Relation to Religion), in Shi Shaopin, ed., *Zhongguo Fengjian Shehui Nongmin Zhanzheng (Peasant Wars in Chinese Feudal Society).* Beijing.

Yang Liansheng
1956 "Laojun Yinsong Jiejing Jiaoshi" ("Annotated Commentary on the Laojun Yinsong Jiejing"), *Bulletin of the Institute of History and Philology, Academia Sinica* 28.

Yoshioka Yoshitoyo
1976 "Rikucho Dōkyō no Shumin Shisō" ("The Idea of the Chosen People in Six Dynasties Daoism"), in *Dōkyō to Bukkyō (Daoism and Buddhism)* 3:223-83. Tokyo.

Zurcher, Erik
1972 *The Buddhist Conquest of China.* Leiden: Brill.

1981 "Eschatology and Messianism in Early Chinese Buddhism," in W.L. Idema, ed., *Leiden Studies in Sinology.* Leiden: Brill.

1982 " 'Prince Moonlight': Messianism and Eschatology in Early Medieval Chinese Buddhism." *T'oung Pao* 68.

Chapter 5

Violence and Buddhist Idealism in the *Xiyou* Novels[1]

Frederick P. Brandauer

Readers of the *Xiyou (Westward Journey)* novels will find it thought-provoking that these works, which consistently project a distinctly Buddhist view of life and the world, are the very same works which in narrative content portray some of the most violent behavior found in all of Chinese fiction.[2] Chinese fiction reflects life, and to the extent that it does so, one would expect it to include descriptions of violence. Indeed with respect to such violence Chinese fiction only takes its place among other great narrative traditions of world literature.[3] Yet as works informed primarily by a Buddhist belief system it might be reasonable to expect less attention to violence and greater effort toward promulgating the message of peace.

From the time of Shakyamuni in the fifth century B.C. to the present, the basic stance of Buddhism has been one of pacifism. Although Buddhist states have maintained armies, and wars have been fought in the name of Buddhism, violence, and particularly the killing of sentient beings, has always been taken to be incompatible with basic Buddhist doctrine. In a long panegyric on the morals of the monks, the Buddha is reported to have stated that he had "given up injury to life" and indeed would not "injure, kill, or put in bonds, or steal, or do acts of violence" (DeBary 1972:33, 35).[4]

Gautama's monks were expected to follow their leader's example and, in an effort to avoid all contact with violent activity, monks in early Buddhism were not allowed to associate with armies nor even to look at soldiers (Nakamura 1972:175).[5] Mahayana Buddhism, the most important form of the religion which developed

115

in China and Japan, inherited this nonviolent orientation. One of the central doctrines of Mahayana Buddhism is that of compassion, and this is directly related to the belief in the need for peace and nonviolence.[6]

Practical applications of this belief are found, for example, in the lay Buddhist movement which became widespread in China in Ming and Qing times. Many lay Buddhists regularly carried on activities designed to free or release life *(fangsheng)*. Releasing life societies *(fangsheng hui)* were organized and releasing life pools *(fangsheng chi)* were constructed. Such pools may still be seen in the front courtyards of temples in China today. Hajime Nakamura claims that nonviolence has been the most important virtue for Buddhists in Asian countries and points out that nonkilling is "the first of the Five Precepts which Buddhist laymen should observe" (Nakamura 1972:173).[7]

Violence in the *Xiyou* novels

In view of the centrality of this belief for Buddhists, the reader of the *Xiyou* novels will surely wonder why these novels portray so much violence. No matter what the arena for action, whether it be the mundane world of Earth or the supramundane world of deities and demons, the activities and relationships in all three works are commonly associated with violence.

Monkey emerges in the *Xiyou ji (Record of the Westward Journey)* through a series of violent acts in Heaven and elsewhere culminating in several grand battle scenes of cosmic dimensions. Peace is only restored when the Buddha imprisons Monkey under the Mountain of Five Elements *(Wuxing Shan)*. In the account of the origin of the westward journey, it is precisely through a violent act, the drowning of Chen Guangrui, that we have the course set for the early life of the pious monk Xuan Zang. Violence is a normal part of the numerous episodes describing the journey itself, and the familiar pattern includes the encountering of a demon, an ensuing battle, and the final overcoming of the demon.

There is also a great deal of violence in the *Xiyou bu (Supplement to the Westward Journey)*. Monkey's dream begins with his wanton slaying of more than fifty innocent women and children in the peony grove. As the novel progresses, more brutal slayings occur with the dream culminating in an intense battle scene in which Monkey's son, Prince Paramita, beheads both Prince Little Moon and the Monk, who has now become a general. The most violent of all episodes in the novel, gruesome and gory in detail, is the trial and punishment of Qin Gui. Here the notorious Song traitor is subjected to a series of eight different kinds of tortures before he is finally judged to be dead.[8]

The *Hou Xiyou ji (Later Record of the Westward Journey)* is highly imitative and, in form, much of its violence is similar to that found in the parent novel. Thus, Little Monkey, a spiritual successor to the great Sun Wukong, must first do battle with the preordained disciples before they can be incorporated into the pilgrim band led by the monk Da Dian. In encountering monsters and demons on the journey, the same episodic pattern of encounter/ battle/submission is maintained.

Although the word *violence* may be used with a wide range of meanings, our framework for understanding this term is quite broad, requiring only the two conditions of the existence of a conflict and the motivation to settle it with force (Harrell, this volume).[9] Sometimes *violence* is understood in a much narrower sense to refer only to physical acts producing harm or insult to human beings.[10] Such a definition may be useful in studies with a focus more limited than that adopted here. In this chapter, I deal with three highly imaginative novels which project fantastic action on a cosmic stage. The narrative scope is limited neither by time nor space, and the cast of characters moves freely across the boundaries of both the mundane and supernatural realms. An understanding of violence here transcends the narrow definition of physical acts producing harm or insult to human beings. Although some sort of conflict and the use of force are always present, violence in these novels often occurs in the domain of the mind and is frequently projected at a cosmic level beyond the boundaries of human affairs.

This chapter has a twofold purpose. First, I analyze the meaning of violence in the *Xiyou* novels with particular reference to Buddhist idealism, which I understand to be the dominant philosophic principle guiding these works. In adopting this approach I am well aware that there are other possible ways to read these novels. The imaginative material in them may be taken more literally and less metaphorically, and readers may appreciate these works with little attention to philosophic principles. The distinction here is not between Buddhist and non-Buddhist interpretations but between high and low culture interpretations.

On the one hand, orthodox Confucian culture, with its abhorrence of physical violence and its emphasis on cultivation of the mind, could easily embrace the Buddhist idealism in these works. This was especially true by the sixteenth century when, in the post-Wang Yangming (1472-1528 A.D.) period, the dominant neo-Confucian philosophy of the *literati* had already absorbed many ideas from Buddhism.[11] Nevertheless, the enormous popularity of the *Xiyou* story cycle in popular folk culture or counterculture suggests that, on the other hand, the novels were often read at a more literal level. For people in the folk culture, who presumably knew very little about Buddhist idealism, the violence in them may well have been appreciated simply for its entertainment value or understood as affirmation, encouragement, or support for their own violent behavior. These popular, nonphilosophic readings could be either low culture Buddhist or non-Buddhist.

Second, I discuss the function of violence in both the narrative and the didactic frameworks of these novels. Although significantly different in purpose, approach, and technique, these works draw from a common Buddhist tradition for their inspiration and orientation and may appropriately be studied together.

Buddhism in the *Xiyou* novels

Recently significant interest has been shown in the influence of traditional religions and religious ideas in Chinese literature, and particularly the influence of Buddhism (Zhang Zhongwen 1984; Ha 1985; Mair 1983; DeWoskin 1983; Idema 1983). In an article on Buddhism and Chinese literature, Wang Enyang suggests that Buddhism has influenced Chinese literature in two ways: (1) by stimulating the imagination of writers, and (2) by revealing the karmic law of retribution (1978:7-13). In Wang's view, when Buddhism entered China, it expanded and renewed the imaginative powers of writers, allowing them to transcend the somewhat narrowly defined scope in which they had previously operated.

Until the advent of Buddhism, Daoist concerns had focused primarily on nature and Confucian concerns on human affairs. With the introduction of the new Buddhist perspective, says Wang, writers' were now stimulated to break free of these perceptual limitations and to exercise their imagination in new ways.[12] Buddhism also introduced into Chinese literature the idea of karmic retribution, an idea which eventually captured the minds of most Chinese to the extent that "today, with the exception of a few who have been influenced by scientific thought and perhaps do not believe in karmic retribution [*sanshi yinguo*, literally 'cause and effect in the three periods,' that is, past, present, and future], there are none who do not believe [in this idea]" (Wang Enyang 1983:9).

Whether one agrees with Wang's conclusions, his analysis is highly useful in assessing Buddhist influence on a great deal of traditional Chinese fiction. Much fiction does show a keen sense of imagination influenced by Buddhist ideas, and many works are guided by a belief in karmic retribution. With regard to the *Xiyou* novels, Wang's analysis is a good starting point for my considerations.

As suggested, a great many readers of the *Xiyou* novels, and many Chinese begin reading the *Xiyou ji* as children, have undoubtedly taken the imaginative material in them primarily, if not exclusively, for its entertainment value. Hu Shi, the great pioneer in *Xiyou ji* studies, interpreted the novel in this way: "Freed from all kinds of allegorical interpretations by Buddhist, Taoist, and Confucianist commentators, *Monkey* is simply a book of good humor, profound nonsense, good-natured satire, and delightful entertainment" (Hu 1958:5). One wonders if Hu Shi did not inadvertently betray a sense for some deeper meaning in the novel with his reference to "profound nonsense." Whatever his underlying views, the recognition of serious Buddhist influence, at least in terms of the place of violence, makes such an entertainment-only interpretation virtually impossible.

If the *Xiyou* novels do, in some significant way, project a Buddhist view of life, the extensive portrayals of violence in them can hardly be dismissed as mere examples of entertaining flights of imagination. Wang Enyang's suggestion of expansion of imagination as a primary Buddhist influence is relevant, yet there is a pressing need to probe more deeply for an understanding of the meaning of the violence described. The problem is that mere reference to Buddhist imagination does not touch on the central issue involved, which is that Buddhist idealism permeates all three novels. This chapter demonstrates that the violence in these works can only be understood adequately when projected against this idealism.

The word *idealism* here is used philosophically and thus has a meaning quite different from that found in ordinary usage. Here it does not refer to the vision of things as they should be or as one might wish them to be, but rather to that set of beliefs which holds that reality consists of ideas, thoughts, or minds, rather than material objects or forces.[13]

To the extend that they are Buddhist works, the *Xiyou* novels assume a belief in karmic retribution. Anthony Yu has interpreted the *Xiyou ji* as "a story of Buddhist *karma* and redemption" (1983:216, 218-22).[14] He sees the pilgrimage as an expiatory experience that Xuan Zang and his disciples must undergo in order to achieve personal redemption. Indeed, the pilgrims have all made some kind of mistake in the past and in an effort to gain immortality are purifying themselves, though often reluctantly, through the journey.[15]

It is the principle of determinism, the basic idea behind *karma*, that is operative throughout the journey. The pilgrims are pre-destined to undergo eighty-one trials, and the journey cannot be completed until the full number has been achieved. Understood as an expiatory pilgrimage, much of the violence in the *Xiyou* novels may be interpreted in terms of karmic cause and effect. The karmic cause may precede the events of the novels or may be found in some experience within the novels. Thus, whereas Tripitaka's trials are taken to be the result of his infraction of the cosmic law in a long-past incarnation, Monkey's agonizing dream experience, which constitutes the bulk of the *Xiyou bu*, is seen to be the result of his amorous involvement with Madam Raksasa in Chapters 59 through 61 of the *Xiyou ji*.

Conforming as they do to this level of Buddhist truth, which affirms the functional reality of the phenomenal world, the *Xiyou* novels do support the idea of karmic retribution. As such they are similar to other novels in the vernacular tradition, such as the *Jin Ping Mei (Golden Lotus)* or the *Xingshi yinyuan zhuan (Marriage that Awakens the World)*, both of which contain plots relying heavily on the idea of *karma*.[16]

Yet with reference to the place of violence, the *Xiyou* novels are also significantly different from these more realistic novels. The imaginative and fantastic context for their plot structures projects an idealistic view of reality in which violence is both internalized and relativized. This context takes much of the action in these works out of the realm of human affairs, in which the laws of *karma* are most easily understood, and locates it in a cosmic realm filled with gods and devils, deities and monsters. Thus, the *Xiyou* novels provide a convenient framework for the exploration of a higher truth in Buddhism, a truth by which, as I will show, the entire phenomenal world, including all *karma*-generated experience of violence, is understood as illusory.

Buddhist idealism as a guiding principle

Although all three novels assume an orientation of Buddhist idealism, the three novels do not project this in the same way. In the *Xiyou ji* idealism as a guiding and operative philosophic principle does not become apparent until the beginning of the pilgrimage. The novel may be conveniently divided into three parts: (1) the story of Monkey and his rebelliousness (Chapters 1 through 7); (2) the story of Xuan Zang and the origin of the mission to India (Chapters 8 through 12); and (3) the mission to India itself (Chapters 13 through 100) (Hu 1958:4). Part One may be further subdivided into the story of the rise of Monkey (Chapters 1 through 3) and the account of Monkey versus the heavenly forces (Chapters 4 through 7). Although much violence is portrayed here, Part One does not convey a distinctly Buddhist view of reality.[17] This section is, rather, a masterpiece of fantasy, humor, and political allegory. The fantastic frame does not contradict the idealism of Part Three, for a consistent point of view is maintained throughout, insofar as the fantastic world of Part One supports the idea of the illusory nature of the world of normal human perception. In Part Two, the mode of the novel shifts to an approximation of realism with the account of the life of Tripitaka and his choice for the Indian mission.[18] With the exception of the murder of Chen Guangrui (Chapter 9), relatively little violence is found here and no suggestion of an underlying philosophic idealism is evidenced.

Part Three is where Buddhist idealism takes on its normative significance. It is the journey and what the journey signifies that conveys a thoroughgoing Buddhist perception of reality, and it is the interpretation of the meaning of the journey that clarifies the place of violence portrayed in it.

Idealism as a guiding interpretive principle is first set forth at the very beginning of the journey. Several days after Tripitaka leaves Chang'an, he comes to the Law Gate Temple *(Famen Si)*, where he is welcomed by the abbot and some 500 monks. In the evening, they all gather to discuss Tripitaka's journey:

> Beneath the lamps the various monks discussed Buddhist doctrines and the purpose of seeking scriptures in the Western Heaven. Some pointed out that the waters were wide and the mountains very high; others mentioned that the roads were crowded with tigers and leopards; still others maintained that the precipitous peaks were difficult to scale; and another group insisted that the vicious monsters were hard to subdue. Tripitaka, however, kept his mouth shut tightly, but he pointed with his finger to his own heart and nodded his head several times. Not perceiving what he meant, the various monks folded their hands and asked, "Why did the Master of the Law point to his heart and nod his head?" "When the mind is active," Tripitaka replied, "all kinds of *mara* come into existence; when the mind is extinguished, all kinds of *mara* will be extinguished" (Yu 1977-1983, Vol. 1:282-83).[19]

Here we have clearly stated the idealist assumptions regarding the journey. All the difficulties to be encountered in it, including its many incidents of violence, are to be interpreted as products of the mind. Because the causes of violence reside in the mind, the solutions to violence will also be found in the mind.[20]

The idealist principle is normative for an understanding of all of Part Three. Although narrative considerations result in a shift from the Monk to Monkey as the knowledgable member of the pilgrim band, still in content and in narrative voice the idealist assumption is maintained. Whether the reader agrees with this philosophic basis for the novel, or is even aware that it exists, a certain mood is produced by it which allows for a lighthearted approach toward events and a great deal of good fun and humor. After all, if the whole material world is illusory, one need not take too seriously such things as physical tortures, brutal killings, and violent cosmic battle scenes.

This lighthearted approach is maintained throughout and is revealed in Buddha's remarkable behavior at the end of the journey. When the purpose of the journey is achieved and the desired scriptures are finally obtained, to their great dismay the pilgrims discover that the scriptures given are all blank scriptures:

> When Sha Monk opened up a scroll of scripture which the other two disciples were clutching, his eyes perceived only snow-white paper without a trace of so much as half a letter on it. Hurriedly he presented it to Tripitaka, saying "Master, this scroll is wordless!" Pilgrim also opened a scroll and it, too, was wordless. Then Pa-chieh opened still another scroll, and it also was wordless. "Open all of them!" cried Tripitaka. Every scroll had only blank paper (Yu 1977-1983, Vol. 4:392).

Here Ananda and Kasyapa, annoyed at not receiving their customary tips, have played a joke on the pilgrims. Ironically, however, the blank scriptures are understood to be true scriptures, for just prior to replacing them, Buddha says to the group:

> Since you people came with empty hands to acquire scriptures, blank texts were handed to you. But these blank texts are actually true, wordless scriptures, and they are just as good as those with words. However, those creatures in your Land to the East are so foolish and unenlightened that I have no choice but to impart to you now the texts with words (Yu 1977-1983, Vol. 4:393).

In contrast to the *Xiyou ji*, in which Buddhist idealism is only apparent in Part Three, the *Xiyou bu* is a thoroughly idealistic work. Written as a supplement intended to be inserted after Chapter 61 of the parent novel, this work tells of a long dream which Monkey experiences after he is caught in the spell of a monster called the Mackerel *(qing yu)*.[21] The novel contains an introduction (Chapter 1), the account of the dream itself (Chapters 2 through 15), and a conclusion (Chapter 16). Because practically the entire novel is an account of the dream, the events described are nearly all ones which take place only in Monkey's mind. Thus, both at the surface level of the dream and also at the metaphorical level of extended meaning, the operative principle is that of idealism.

The author makes this idealism clear in the narrative. At the very beginning of the novel, Monkey sees a grove of beautiful red peonies. He does not realize it, but he is now entering the spell of the Mackerel. This is shown by the disagreement Monkey has with the Monk over the redness of the peonies, a disagreement which ends only when the Monk recites the following *gatha*: "It isn't the peonies that are red, but the mind of the disciple that is red. When all the flowers of the peonies have fallen, it will be just as before they had opened" (Dong 1955:47-48; trans. Brandauer 1978:82).

The dream thus begins when Monkey sees the peonies, and it does not end until Monkey is awakened by the Buddha, the Venerable One of the Void, in the last chapter. The various episodes of violence which occur in the dream are therefore only figments of Monkey's mind. This is made very clear in the concluding section of the novel. There, the narrator, presumably the author himself, offers the following comment:

> In fact, the Mackerel Spirit deluded the Mental Monkey just in order to eat the flesh of the T'ang Monk. Therefore, on one hand he befuddled the Great Sage and on the other hand he disguised himself in the form of a little monk, playing a trick on the T'ang Monk. Who would have known that the Great Sage would be awakened by the Venerable One of the Void? Truly,
>> Monsters and wicked ones may endure
>> a thousand schemes,
>> But one whose mind is right has never
>> had to fear the demons.
> (Dong 1955:308-09; trans. Brandauer 1978:86)

The clearest statement of the idealist interpretation comes, however, in the story itself. After Monkey is awakened, the Buddha explains the meaning of his dream, and the explanation comes in the form of a long *gatha* composed of twenty-two couplets. The *gatha* begins as follows: "And there were no spring-time boys and girls, for these were the roots of the Mackerel; and there was no new Son of Heaven, for this was the power of the Mackerel." The *gatha* continues by listing in the first line of the couplet elements from Monkey's dream which are said to be nonexistent and then identifying in the second line these elements with some part of the Mackerel and its activity. The last couplet sums up the meaning of the entire dream: "And there was no Mackerel, for this was Monkey's desire" (Dong 1955:301-07; trans. Brandauer 1978:92-93).

Thus, the violence in this novel—be it the killing of innocent boys and girls (Chapter 1), the beheading of Beauty Yu (Chapter 6), the slaying of the Six Thieves (Chapter 8), the punishments meted out to the traitor Qin Gui (Chapter 9), or the killing of Prince Little Moon and the Monk by Monkey's son, Prince Paramita (Chapter 15)—is all generated out of Monkey's own mind. Furthermore, all the psychological violence done to Monkey's psyche, which causes him such anxiety and finally unbearable anguish, is the product of nothing other than Monkey's own mental process.

When we turn to the *Hou Xiyou ji*, we find that we are working with a very different kind of novel. In form and general plot outline it resembles the parent novel almost to the point where the reader will wonder if there is any originality in the novel at all. The novel gives the account of a second journey to the West, taking place just before the great suppression of Buddhism of 843-845 A.D. The novel follows the same tripartite outline of the *Xiyou ji*. Part One (Chapters 1 through 4) gives the account of the birth and enlightenment of Little Monkey (commonly known as Little Sage) who is a spiritual descendant of the great Sun Wukong. Little Monkey is closely modelled on his famous ancestor; he too is produced from a stone egg and desires cultivation; he too finally achieves enlightenment after a long quest; he too first goes to Hell and then later to Heaven, where he creates a disturbance and is finally subdued.

Again following the parent novel, we have in Part Two (Chapters 5 through 9) the story of the origins of a second mission to the West. We are told how Tripitaka and Sun Wukong, both now Buddhas, after surveying the situation in China decide that the first journey to the West was not enough. Buddhism in China has degenerated to such an appallingly low level that something drastic needs to be done. The problem is that, although scriptures were obtained from the West on the first journey, no one now knows what these scriptures mean. A second journey is thus required to obtain the true interpretations. The well-known monk Da Dian,[22] a friend of Han Yu, the leading critic of Buddhism, volunteers for the mission.

Part Three (Chapters 10 through 40) gives an account of the second journey, predictably closely following the pattern of the first. In a sequence of twenty separate episodes, the Monk, who now goes by his religious name of Banjie, first is given disciples (Little Monkey, Zhu Shouzhuo, who is a son of Zhu Wuneng, and Sha Mi, a disciple of Sha Wujing), and then overcomes a variety of monsters, demons, and temptations. The true interpretations are finally obtained, and the pilgrims return to China and a grand reception by Emperor Muzong (r. 821-825 A.D.). Thereupon they return again to the West, report to the Rulai Buddha, and are given appropriate promotions.

The important point here is that the purpose of the second journey is to obtain true interpretations of Buddhist sutras. Although the reader is never told specifically what these are, it is clear in episode after episode that the author desires for China a return to pure, orthodox, idealistic Buddhism. As in the parent novel, the temptations invariably generate or at least threaten violence, and, as in both earlier *Xiyou* novels, it is assumed that the causes as well as the solutions for violence are to be found in the mind.

The idealistic basis for the novel is established in Little Monkey's experience of enlightenment. Here the account differs from that found in the parent novel. Little Monkey goes out to seek enlightenment, but after studying with a Daoist patriarch and several others, he is disillusioned by their corruption and com-promising behavior. He returns to his home, the same Flower Fruit Mountain as in the *Xiyou ji*. There, in a deep cave, he engages in mind purifying exercises and meditation for forty-nine days. Finally a spiritual light permeates his being, and an old monkey with bright, fiery eyes appears. From behind his ear the old monkey takes out a cudgel with golden rings, which he hands to Little Monkey. The old monkey, clearly intended to be Sun Wukong, then disappears, and Little Monkey experiences enlightenment:

It was just as if his heart were sprinkled with sweet dew and his mind filled with [Buddhist] wisdom.[23] In a moment he had transcended the world and attained spirituality. He urgently wanted to ask about this but the old monkey had already moved toward him and become one with himself. Greatly enlightened the Little Stone Monkey said, "In fact people have the True Master within their own minds, but they just don't know how to find him." All of a sudden his whole body felt light in weight, and he was filled with an abundance of spiritual strength (*Hou Xiyou ji*:2.13a-b).

Little Monkey's self-enlightenment establishes the idealistic principle for the entire novel. To reinforce this we have the principle restated at the very beginning of the journey. In an episode in many ways similar to the Law Gate Temple episode of the *Xiyou ji*, Monk Banjie and Little Monkey, soon after leaving Chang'an, come to a certain Heavenly Flower Temple (Tianhua Si), where they discuss their journey with the resident monks. At one point Banjie says to the assembled group: "Purity and nonbeing are the truths of Buddhism, whereas adornments and extravagances are the demons of Buddhism" (*Hou Xiyou ji*:10.3a). Here we have not only a statement of the motivation behind the second mission but also a clue given to the reader on how the events of the journey, many involving violence, should be interpreted.

In all three *Xiyou* novels, Buddhist idealism is the basic guiding principle whereby the meaning of violence must be understood. Violence is never to be taken at face value. It is always an indication of a deeper truth operative at all levels of the narrative. In addition, violence in the *Xiyou* novels serves many functions. The remainder of this chapter addresses several of the novels' specific narrative and didactic functions.

The narrative functions of violence

In all three novels, violence, or the threat of violence, serves as a device to propel the plot forward. This is certainly true of the journey episodes in the *Xiyou ji* and the *Hou Xiyou ji*. Because the *Xiyou bu* is presented as simply one more such episode, the same function is also served here.

By my calculation, forty-one separate episodes comprise the

Xiyou ji journey, giving an account of seventy-seven of the eighty-one prescribed calamities.[24] Nearly all of these calamities have a relationship to violence, either directly by describing some kind of violent behavior or indirectly by describing the results of violent behavior.[25] Furthermore, twenty-eight of the journey episodes involve encountering one or more monsters. Most of the male monsters want to eat Tripitaka,[26] and the female monsters usually want either to seduce or marry him.[27] Some monsters are simply in the unfortunate position of somehow hindering the westward journey, and contact with them results in violence.[28]

As I mentioned earlier, the pattern in the *Xiyou ji* is for a monster to be encountered, some form of battle or struggle to follow, and one or more of the disciples to kill or subdue the monster. It is violence or the threat thereof that introduces a new episode, and it is the resolution of the violent situation that ends an episode. The *Xiyou bu* fits this pattern perfectly. The Mackerel is a monster who wants to eat the monk, and the novel, in the form of another journey episode, ends when the monster is killed.

In the journey of the *Hou Xiyou ji*, twenty episodes are covered in thirty-one chapters, and thirteen of these episodes involve violence.[29] Although the pattern of the parent novel is maintained, the strong and varied allegoric thrust of many episodes results in a greater range of threats and temptations. Monsters here do not neatly fit into the cannibal and seductress categories. Still, it is frequently violence or its threat that advances the narrative.

A second narrative function may be seen in the first two *Xiyou* novels. Violence here is the device for establishing a conflict between Monkey and the Monk, a conflict that generates tension and lively interplay between the two characters and critical activity in the plot. It also serves an important didactic purpose, which I discuss later.

In Part Three of the *Xiyou ji*, Monkey and the Monk represent two different levels of Buddhist understanding regarding violence. The Monk abhors all violence and is repeatedly critical of Monkey for engaging in violent activities, particularly the killing of monsters. Monkey, on the other hand, possesses superior intelligence and insight and is able to detect danger and recognize the presence of monsters, even those in disguise. As a defender of his Master, he is quick to take action against all forms of threats against the success of the journey.

On two occasions, the dispute over violence results in the dismissal of Monkey from the pilgrim band. In Chapter 27, the White Bone Demon tries to get at the Monk through the Pig. The object, as usual, is to gain immortality by eating the flesh of the pure Monk, and the technique is to approach the disciples in disguise. The demon first takes the form of a beautiful young girl. Monkey, who has been away picking peaches, returns and slays the girl, but the monster escapes and returns, disguised now as an old woman. Again Monkey detects the evil aura and slays the old woman.

By this time the Monk is becoming increasingly angry with Monkey, a situation aggravated by the Pig's deliberate efforts to create trouble. The monster returns a third time disguised as an old man, and when Monkey kills it again, this time with the help of local deities, it turns into a pile of white bones. A prolonged and heated argument follows, which ends only when the Monk writes a letter banishing Monkey. The disciple's words to the Monk are revealing: " 'Master,' said Pilgrim, 'you have really wronged me. This is undeniably a monstrous spirit, bent on hurting you. I have helped you to ward off danger by killing her, but you can't see it' " (Yu 1977-1983, Vol. 2:30).

Monkey is dismissed a second time in Chapter 56, and once again this is the result of disagreement with the Monk over the use of violence. One evening, the pilgrims are attacked by a group of more than thirty bandits, who capture the Monk and hang him from a tree. Despite their brutality, the Monk seeks conciliation. Monkey, however, defies the Monk's orders against killing, and in a particularly gory scene slays the two bandit leaders, literally beating out their brains, which gush forth like "bean curd." Later, a battle ensues in which many bandits are killed, including one who is the son of a friendly old man named Yang.

> Pilgrim went forward to pick up a knife and beheaded the one in yellow. Holding the bloody head in his hand, he retrieved his iron rod and, in great strides, caught up with the T'ang monk. As he arrived before the horse, he raised the head and said, "Master, this is the rebellious son of old Yang, and he's been beheaded by Monkey." Paling with fright, Tripitaka fell down from the horse, crying,

"Wretched ape! You've scared me to death! Take it away! Take it away!" Pa-chieh went forward and kicked the head to the side of the road, where he used the muckrake to bury it (Yu 1977-1983, Vol. 3:101).

Tripitaka is furious and begins to recite the spell tightening the fillets on Monkey's head. He then berates his disciple, and his words provide a good summary of his views:

"Brazen ape," said Tripitaka, "you're just too vicious! You are no scripture pilgrim. When you slaughtered those two bandit chiefs below the mountain slope yesterday, I took offense at your want of human kindness. When we reached that old man's house last night, he was good enough to give us lodging and food, and moreover, it was he who opened his back door to let us escape with our lives. Though his son is no good, he has not done anything to deserve this kind of execution. As if that's not enough, you have taken so many lives that you have practically destroyed the sentiment of peace in this world. I have tried to admonish you so many times, but there's not a single thought of kindness in you. Why should I keep you? Be gone, quickly! Or I will start reciting the magic words once more!" (Yu 1977-1983, Vol. 3:102).

Essentially, the two opposing views of violence reflect two levels of Buddhism. The Monk represents a lower level of truth, or "common" truth, which is that level of truth seen most clearly in popular Buddhism. Here, the surface reality is affirmed, or at least not totally denied, and the Buddha's injunction not to kill is interpreted literally in the context of this reality. Monkey represents a higher perception of truth, in which all surface reality is understood to be illusory, and ultimate reality is seen exclusively in idealistic terms. The debate over these two views has a long history, and I believe it is appropriate to see the Monk and Monkey standing for the "two truths" of Buddhism, a dichotomy which became widely accepted after the fifth century.[30]

With regard to the *Xiyou bu*, although the two views of higher and lower Buddhism are still represented by the Monk and Monkey, curiously the roles are reversed. Now it is the Monk who is wise and Monkey who is confused. The issue still involves violence—in this case the threat from the Mackerel monster—but here it is Monkey who is deluded, not the Monk. The goal of the monster is, of course, to get the Monk, but the violence of the dream is all directed at Monkey. When approaching the peonies it is Monkey who takes the unreal for real, and in the dispute which follows it is the Monk who demonstrates superior wisdom:

> When the Priest heard Monkey mention sunlight, he decided that his disciple's concept was even farther off. "Stupid ape!" he scolded. "It's you who's red! You talk about the peonies and then about sunlight—you certainly drag in trivialities!"

> Monkey said, "You're joking, Master. All the hair on my body is mottled yellow, my tiger-skin kilt is striped, my monk's robe is gray. Where do you see that I'm red?"

> The Priest said, "I didn't say that your body is red. I said that your heart is red" (Lin and Schulz 1978:25).

Although the roles are reversed, the place of violence, or more specifically its threat to the well-being of the pilgrims, serves the same narrative function in both novels. It establishes a controversy between Monkey and the Monk which introduces a new episode, and indeed in the case of the *Xiyou bu*, a whole new novel.

Violence and didactic purpose

In addition to narrative functions, violence also serves certain didactic purposes in the *Xiyou* novels; I discuss two of these together with the chief teaching device employed. The three novels are quite different in didactic thrust. As mentioned, although all three novels are written from an idealistic point of view, they do not convey this idealism in the same way. Whereas the *Xiyou bu* and the *Hou Xiyou ji* show a serious and sustained teaching purpose, the parent novel is less overtly didactic. In it, through the ongoing conflict over violence between Monkey and the Monk we see two views regarding Buddhist idealism compared. In contrast, both the *Xiyou bu* and the *Hou Xiyou ji* are thoroughly didactic works: the first describes a classic Buddhist enlightenment experience through the account of Monkey's dream, and the second elucidates the correct meaning of Buddhism by telling of a journey to obtain true interpretations of scriptures. In terms of didactic motivation, in the *Xiyou ji* we see idealism contrasted; in the *Xiyou bu* we see it analyzed; and in the *Hou Xiyou ji* we see it defended.[31]

The three novels share at least two common didactic functions of violence. The first is that violence is repeatedly used to teach the truth of the illusory nature of the phenomenal world. Violence is seldom what it appears to be in these works, and the reader is continually kept in doubt with regard to how it is to be interpreted. Violence is used to raise the question of what is true and what is false, and what the difference is between reality and appearance. Because Buddhism denies the ultimate external reality of the phenomenal world, and violence is a part of this world, the message is that the meaning of violence is to be interpreted internally, not externally.

This is most clearly demonstrated in the *Xiyou bu*. Here the violence portrayed, beginning with the slaughter of the innocents in the peony grove and ending with the final battle scene, is all a dream or figment of Monkey's own mind.

In contrast, the parent novel seldom overtly internalizes violence. Yet, the way in which it portrays violence reveals the same idealistic orientation. Some readers may find it difficult to understand how violence in the *Xiyou ji* can be treated with such flippancy, or even playfulness. Not only is Monkey quick to kill off demons, monsters, and any others who stand in his way, but on occasion he has to kill the same one several times, the White Bone Demon in Chapter 27, for example. Here the demon is killed three times, first as a young girl, then as an old woman, and finally as an old man. Clearly we are involved here in a dimension of reality which is different from that governed by the laws of the material, phenomenal world.

Similar to the *Xiyou bu* we find that the overt didactic thrust of the *Hou Xiyou ji* is so strong that violence is almost always interpreted internally. A good example is found in Chapters 28 through 30, an account of how the two kings of the Yin-Yang Mountains try to kill the pilgrims. After much battling, the Monk and his disciples are all caught in the snares of a certain Young Son of Creation (Zaohua Xiao'er), who controls such things as life and death, poverty and wealth, etc. Little Monkey is easily able to get free of the first ten snares,[32] but when the eleventh and last snare is thrown at him, he is firmly caught in it. This is the wish-to-win snare *(haosheng quan)*, and no matter how hard Little Monkey struggles, he cannot break free. Finally, Lao Zi arrives and explains the meaning of the snares: "Let me clarify this for you. How could the Young Son of Creation have any snares to trap you? You've just trapped yourself with your own snares" (14b).[33] When Little Monkey finally understands that the snares are all in his own mind, he gives up his wish to win and is freed immediately. He then goes and releases the others, and after a grand reunion, the pilgrims proceed on their way again.

Violence is also used in these novels to support a view of reality which is functionally monistic.[34] Not only is violence internalized and idealized to support a view of the material world as illusory, it is also relativized within the context of a monistic universe. There is no sharp distinction in these works between the natural and the supernatural worlds, between good and evil, between heaven and hell, between deities and demons or between gods and devils.

This is best known in the *Xiyou ji* with reference to the origin and purpose of the eighty-one trials encountered on the journey. The trials, most of which involve some kind of violent behavior, are all preordained by the Bodhisattva Guanyin herself. At the end of the journey, when Guanyin reads out the list of ordeals undergone, she discovers that one more is still required:

> After the Boddhisattva had read through the entire registry of ordeals, she said hurriedly, "Within our order of Buddhism, nine times nine is the crucial means by which one returns to immortality. The sage monk has undergone eighty ordeals. Since one ordeal, therefore, is still lacking, the sacred number is not yet complete."

> At once she gave this order to one of the Guardians: "Catch up the Vajra Guardians and create one more ordeal." Having received this command, the guardian soared toward the east astride the clouds (Yu 1977-1983, Vol. 4:402).

The final ordeal to complete the magic number involves the dunking by White Turtle in the River That Leads to Heaven (Chapter 99). The interpretation given of these eighty-one trials is that they represent a divine effort to help the pilgrims purify themselves in preparation for Buddhahood and immortality. The point is that here a kind of reality is assumed that is functionally monistic, and this is consistent with prevailing Buddhist views.

The narrative of the journey fully supports the monistic view. Repeatedly demons encountered are sent by deities to test the pilgrims, or turn out somehow to be related to deities, or to be members of the household of a deity, or even to be deities themselves in disguise (Campany 1985). Thus, for example, the Golden Horned King (Jinjiao Dawang) and the Silver Horned King (Yinjiao Dawang) that appear in Chapters 32 through 35 are really the helpers of Lao Zi sent by the Boddhisattva to test the pilgrims, and the monster king of Black Cock Kingdom (Wujiguo Yaoguai Guowang), seen in Chapters 36 through 39, is Manjusri's green-haired lion, also sent to test the pilgrims.

In considering the didactic function of violence in these novels, the literary device most commonly used is clearly that of allegory.[35] The *Xiyou bu* as a whole is itself an allegory in which the violence done to Monkey by the Mackerel stands for the psychological violence we inflict on ourselves by our desires. Whether or not we are willing to accept the *Xiyou ji* and the *Hou Xiyou ji* as full-fledged allegories in themselves, they are definitely filled with short, self-contained allegories, often appearing as journey episodes.

In the *Xiyou ji* we have, for example, the slaying of the Six Thieves in Chapter 14;[36] the temptation of the Pig by the Old Lady of Mount Li and her three helpers, an allegory on sexual lust that appears in Chapter 23; the attempted seduction of the Monk by the cultured tree spirits, an allegory on temptation through refinement and culture in Chapter 63; and the temptation by the spider demons, an allegory on the seven passions from Chapter 72. And in the *Hou Xiyou ji* we have the Great Deficiency King with his many dangerous pits in Chapters 13 through 15; the Great King of Liberation (Jietuo Dawang) with his thirty-six ditches and seventy-two pits (Chapters 16 through 18);[37] the two kings of the Yin-Yang Mountains, an allegory on the duality of the cosmos in Chapters 28 through 30; and the battle between Eternal Woman (Bulao Popo) and Little Monkey, an allegory on sexual temptation from Chapters 32 through 33. These are all episodes in which violence is used to serve a didactic function, and the literary device employed is that of allegory.

The three *Xiyou* novels contain a large amount of violence, and the meaning of this violence can only be satisfactorily understood in terms of the principle of Buddhist idealism on which these works are based. When the importance of the underlying idealism is understood, then some of the narrative and the didactic functions of violence become clear. Buddhist idealism is very different from most prevailing Western or Marxist views of reality; upon encountering it in novels such as these, we may be tempted to dismiss it or treat it lightly, assuming that the authors could scarcely have intended for us to treat life and the world in this way. Yet, if we can accept that these works are informed by a genuinely Buddhist point of view, then it is essential that we take seriously the philosophic presuppositions upon which this view is based. We may not find these congenial to our way of thought, yet we surely err if we impose on these works our own expectations.

Notes

1. This is the revised version of a paper presented on May 14, 1986, to the University of Washington Asian Literature Colloquium. I am grateful to all who helped me improve the original draft, especially my colleagues Professors Colett Cox, Stevan Harrell, and David Knechtges, who made important corrections and suggested appropriate revisions.

2. This essay is limited to consideration of the three most familiar traditional novels based on the story of the journey of the Chinese monk Xuan Zang (602-664) to India. The following texts of the novels have been used: Wu Cheng'en 1961; Dong Yue 1955; and *Hou Xiyou ji* 1975. I have also used the following translations: for the *Xiyou ji*, Yu 1977-1983; and for the *Xiyou bu*, Lin and Schulz 1978. The *Hou Xiyou ji* has never been translated. There is much dispute over the authorship of the *Xiyou ji*. Wu Cheng'en's dates are c.1506-c.1582, and the earliest extant 100-chapter version of the novel is the 1592 Shide Tang edition. Dong Yue's dates are 1620-1686. The *Hou Xiyou ji* was written by an anonymous Qing author, probably sometime before 1715, and the earliest recorded edition is dated 1783. A heretofore relatively unknown fourth *Xiyou* novel, possibly dating from Ming times, has recently been published and awaits study by scholars. This is the *Xu Xiyou ji*. Two editions are now available, both dated 1986. There is also a modern comic-satiric novel, *Xiyou xinji*, based on the *Xiyou* story.

3. For a study of violence in contemporary Indian literature, see Kohli 1973; for a quantitative analytic study of violence in French and American fiction, see Morrell 1971.

4. Although this quotation is not necessarily reliable as an actual record of the words of the founder of Buddhism, for all sutras claim to contain the words of the Buddha, it does indicate the importance of pacifism in the tradition.

5. Warder attributes the demise of Buddhism in India to its inability to deal with the violence of a militant Islam: "The teaching of Buddhism, especially its social programme of nonviolence and its exploration of the problem of freedom, has always been relevant to humanity. It has not always been practicable. It was swept out of India a few centuries ago because it had no immediate answer to the violence of Islam" (1980:519).

6. Despite Mahayana pacifism, Chinese history provides numerous examples of Buddhist activities associated with violence (Shek, this volume). The vituperative debates and philosophical attacks between opposing Buddhist schools may at times also be characterized as *violent*.

7. The five cardinal precepts of Buddhism are: not to kill, steal, commit adultery, tell lies, or drink intoxicating liquor (Ch'en 1973:55).

8. In succession Qin Gui is (1) pricked with needles, (2) slapped across the mouth, (3) placed on a "mountain of knives" so that blood pours from his body, (4) is pulverized with a sledge hammer, plunged in the ocean, has both sets of his ribs torn open and spread out in the form of two pairs of wings of a dragon-fly and beaten with iron whips, (5) has a jar of human pus poured down his throat and then has his body sawed into many pieces, (6) has an iron Mt. Tai lowered on his back, (7) is turned into a horse and then beaten, whipped, and made to run fast, and finally (8) has his body cut into strips which are thrown into a blazing furnace (Chapter 9).

9. Most dictionaries give a list of several definitions covering a range all the way from intense physical acts to the extreme exercise of force in any context. In his introduction to a volume of essays on violence, Wiener discusses the problem of defining the word:

> The reader of our participants' essays will be struck by the wide range of meanings given to the term *violence* in the ancient philosophical and religious sense of the perpetual war between the forces of good and evil, in civil disobedience or violation of the laws, in violence to truth and political freedom, in violence to democratic ideals, in the pursuit of utopias, in civil resistance in international relations, in paternal colonialism and the battered child, in the conflict of spiritual values and human aggressiveness, and finally, in the Marxist and Leninist ideas of revolutionary violence. We run the logical risk of stretching the term too far beyond its ordinary physical meaning, but there is ample justification for accepting the extended usage because of the very pervasive applications of violence in all the fields represented by our participating authors, in this age of worldwide strife (1972:x-xi).

10. Morrell acknowledges the wide range of usage but chooses a fairly narrow definition: "In this study I have limited the definition of violence to a physical act presented by the author as an actual occurrence which is caused by man, animals, or inanimate forces and which produces physical harm or physical insult to a human being, dead or alive" (1971:1).

11. In a recent book, Plaks interprets all four of the great Ming novels —*Sanguo zhi yanyi, Shuihu zhuan, Jin ping mei,* and *Xiyouji*—in terms of post-Wang Yangming neo-Confucianism (1987).

12. This is the same argument used by Mair (1983). Although he cites Chen Shouyi and Lai Ming to support his views (1983:12, n. 45), he makes no mention of Wang's important work.

13. On the meaning of idealism in philosophy and the range of views included in it, see Titus and Smith 1974:422-38.

14. Yu proposes that the Chinese novel be read on at least three levels: (1) as a tale of physical travel and adventure; (2) as a story of Buddhist *karma* and redemption; and (3) as an allegory of philosophical and alchemical self-cultivation.

15. Tripitaka is the Elder Golden Cicada who had been inattentive to a sermon given by the Buddha and has now undergone ten reincarnations to achieve a level of purity which makes him a desirable meal for monsters. Tripitaka's identity is revealed by the White Bone Demon in Chapter 27 (Wu 1961, Vol. 1:305). In Chapter 81 Monkey and the Pig discuss Tripitaka's transgression of the Law and his subsequent incarnations (Wu 1961, Vol. 2:923). Wuneng had been a heavenly general, banished because he flirted with the Moon Goddess, and Wujing a celestial general, banished because he broke a glass cup.

16. For a discussion of the place of the ideas of *karma* and retribution in the structure of *Jin ping mei*, see Hsia 1968:180-83. For the *Xingshi yinyuan zhuan*, see Plaks 1985:543-80. He writes: "Finally, the most difficult critical problem in dealing with *Hsing-shih yin-yuan chuan* is undoubtedly the question of how to interpret the didactic framework of karmic retribution which forms the structural skeleton of the work" (1985:575).

17. For violent behavior in Part One, see how Monkey saves his companions from the demon Hunshi Mo (Chapter 2), steals weapons from the Kingdom of Aolai (Chapter 3), battles with Tuota and Nuocha (Chapter 4), engages in riotous behavior in Heaven (Chapter 5), battles first with Guanyin's disciple Huian and then with the mighty god Erlang (Chapter 6), and is finally overpowered and confined in the Mountain of Five Elements (Chapter 7).

18. Hsia writes that the Tripitaka of the novel is at least three different persons: (1) the saintly monk of popular legend; (2) a potential Buddha; and (3) an ordinary mortal undertaking a hazardous journey (1968:125-30). Part Two gives the account of the legendary monk.

19. Yu explains *mara* as follows: "In Buddhism, *mara* has the

meaning of the Destroyer, the Evil One, and the Hinderer." For the original of this passage, see Wu 1961:143. The Chinese word *xin* is hard to translate; Yu translates it first as *heart* and then as *mind*. It is, however, one and the same word in Chinese.

20. Anthony Yu warns against an exclusively idealistic interpretation:

> In view of the prominence given to the images of the mind, the temptation to read the entire narrative as a late Ming allegory on idealism with preponderant neo-Confucian overtones is enormous. But to do so with Chang Shu-shen, one of the mid-Ch'ing editors of this narrative, is to miss a good deal of the other elements woven into the polysemous fabric of the work (1983:215).

Without denying the polysemous nature of this novel, it is important to understand what it means as a Buddhist work. In view of the novel's avowedly Buddhist presuppositions, its stated idealist assumptions regarding the journey described must be taken seriously.

21. Allegorically standing for desire (*qing* for "mackerel, equivalent to *qing* for "desire"); see Brandauer 1978:59-60.

22. Da Dian is an historical person (731-824 A.D.) mentioned in both the writings of Han Yu and in a local gazetteer for Chaozhou. His name was Chen or Yang Baotong, and he was a monk in the southern Chan school. Han Yu learned to know him when banished to Chaozhou. See Ci Yuan 1984, Vol. 1:676. For a discussion of Han Yu's relationship with Da Dian and the translation of relevant documents, see Hartman 1986:93-99.

23. The Chinese reads *tihu guanding*, a four-character phrase used in Buddhism, meaning "the pleasure of understanding or receiving wisdom" (such as 'pouring rich liquor over one's head') (Lin Yutang 1972:509). *Tihu* is 'clarified butter,' and as an alcoholic drink it would be akin to kumiss. For this information I am indebted to David Knechtges.

24. For a listing of all but the last calamity, Wu Cheng'en 1961: Chapter 99.

25. The one exception, it seems, is calamity number eighty (Chapter 98), in which Tripitaka discards his mortal body upon entering the realm of Buddha. Calamity number eight (Chapter 14) is the freeing of Monkey from Wuxing Shan. Although this does not involve violence, it is the consequence of the violent imprisonment of Monkey in the mountain (Chapter 7).

26. These include: (1) the Black Wind Monster *(Heifeng Guai)*, (2) the White Bone Demon *(Baigu Jing)*, (3) the Yellow Robed Monster

(Huangpao Guai), (4) the Red Boy *(Hong Hai'er)*, (5) the Black Water River Demon *(Heishui He Guai)*, (6) the Great King of Inspiration *(Linggan Dawang)*, (7) the Great Unicorn King *(Dujiao Dawang)*, (8) the Old Yellow-Browed Buddha *(Huangmei Laofo)*, (9) the Three Monsters— Lion, Elephant, and Roc *(Sange Motou)*, the Old Monster *(Lao Yao)*, the Nine-Spirited Primordial Saint *(Jiuling Yuansheng)*, and the Three Great Kings of Avoidance—Cold, Heat, and Dust *(Bihan, Bishu, Bichen Dawang)*.

27. See, for example, the Female Scorpion Monster *(Nü Guai)*, the Pine, Cypress, Juniper, Bamboo, and Apricot Monsters *(Song, Bo, Huai, Zhu, Xing Jing)*, and the Princess of She Wei Kingdom *(Shewei Guo Gongzhu)*.

28. For example, the Bull Monster King and Lady Rakshas *(Niu Mo Wang* and *Luocha Nu)*, and the Snake Monster *(Dashe Yaojing)*.

29. The episodes, by chapter covered, are as follows: 10, 11-12*, 13-15*, 15-16*, 16-18*, 19*, 20-21*, 22, 23-24*, 25, 26, 27*, 28-30*, 31*, 32-33*, 34*, 35, 36-37, 38*, 39-40. Episodes involving violence are marked with an asterisk.

30. Stcherbatsky 1962, Vol. 1:9. In his "Introduction," Stcherbatsky discusses the three periods in the history of Buddhist philosophy. In the first period (fifth through first centuries B.C.), Buddhism stressed a radical pluralism and the "four noble truths;" in the second period (first through fifth centuries A.D.), a radical monism and the "two truths;" and in the third period (fifth through tenth centuries A.D.), a thoroughgoing critical or transcendental idealism. Of the kind of Buddhism developed in the second period, Stcherbatsky writes:

> However, the new Buddhism did not repudiate the reality of the empirical world absolutely, it only maintained that the empirical reality was not the ultimate one. There were thus two realities, one on the surface [and] the other under the surface. One is the illusive aspect of reality, the other is reality as it ultimately is. These two realities or "two truths" superseded in the new Buddhism the "four truths" of the early doctrine.

In a recent book on Buddhism and medieval Japanese literature, LaFleur refers to the same two ways of viewing the world. Both are Buddhist, and LaFleur designates them as (1) cosmology, and (2) dialectic (1983:ix-x, 125). In an excellent article on the Huayan system of classification of Buddhist doctrines, Liu Ming-wood shows how Fa Zang (643-712 A.D.) developed the idea of the "five teachings" of the Buddhist tradition.

Although the classification is in terms of five separate categories, Fa Zang's view was that there are only two basic aspects of being: (1) the noumenal or absolute aspect, in which the mind is understood in terms of *tathata*; and (2) the phenomenal or mundane aspect in which the mind is understood in terms of birth and death. The two aspects are nondual and merge freely with each other. One is obscure and the other distinct, yet they complement each other without obstruction (1981:10-46).

31. The editors of a recent reprint acknowledge the didactic purpose of the *Hou Xiyou ji* with reference to its satire, but seemingly fail to recognize its strong defense of Buddhist idealism: "The aim of the *Hou Xiyou ji* is to ridicule Buddhists and satirize Confucians, and in mythological and supernatural fiction, this is a comparatively good work" (*Hou Xiyou ji* 1985).

32. The ten snares are divided into four groups: (1) fame *(ming)*; (2) prosperity *(li)*; (3) wine *(jiu)*, sex *(se)*, wealth *(cai)*, anger *(qi)*; and (4) greed *(tan)*, harsh words *(chen)*, infatuation *(chi)*, and passion *(ai)* See the *Hou Xiyou ji* 1975:30.13b-14b.

33. It is significant that it is Lao Zi, founder of Daoism, who explains the meaning of these snares. Through the *Xiyou* novels there is a strong eclecticism demonstrated regarding the three traditional religions of China. The basic unity of these religions is assumed.

34. Here I adopt the terminology used by Sung-peng Hsu and make a distinction between functional monism and ontological monism. In discussing the thought of Hanshan Deqing, a leading Buddhist monk active at the time when the *Xiyou ji* was probably written, Hsu points out that it is problematic to label Hanshan's concept of the universal Mind as "monistic" because there is in it no ontological commitment. Nevertheless some sort of universalism is implied: "Thus the term *nondualism* is probably more appropriate than *monism* for the purpose of categorizing Han-shan's philosophy of Mind. yet one can still say that his philosophy is a monism in practical function even if it is not a monism in theoretical commitment" (1979:108). The view of reality in the *Xiyou* novels is based on a functional monism even if, from the strictly orthodox Buddhist point of view, it does not project an ontological monism.

35. Most traditional didactic interpretations of the *Xiyou ji* are allegorical, showing how the work promotes Buddhist, Daoist, or neo-Confucian ideas. The early missionary-scholar Timothy Richard even saw the work as a Christian allegory, advocating not Confucianism, nor

Daoism, nor Primitive Buddhism, but something superior to all three—Mahayana Christianity (1913). For a recent explanation of the work as allegory, both Buddhist and Daoist, see Xiao 1978. For recent Western studies of the work as allegory, see Anthony Yu 1977-1983:36-62 and Plaks 1977:163-202. For a masterfully written and comprehensive neo-Confucian allegoric interpretation, see Plaks 1987:183-276.

36. These Six Thieves stand for the six sense organs: eye, ear, nose, tongue, mind, and body, and appear allegorically also in the *Xiyou bu* (Chapter 8) and the *Hou Xiyou ji* (Chapter 14). For a discussion of the allegory of the Six Thieves, see Hsia 1968:129-30.

37. This is an allegory on the problem of human suffering and emotions. In Buddhism, *jietuo* means a "release," or "liberation from worldly cares" (Lin Yutang 1972:1376).

References

Brandauer, Frederick P.
1978 *Tung Yueh*. Boston: Twayne.

Campany, Robert F.
1985 "Demons, Gods, and Pilgrims: The Demonology of the Hsi-yu Chi," *CLEAR* 7:95-115.

Chen, Kenneth K.S.
1973 *The Chinese Transformation of Buddhism*. Princeton, N.J.: Princeton University Press.

Ci Yuan
1984 Beijing: Shangwu Yinshuguan.

DeBary, William Theodore
1972 *The Buddhist Tradition in India, China, and Japan*. New York: Vintage.

DeWoskin, Kenneth J.
1983 "On Narrative Revolutions," *CLEAR* 5:29-45.

Dong Yue
1955 *Xiyou bu*. Beijing: Wenxue Guji Kanxing She. (Photo reprint of woodblock edition, preface dated 1641.)

Ha Longwen
1985 "Zhongguo Zongjiao yu Zhongguo Wenxue" ("Chinese Religion and Chinese Literature"), *Zhishi Fenzi* (The Chinese Intellectual) 1(4):84-89.

Hartman, Charles
1986 *Han Yu and the T'ang Search for Unity*. Princeton, N.J.: Princeton University Press.

Hou Xiyou ji
1975 3 vols., in *Hanben Zhongguo Tongsu Xiaoshuo Congkan*, Series No. 4. Taibei: Tianyi Chubanshe. (Photo reprint of Qing woodblock edition.)

1985 Liaoning: Chunfeng Wenyi Chubanshe. (Typeset reprint of Qing edition.)

Hsia, C.T.
1968 *The Classic Chinese Novel: A Critical Introduction*. New York: Columbia University Press.

Hsu, Sung-peng
1979 *A Buddhist Leader in Ming China: The Life and Thought of Han-shan Te-ch'ing*. University Park: Pennsylvania State University Press.

Hu Shih
1958 "Introduction to the American Edition," in Arthur Waley, trans., *Monkey*. New York: Grove Press.

Idema, W.J.
1983 "The Illusion of Fiction," *CLEAR* 5:47-51.

Kohli, Suresh
1973 *Sex and Violence in Literature and the Arts*. New Delhi: Sterling.

LaFleur, William
1983 *The Karma of Words: Buddhism and the Literary Arts in Medieval Japan*. Berkeley and Los Angeles: University of California Press.

Lin, Shuen-fu and Larry Schulz
1978 *Tower of Myriad Mirrors*. Berkeley and Los Angeles: University of California Press.

Lin Yutang
1972 *Lin Yutang's Chinese-English Dictionary of Modern Usage*. Hong Kong: Chinese University of Hong Kong.

Liu, Ming-wood
1981 "The P'an-chiao System of the Hua-yen School in Chinese Buddhism," *T'oung Pao* 67(1-2):10-46.

Mair, Victor H.
1983 "The Narrative Revolution in Chinese Literature: Ontological Presuppositions," *CLEAR* 5:1-27.

Morrell, Karen Lee
1971 *A Computerized Content Analysis of Violence in Nineteenth and Twentieth Century French and American Novels*. Unpublished Ph.D. dissertation, University of Washington.

Nakamura, Hajime
1972 "Violence and Non-Violence in Buddhism." In Philip P. Wiener and John Fisher (eds.), *Violence and Aggression in the History of Ideas.* New Brunswick, N.J.: Rutgers University Press.

Overmyer, Daniel L.
1976 *Folk Buddhist Religion: Dissenting Sects in Late Traditional China.* Cambridge, Mass.: Harvard University Press.

Plaks, Andrew H.
1977 "Allegory in *Hsi-yu Chi* and *Hung-lou Meng,*" in Andrew Plaks (ed.), *Chinese Narrative: Critical and Theoretical Essays.* Princeton, N.J.: Princeton University Press.

1985 "After the Fall: *Hsing-shih yin-yuan chuan* and the Seventeenth Century Chinese Novel," *Harvard Journal of Asiatic Studies* 45:543-80.

1987 *The Four Masterworks of the Ming Novel: Ssu Ta Ch'i-shu.* Princeton, N.J.: Princeton University Press.

Richard, Timothy
1913 *One of the World's Literary Masterpieces, A Mission to Heaven: A Great Chinese Epic and Allegory by Ch'iu Ch'ang-ch'un.* Shanghai: Christian Literature Society.

Stcherbatsky, F. Th.
1962 *Buddhist Logic.* New York: Dover. (Reprint of ca. 1930 edition.)

Titus, Harold H. and Marilyn S. Smith
1974 *Living Issues in Philosophy.* New York: D. Van Nostrand.

Wang Enyang
1978 "Fofa yu Zhongguo zhi Wenxue" ("Buddhist Doctrine and Chinese Literature"), in Zhang Mantao, ed., *Fojiao yu Zhongguo Wenxue (Buddhism and Chinese Literature).* Taibei: Dacheng Wenhua Chubanshe.

Warder, A.K.
1980 *Indian Buddhism* (2nd Rev. Ed.). Delhi: Motilal Banarsidass.

Wiener, Philip P. and John Fisher, eds.
1972 *Violence and Aggression in the History of Ideas.* New Brunswick, N.J.: Rutgers University Press.

Wu Cheng'en
1961 *Xiyou ji* (2 Vols.). Hong Kong: Shangwu Yinshuguan.

Xiao Jianqing
    1978 "Xiyou Ji yu Xuan Zang" ("Xiyou ji and Xuan Zang"), in Zhang
Mantao (ed.), *Fojiao yu Zhongguo Wenxue (Buddhism and Chinese
Literature)*. Taibei: Dacheng Wenhua Chubanshe.

Yu, Anthony
    1977-83 *The Journey to the West* (4 Vols.). Chicago: University of
Chicago Press.

    1983 "Two Literary Examples of Religious Pilgrimage: The *Commedia*
and the *Journey to the West*," *History of Religions* 22(3).

Yu Chun-fang
    1981 *The Renewal of Buddhism in China: Chu-hung and the Later
Ming Synthesis*. New York: Columbia University Press.

Zhang Zhongwen
    1984 *Fojiao yu Zhongguo Wenxue (Buddhism and Chinese Literature)*.
Hefei: Anhui Jiaoyu Chubanshe.

Chapter 6

Urban Violence During the Cultural Revolution: Who Is to Blame?

Anne F. Thurston

On August 18, 1966, at a rally a million Red Guards strong, Chinese Communist Party Chairman Mao Zedong descended from the podium overlooking Tiananmen Square and joined the crowd. Among the many young revolutionaries he met that day was a female middle school student, who presented him with a Red Guard armband. "What is your name?" Chairman Mao asked. "Song Binbin," the young girl responded, explaining that the characters of her name meant "gentle." "We don't want gentleness," Mao is said to have responded. "We want war." Song Binbin changed her name. She became Song Yaowu, "Song wants war" or "Song wants violence." It is said that after changing her name Song Yaowu herself engaged in violence, going so far as to kill (Karnow 1972:203).

Song Yaowu was not alone. Violence was pervasive during China's Great Proletarian Cultural Revolution. Just how many died in that violence is uncertain, but current estimates point to a figure in excess of one million. The Gang of Four alone was charged with causing the deaths of nearly 35,000 people (A Great Trial 1986:20-21). People died of beatings, torture, execution, and murder. They died in factional violence between rival Red Guards. They died by suicide and from the refusal to grant medical aid to those labelled counterrevolutionaries. They died when the state intervened to reestablish order. Many of those participating in violence believed that they were acting with the blessing and encouragement of their highest and most beloved leader. Moreover, the system of values upon which permission to engage in violence was based persuaded many, particularly the young, that violence, even when it resulted in death, was morally good.

Not everyone engaged in violence. Most Chinese did not. The reasons some participated enthusiastically and others shunned violence lie deep in the individual psyche. Without access to individual explanations of behavior, the violence of the Cultural Revolution can never be fully comprehended. Much of the information for this inquiry comes from interviews with Chinese who either engaged in violence or were victims of it. Their perspectives are invaluable for understanding the breakdown of order during the period which has come to be known as the Ten Years of Great Disaster (Thurston 1987).

This chapter asks why the violence of the Cultural Revolution was possible. The causes are explored at three levels of analysis: the permissive—the long-term, underlying factors that render violence possible; the proximate—the social and ideological conditions that foster and legitimate violence; and the immediate—the conditions that actually lead individuals to act violently. In addition, the inquiry raises a fundamental question of the twentieth century, that of individual responsibility in a political system that condones or even encourages behavior that much of the world would regard as immoral and punishes behavior that most moral codes would regard as good.

Permissive causes

Many of those who have studied instances of human inhumanity would argue that the seeds of violence are in us all, that deep in human nature is a propensity to do others harm, and that a fundamental role of the state is precisely to prevent war of all against all. The veneer of civilization, according to this argument, is very thin. Aldous Huxley, writing of the mass hysteria of the Loudun witch trials, reminds us:

> Civilization, in one of its aspects, may be defined as a systematic withholding from individuals of certain occasions for barbarous behavior. In recent years we have discovered that when, after a period of withholding, those occasions are once more offered, men and

women, seemingly no worse than we are, have shown themselves ready
and even eager to take them (1952:18).

What most men need, Huxley argued, is authoritative permission to
do others ill.

Stanley Milgram's seminal experiments seem to confirm Huxley's argument. Testing the limits of Americans' subservience to
authority, Milgram found them willing, in the name of science and
out of deference to authority, to administer what they thought were
harmful, even potentially lethal, electric shocks to their fellow
subjects (Milgram 1974). China's Cultural Revolution stands as an
all too real occasion when permission to engage in barbarous
behavior was once more authoritatively granted, beginning with
Mao's admonition to Song Binbin. Once such permission was
granted, the shackles of civilization were lifted, and otherwise
ordinary Chinese engaged in unprecedented violence. There was, of
course, much in traditional Chinese culture and the recent Chinese
past that disposed Chinese people to an acceptance of violence as
necessary or even inevitable. The Cultural Revolution's violence
had roots deep in Chinese history (Harrell, this volume).

Proximate causes

Both the charismatic authority and the political ideology of Mao
Zedong served as proximate causes for the breakdown of order in
the Cultural Revolution. By 1966, when the Cultural Revolution
began, Mao had become a paradigmatic example of charismatic
authority. The people of Chinese—most of them at least—had
elevated their leader beyond emperor to deity, exhibiting before him
a slavish subservience, blind obedience, and unquestioning faith,
offering him the willing sacrifice of their own freedom and
independence of judgment. So much did so many people love
Chairman Mao, so greatly did they admire the Communist Party,
so timorous were they before authority that, faced with conflicts
between their own perceptions and what the authorities told them
was happening, many doubted not the Party or the Chairman but
themselves. The capacity for independent human judgment was
grotesquely, pathetically maimed.

During the Cultural Revolution, Maoist ideology served to render violence legitimate. Mao proposed that violence was not only necessary but also morally good. There was resonance between this Maoist exhaltation of violence and the flamboyant bravado of China's traditional folk heroes (Harrell and Brandauer, this volume). But the hero and villain had gone through something of a metamorphosis (Kraus 1982).

The distinction between friend and enemy, people and non-people, is basic to Maoist thought. At any point, Mao argued, 95 percent of China's people could be classified as "friend" or at least potential friend, with the remaining 5 percent falling into the ranks of the enemy. Toward friends, nonviolent persuasion was the only acceptable exercise of power. Toward enemies of the people, coercion and force were often, though not always, acceptable means.

Moreover, Mao based his distinction on the Marxist notion of class. Individuals of "good classes," by definition, led good lives; individuals of the "bad," exploiting classes inevitably engaged in evil. People became enemies not for their deeds but for their class. This represented a significant redefinition of the meaning of human relationships in China, prescribing conflict in interactions that may traditionally have been suffused with tension but which were not held to be inherently conflictual.

The concrete composition of "enemies" and "friends" changed as the Chinese revolution progressed. During the war against Japan, for example, the Japanese invaders were seen as the primary enemy. During the civil war of the late 1940s, the Guomindang "reactionaries" assumed that role. During land reform (1949-1952), the landlords were the main enemy.

The categories of class became substantially muddled after 1952, as the economic system evolved toward socialism. In 1956, after major changes in the economy—transfer of industrial owner-ship to the state and land ownership to agricultural collectives— Mao announced that the transformation of China from capitalism to socialism was, in the main, complete. Orthodox Marxist theory holds that, at this point, classes (defined in terms of relationship to the means of production) disappear. In socialism, everyone stands equal before the means of production. With the end of capitalist exploitation in the cities and landlord exploitation in the country-side, class struggle, and hence the domestic use of force against enemies of the people, should also have come to an end.

Yet Mao gradually came to see class not only in material terms of relationship to the means of production but also as a state of mind. He recognized correctly that one's state of mind could persist long after socialization of the means of production. What is more, Mao eventually concluded that the capitalist state of mind was somehow contagious, that it had taken hold even in the ranks of the Communist Party. As long as the capitalist state of mind persisted, so did classes. And so, Mao argued, did class struggle.

The need to carry on class struggle, to bring it to its logical conclusion, stood as the ultimate justification for the revolution and for many of the political campaigns which swept China after 1949, including the Cultural Revolution itself. Revolutions based on class struggle were seen as both violent and good. As Mao wrote, in a quotation often cited during the Cultural Revolution:

> A revolution is not a dinner party, or writing an essay, or painting a picture, or doing embroidery; it cannot be so refined, so leisurely and gentle, so temperate, kind, courteous, restrained and magnanimous. A revolution is an insurrection, an act of violence by which one class overthrows another (1967:30).

By 1966, not only had this Maoist morality of class violence become the dominant ethical code but also all other moral codes had come to be regarded, officially at least, as illegitimate. This is not to say that no one believed in old codes of morality. But the price of public expression of alternative beliefs was often quite literally one's life. Even those who did not believe had to behave publicly as though they did. Thus, once Mao gave permission for violence during the Cultural Revolution, there was no reasoned way, apart from quoting Mao to refute Mao, to argue against it.

Immediate causes

While the stage thus was set for an outbreak of violence during the Cultural Revolution, the actual outbreak can only be understood through an examination of immediate circumstances. We need to explore what led specific individuals to engage in violence while others eschewed it. No single cause serves to explain the widespread outbreaks of violence; individuals participated for many reasons. The forms that violence took, the variety of participants, and the circumstances under which violence took place all need to be understood.

The public struggle session

The primary and most frequent form for attacking the accused during the Cultural Revolution was the public struggle session. Always dehumanizing and often violent, these sessions spared few individuals the verbal and physical abuse that were their hallmark. Usually held in the work unit of the accused, in classrooms, offices, or auditoriums, the public struggle session consisted of attacks by colleagues, students, friends, and sometimes even relatives—people one knew and saw every day. Subordinates were pitted against superiors, students against teachers, friends against friends, colleagues against colleagues, and even spouse against spouse, rending the basic fabric of Chinese social relationships.

If the accused were famous or important enough, struggle sessions became spectacles convened in huge, open sports stadiums. Crowds numbered in the tens or hundreds of thousands. Wang Guangmei, the wife of Liu Shaoqi, was publicly humiliated before thousands at Qinghua University (Ling 1972:198-214; Karnow 1972:326-331; Rice 1972:344-347; Dittmer 1978:103-04), and 10,000 are said to have watched as Ba Jin, China's most famous contemporary novelist, was forced to kneel on broken glass. Thousands watched, too, at the execution of 28-year-old Yu Luoke.

For many urban adult Chinese, the Cultural Revolution was not the first time they had joined in attacks against colleagues and friends. Earlier campaigns had served both to socialize China's adults into a new culture that condoned struggle and violence and also to draw individuals into actual participation in struggle. The thought reform campaign and land reform, the campaign against counterrevolutionaries and the campaign against Hu Feng, the campaigns against bureaucracy and waste, the antirightist campaign and the anti-right-deviationist campaign, the campaign to root out the white flags, and the four cleans campaign, all rested on the struggle session—the mobilization of the Chinese people in attacks against their colleagues and friends.

For many, the 1957 antirightist campaign had been a major turning point, the first time they had publicly stepped forward to accuse colleagues or friends, many of whom they knew to be innocent and good. It was difficult or downright impossible, many Chinese would argue, to remain silent during this campaign. To remain silent was to risk being attacked oneself. At best, people attacked to avoid being attacked. At worst, they slandered to get ahead, to climb the ladder of success. The road to political success was strewn with the bodies of the innocent. For many, the antirightist campaign, not the Cultural Revolution, represented the end of innocence, the end of the golden years of Chinese socialism. The Cultural Revolution was different less in form than in scope, with its vastly larger number of participants and greatly escalated violence.

While earlier campaigns had conditioned China's adults to the inherent violence of the struggle session, motivations for participating in the Cultural Revolution were nonetheless varied. In fact, not everyone participated. Some were able, by virtue of retirement or simply by staying at home, to avoid participation altogether. Of those who did take part, many participated, initially at least, out of genuine conviction. Of the true believers, many were convinced not only that struggle and violence were necessary for the achievement of revolutionary goals but also that the sacrifice of a few innocent people was the inevitable price to be paid.

Some people were forced to participate, as when wives were compelled to witness attacks on their husbands from front row seats. Others participated out of fear that if they held their peace, they would themselves be attacked. One lesson of the 1957 antirightist campaign had been the peril of silence.

Some participated because they were evil. Many Chinese note that the Cultural Revolution provided an unprecedented opportunity for evil people to come to the fore without fear of retribution. Indeed, they are correct. Those with pasts unlikely to bear public scrutiny attacked in order to discredit their potential accusers. One case of a petty party official who had been dipping into the till is typical. During the Cultural Revolution, he led the attacks against the woman who had discovered him in the act, accusing her of being a habitual liar with a vendetta against the party.

Others participated out of rank opportunism, recognizing that the path to upward mobility lay in attacks on those in power. The Cultural Revolution, involving as it did the overthrow of people in power at every level of Chinese society, opened wide new avenues of upward mobility, which many were eager to seize.

For many, however, the reasons for participation were more prosaic and petty, demonstrating anew the tragic banality of evil. One must suppose that large numbers of people participated in struggle sessions mindlessly, unquestioningly, for the spectacle they provided. The struggle session was, after all, a form of entertainment, of what the Chinese call *renao*. Politics as spectacle was not new to China. Criminals condemned to execution were and are paraded through the streets on the way to their deaths, as public examples to those who might be tempted to crime. Traditionally, the condemned were expected to entertain the crowds by singing verses from local operas. Lu Xun, whose satires were sometimes directed at his countrymen's fascination with spectacle and gore, gave up medicine and turned to writing when he saw a picture of a Chinese being executed by the Japanese for having served as a Russian spy. The scene is intensified by a crowd of healthy but apathetic Chinese "come to the enjoy the spectacle" (Lu 1972:2-3).

"I think it is because their lives are so boring," said one young man, attempting to explain the seamy spectacle the Cultural Revolution became and why so many participated in it. He remembers the curiousity, the fascination with which the struggle sessions were watched:

> When they were the leaders, everyone was very respectful to them. But when they came under attack, everyone wanted to come and see the leaders. Not necessarily to attack them themselves, but to see them being attacked. There is a strain in the Chinese national character that loves *renao*, loves excitement. It is a strain that Lu Xun has written about, a strain that has existed traditionally and that continues to exist even now. When people fight on the street, everyone comes to gather around, to stare, to watch. Or if there is an accident. Sometimes there

are public executions on television, and people turn on to watch. When the trial of the Gang of Four was televised in China, everyone who had access to a television watched. Everyone.

Most people don't find their work very interesting . . . so if there is a game of chess, a small crowd will gather around. I don't find chess very interesting, but some people seem to find it interesting just to watch. At some of the small shops where you go to eat dumplings, people will wait for two hours to buy some dumplings. They just stand in line for two hours and chat with their friends and smoke and wait for the dumplings. The cook will stand there with all the people waiting and slowly, casually, wrap the dumplings, pinch the skins together until there are enough to fill the steamer. Then after they are in the steamer it takes half an hour for the dumplings to cook. After half an hour, maybe some people will buy three pounds, some five pounds, and after ten people are served, there are no more dumplings. But there are still thirty people waiting. So it takes two hours, and people just wait patiently.

Life in China, before the grand spectacle of the Cultural Revolution, was boring indeed. Alternative forms of entertainment were rare. With the campaign against the Four Olds prohibiting any traditional forms of entertainment, the enormously popular local operas—time-honored sources of relaxation for workers, peasants, and intellectuals alike—were banned. The attack on bourgeois capitalism excluded Western entertainment, including music and films. Official revulsion against Soviet revisionism stopped imports from the former Elder Brother, so Soviet ballet could no longer be performed. Teahouses, where old men used to spend their days in reminiscence of times gone by, playing cards and listening to storytellers recount legends of the past, were closed. Chess and cards were forbidden. Mahjong, boisterous and always good for a little bet, had long been declared illegal along with other forms of gambling.

For entertainment in the mid-1960s, the people of China had only the eight model operas sanctioned by Mao's wife, Jiang Qing, in which heroes were perfect and villains despicable, with no characters in between. Nearly everyone agreed that they were unbearably dull. Or people could join the carnival of the Great Proletarian Cultural Revolution, entertainment that was both exciting and real. The young toured the country in the "great revolutionary link-ups," participated with joyous abandon in the destruction of the Four Olds, engaged in wanton attacks against the so-called ox ghosts and snake spirits who had been their leaders, teachers, even parents. Adults cheered and shouted as ox ghosts and snake spirits were herded through the streets. They visited the "living museums" in the homes of the bourgeoisie. Or they joined the crowds who came to watch, spit, and jeer at the struggle sessions, which the public was encouraged to attend.

The violence of the young

The quintessential Western image of violence during the Cultural Revolution is not the public struggle session of adults versus adults. Rather, it is the picture of exuberant and unrestrained young Red Guards sacking, looting, beating, killing, and warring with one another. The Red Guard violence takes a place with Nazi Germany and the Kampuchean Revolution as yet another example of the contagious mass psychoses to which the young apparently succumb more easily than adults. The violence of the young began very early in the Cultural Revolution—during the summer and fall of 1966— with physical attacks on individuals, house searches, widespread destruction of both personal property and of sundry manifestations of the Four Olds. It culminated in the outbreak of factional fighting between rival Red Guard groups and revolutionary rebels.

Adults and youngsters had different motivations for violence in the Cultural Revolution. Whereas adults had had experience in previous campaigns, most of the young had not. The young had been socialized as children into the values of Maoism, and the values they learned strongly correlated with their behavior in the Cultural Revolution. First, for the young even more than the adults, Chairman Mao held charismatic authority and deserved blind, unquestioning, near-total obedience. One young man, who was thirteen years old in 1966 and an ardent supporter of Mao and the Cultural Revolution, remembers:

> We were young. We were fanatics. We believed that Chairman Mao was great, that he held the truth, that he was the truth. I believed in everything Mao said. And I believed that there were reasons for the

Cultural Revolution. We thought that we were revolutionaries and that because we were revolutionaries following Chairman Mao, we could solve any problem, solve all of society's problems.

Second, the young people of China believed both in the Maoist distinction between enemies and friends and that violence against enemies was necessary and good. From childhood they had been taught that landlords, reactionaries, counterrevolutionaries, rightists, bad elements, ox ghosts and snake spirits, traitors, spies, and a whole host of class enemies were less than human, legitimate objects of violent attack. Recalling how one of his students participated in beating to death a colleague during the Cultural Revolution, an elderly professor remarked, "I can almost understand how it happened. The landlords were the enemies then. They weren't people, really. You could use violence against them. It was acceptable."

Third, young people had learned that revolutions were both violent and good. They believed that the Great Proletarian Cultural Revolution was indeed a revolution. With a concreteness that became all too evident as events progressed, the link in young minds between revolution, violence, and moral good became indivisible. Too young to have proved themselves in earlier political struggles, the young saw the Cultural Revolution as an opportunity to demonstrate their revolutionary ardor. But the opportunity to prove themselves revolutionary was also a chance to demonstrate that they were good. If there was anything upon which the young agreed, it was that revolution was good and that revolutionaries were good people.

Thus violence, too, was seen as good, because closely linked to the concept of revolution as good was the conception of revolution as violence, for Mao had defined it as "an act of violence whereby one class overthrows another." "Of course there was violence," said one youthful participant, recalling Mao's influence on young people's behavior.

But even this predisposition, ideological and social, does not explain actual behavior. An overwhelming reason for widespread violence among young Chinese lay in peer pressure. So intense was that pressure, and so high the psychic price of nonparticipation, that avoidance was nearly impossible. In fact, the young could only avoid taking part by staying home or running away, as many did. The "great revolutionary link-ups," with millions of youths traversing the length and breadth of China on free trains, and the Long Marches through the countryside designed to duplicate the party's history and to "learn from the poor and lower-middle peasants," served multiple purposes. To be sure, youthful rebels exchanged revolutionary experience with comrades from other cities. Long Marches permitted the young to share weal and woe with poor peasants. But free train rides were also an unprecedented opportunity for national sight-seeing and a means of escape from the upheavals of the cities, a way to avoid participation.

Although young participants were united in the belief that revolution and revolutionaries were good, individual motivation nonetheless varied. Children of workers and children of leading cadres, children of models and children of rightists, all found legitimate reasons for joining. For example, one young woman whose father was a high-ranking cadre joined when she heard that there were still counterrevolutionaries in China. Given her father's long-term commitment to their eradication, she wanted to continue his work:

> My father had made the Chinese revolution. He had wanted to wipe out the counterrevolutionaries and to establish a new China. So when my friends and I heard that there were still counterrevolutionaries in China, of course we immediately wanted to join the movement to wipe them out!

She never doubted that this "wiping out" would be violent:

> All that time, Mao's personality cult was very strong. All we knew was that socialism was good, capitalism was bad. We were revolutionary rebels. We organized the Red Guards to pull down the capitalist roaders. We were told that all things in a capitalist roader's family were capitalist things. The homes of the capitalist roaders had to be occupied by the revolution, so we, the revolutionaries, had to take over their houses. We were told that we must use the revolutionary ax against the counterrevolutionaries. The house search was considered one of those acts, one way of using the revolutionary ax against the counterrevolutionaries.
>
> When the day came [to carry out the house search], we all got

together in our offices. We were all wearing army uniforms, because it was considered very glorious then to wear army uniforms. All the girls put on caps, like the boys, and we tucked our hair up under our caps so we looked like boys. We rolled up our sleeves. And we all took off our belts and wore them around our waists, on the outside of the uniform. The belts were our weapons. When we wanted to beat someone, all we had to do was take off our belts. We all agreed that we would use the revolutionary ax against [the minister whose house they were searching], that we would treat him as the enemy because he opposed Chairman Mao. We knew we would beat him, too.

And they did.

Young people with decidedly nonrevolutionary backgrounds found the Cultural Revolution an opportunity to demonstrate that, despite their family history, they were themselves revolutionary. The son of a Guomindang official, never fully trusted by the People's Republic, became an early and enthusiastic activist in the attacks on the authorities. As he explained:

I was excited when the Cultural Revolution began, happy to participate. Because the Cultural Revolution was a revolution, and revolution was good, revolutionaries were good people. My generation had never participated in a revolution. We hadn't participated in the War of Resistance against Japan or in the struggle for Liberation. So we all wanted an opportunity to become real revolutionaries ourselves.

But for many who participated, violence was less a conscious choice than the initially unwitting product of circumstances that had their own momentum, compelling behavior based more on mass contagion than on conscious forethought. This is particularly true of the factional fighting between rival Red Guard groups, which began later in the Cultural Revolution and was, as one participant described it, "a gradually escalating thing." He tells his story thus:

At first, like when we took over the newspaper, there were no weapons. We just pushed our way in, using our fists if necessary, so no one was hurt. Certainly no one died. Maybe a few people used sticks or clubs at that time, but very few. Later, though, we began to use clubs and pipe swords more and more. And then we began to use knives. Some people died in the knife fights, not immediately but two or three days after the fight. When you know someone is using knives, you are very careful, and I was always very careful to avoid people with knives.

But the level of violence gradually increased so that people were using guns. The level of violence really increased after we had guns. I saw many people killed. Many people. Four of my best friends, three boys and girl, were killed, one when he was standing right next to me.

It's hard to say what started the violence, really. Nothing sometimes, or just an apparently little thing like a big character poster attacking the other side that the other side didn't like. But there was violence, and we did have guns and hand grenades, and I was involved in it. I had a gun.

At first it just seemed like a game, as though it wasn't real, that it was just something exciting. But then, in August 1967, I was in a big battle with my friends, and we were using guns, and one of my friends was shot. He was standing right next to me, just like this, and he was shot. We tried to save him, tried to use emergency measures, but there was no life in him. His eyes had rolled back so all you could see was white, and there was dark blood coming out of his head and the brain tissue, because he had been hit in the head. As we tried to save him I could feel that his body was already getting cold, that he was already dead. We pulled him inside, because the battle was still going on outside. I was very angry, and I began to shoot, to fire my gun. I can still see my friend's face after he was dead. Sometimes it still comes back to me in my dreams.

I don't know whether I killed anyone or not. When you are firing a gun and everyone else around you is firing a gun and people are being killed, you don't know who is doing the killing. It's easy to fire a gun. No one had to teach us then. We all received military training in schools, girls and boys alike, and in college. We knew how to use guns, and we knew how to repair them. Besides, it's easy to fire a gun. Anyone could learn.

Violence against the self

A third form of violence typical of the Cultural Revolution was violence against the self, ranging from the humiliating self-criticism of the public struggle sessions to literal self-destruction. The suicide rate rose dramatically during the Cultural Revolution.

A major purpose of public struggle sessions and of incarceration, which many endured, was solicitation of a confession, a recognition of guilt. Leniency was generally promised to those who confessed. Many were, in some sense, guilty of the accusations against them, having claimed special privileges for themselves and their families, having genuinely admired Liu Shaoqi, or having failed fully to support party policies. Not only were many of the party members genuinely guilty of the bureaucratism the Cultural Revolution was supposed to attack, but also many of them were petty tyrants, grossly unfair to their subordinates and often downright corrupt.

But in most cases, accusations were either exaggerated beyond all semblance of accuracy, or the "crimes" committed would not, in ordinary circumstances, have been considered crimes at all. In numerous cases, the accusations were simply false. Thus, one of the hallmarks of the Cultural Revolution was the false confession. Numerous people testified to crimes which they had not committed. An overwhelming lesson of this period lies in the rapidity with which integrity is sacrificed to expediency.

The reasons for confession are several. First, even if people knew they were innocent of the exaggerated claims made against them, they nonetheless considered themselves guilty of "mistakes." As one person put it:

> At the beginning of the Cultural Revolution, I thought maybe it was right. I thought maybe we did have too much privilege. I thought a lot during those days, and I really examined myself to see if I had committed any mistakes. I really loved Chairman Mao and socialism and communism, and I believed in them. I thought that maybe I was backward, that I should study the Cultural Revolution because I wanted to be more and more revolutionary.

A more frequent reason for confessing, particularly as the movement progressed and the accusations grew ever more exaggerated, was simple expediency. The promise of leniency was often kept, and, subject to persistent verbal abuse and often physical torture, the majority of people chose comfort over integrity:

> By confessing, people could avoid the most severe punishment. People couldn't stand the torture. By confessing falsely, they at least got temporary relief. During those persecution movements, there was no right or wrong. Everything was upside down, in confusion. So people did the immediate thing, the thing that at the moment seemed right,

excusable. So why not just confess instead of suffering for an utterly ridiculous cause? It was a way to survive, a way to get through a certain period of time.

Others confessed not out of conviction or expediency but out of disorientation that bordered on mental breakdown. Subject to repeated verbal and physical abuse, not permitted to sleep for days on end, finding their own identities assaulted at every turn, some people literally lost their sense of identity and came to believe that they really were the evil people their accusers claimed them to be. The images invoked in Chinese minds by the appellation *ox ghost and snake spirit* are vivid and real, and many Chinese write or speak about coming to feel that they were literally what their labels said they were. In fact, so extreme could the disorientation become that even after rehabilitation and the removing of labels, some continued to insist that they really were the ox ghosts and snake spirits they had confessed to being.

The most extreme form of violence against the self was suicide. While it is obviously impossible to say with certainty why any individual takes his or her own life, reports of colleagues and friends can contribute to our understanding. No single factor can explain the high rate of suicide during the Cultural Revolution; people took their own lives for a variety of reasons.

Officially, suicide represented an admission of guilt, and in such cases memorial services traditionally held for the dead were often replaced by a struggle session against the deceased. In some cases, suicide may indeed have been an admission of guilt, and friends and relatives of suicide victims report continuing uneasiness about the possibility that the victim was guilty after all.

In many cases, however, suicide during the Cultural Revolution derived from the depression and despair brought on by persistent attacks and an inability to respond satisfactorily to tragically adverse circumstances. As one observer recalls, "People committed suicide because they were not optimistic enough. There was no bright future." In the hopelessness born of depression, some people came to see life as no longer worth living. It is significant, for instance, that many people reported their friends' suicides as taking place in the early morning, hours before others were awake. One of the symptoms of clinical depression is early waking, when the sense of depression is strongest.

For others, suicide was born of fear, a means of escape from a terrifying situation. One man describes the suicide of a classmate:

> There was a group at the school who were under a lot of pressure for having opposed the army, and they were trying to shift the blame to others by putting up big character posters on the dormitory where my classmate lived. It said all sorts of things—"you female ox ghost and snake spirit, you betrayer of our country, you who lost the face of our great nation, you must confess in three days or otherwise revolutionary action will be taken." Lots of people got such ultimatums. But this was the first for her, and she jumped out of the window just a few minutes after those boys left. I rushed to the spot just one or two minutes after she leaped. I saw her wriggling on the ground with one leg just broken. No blood. Just one or two drops out of her mouth. She died a half-hour later in the hospital. The doctor said her heart had been shaken out of position.

Finally, suicide was sometimes a form of protest against an unjust government. In explaining the suicides of colleagues, Chinese intellectuals quote the aphorism that intellectuals would rather kill themselves than suffer humiliation. The suicide of protest has deep roots in traditional China, exemplified in the death of Qu Yuan, a patriotic poet who is said to have drowned himself in protest when the emperor refused to heed his advice. Fu Lei, the erudite Chinese translator of Balzac, a flamboyant scholar conversant with music, literature, and art, is only one of many intellectuals who killed himself, together with his wife, in 1968 in just such a suicide of protest (Fu 1981).

Violence by the state

One final form of violence characteristic of the Cultural Revolution remains little understood outside China and little discussed within. It is the violence that occurred when the state moved to reestablish order then sought to maintain it through routinized repression. The state engaged in violence, for example, when the military intervened to end factional fighting between rival Red Guard groups, often rounding up young people by the tens of thousands, first confining them within the cities and then dispatching them to the countryside. Between 1968, when this policy began, and 1975 some twelve million young people were sent to the countryside in what was surely the largest forced migration in the history of humankind (Bernstein 1977).

Violence also occurred when university campuses were taken over by the so-called worker-soldier propaganda teams. Many in China argue that the worst violence took place at this point, not at the time of youthful rebellion. During this stage, numerous young people were executed. More research is needed before this period can be fully understood. In the end, however, the state emerged victorious in the Cultural Revolution—first in the form of the military and later in the form of the party. The revolutionary rebels, many of whom believed they had been acting on behalf of Mao and in the interests of democracy and justice, became new victims. Throughout China, party cadres who had been victims in the early stages of the Cultural Revolution, many of whom had indeed been guilty of varying degrees of abuse of power and outright corruption, returned, officially exonerated, to their former posts.

The legacy of the Cultural Revolution

The legacy of the Cultural Revolution is thus extremely complex. Harold Lasswell (1971:42) has argued that "revolutions are ruptures of conscience," that violence against existing symbols of authority demands that participants inevitably face a crisis of conscience. Mao Zedong would agree. A rupture of conscience lay at the heart of his revolutionary redefinition of human relationships, a fundamental goal of Maoist politics. The movement was often called a "revolution that touches people to their very souls." Whole classes of people traditionally viewed as benign were transformed into enemies, for the Cultural Revolution self-consciously aimed to break connections with the Chinese past. Political campaigns and struggle sessions had long been used to further a rupture of conscience. Through participation, the reasoning went, comes belief. Participation in struggle can both demonstrate the efficacy of struggle and foster a belief in the legitimacy of the judgment against the objects of attack.

The Cultural Revolution did indeed touch people to their very souls; but for many adults, participation was less a rupture of conscience than an abrogation of conscience, sacrifice of their own independent judgment to a charismatic leader and a system of values in which they did not entirely believe. During both the antirightist campaign and the Cultural Revolution, many people knew both that their victims were innocent and that, by their own moral standards, they were doing wrong. They knew that they acted out of expediency. Hence for many adults, a legacy of the Cultural Revolution is a lingering sense of guilt—a recognition that, although they could still distinguish right from wrong, they acted in their own immediate self-interest rather than on the basis of moral principles:

> None of us is innocent. Not really. Not completely. Not even those of us who were victims. Perhaps somewhere in China is someone, are some people, who have always been honest, who have always told the truth, always spoken what was in their hearts, who have never had to speak words that they did not feel. Who they are, where they are, I couldn't say. For all of us, at one time or another, have had to speak words that we did not really believe. Because the political line has changed so often, so dramatically. Only people who did not think at all, who have lost the capacity for thought, could follow all those changing lines, could believe all the shifts in line. There are people like that, people who blow with the wind, without ever questioning or thinking. But they have lost the capacity for thought and therefore, perhaps, the capacity to be human. They are torpid.

For those who engaged in attacks against the self, who confessed to crimes of which they were not guilty, this guilt is compounded by a more or less profound loss of self-respect, a sense of having betrayed themselves and anger against those who "made them do it."

While many adults knew that they acted not out of morality but out of expediency in the Cultural Revolution, many of the young people both believed their behavior to be good and were unaware of alternative moral standards which might judge them wrong. Basic standards of right and wrong, apparently, are less innate than instilled. In 1980, when the Cultural Revolution had ended and an American teacher in China had occasion to teach her class the Ten Commandments, there was one commandment her students simply did not understand: "Thou shalt not bear false witness against thy neighbor." Products of the Cultural Revolution, they had grown up steeped in false witness. They had never learned that it might be wrong.

Nonetheless, today many feel guilty for their behavior as youthful rebels. Socialization into Maoist values was never perfect, and the family and community often exerted an influence at odds with the official line. Thus, one early participant expressed his guilt by saying:

> I feel I must apologize to my country and my people. I must fall on the ground on my knees and beg for their forgiveness. Because if we fanatic young Red Guards had not done what we did, the country would not have been paralyzed. If we had not done what we did, what happened . . . would never have happened. On the one hand, it is true that we were used by the Gang of Four. But on the other hand, in terms of the entire history of what happened, we, I, my generation, still have a share of the responsibility. We doubted. We recognized they were evil. We opposed them in our hearts. But we did not oppose them openly.

But the dominant legacy among those who were young during the Cultural Revolution seems less guilt and more feelings of betrayal and consequent anger and cynicism. The man who had taken up guns during factional fighting, who lost several friends to violence during the Cultural Revolution, concludes:

> When I first joined the Cultural Revolution, I believed in the ideals of Mao Zedong. I thought I was fighting for Mao and against Liu Shaoqi, and I thought that the conservatives represented Liu Shaoqi and were the enemy. But I gradually came to realize that the conservatives weren't the enemy. It was Chairman Mao who made us do that as part of his own struggle for power. He had used all the Red Guards, both the conservatives and the revolutionary rebels. It was Chairman Mao who was the enemy.

Many of the young have overcome their guilt and feelings of betrayal to make positive contributions to their society. But many others remain cynical and more preoccupied with their own advancement and material comfort than with contributing to their country. The major legacy of the Cultural Revolution among the young is a profound sense of anomie.

But one must speculate (and it can only be speculation because most Chinese are inaccessible to interviewers) that for the vast majority of participants in the spectacle of the Cultural Revolution, that episode was not a revolution that touched them to their very souls. The vast majority must have been those torpid individuals who always blow with the wind, never questioning or thinking, those apathetic individuals Lu Xun so deplored, who joined the movement for the excitement of *renao* or from a deeply ingrained tendency to follow. These individuals neither understood the Cultural Revolution when it happened nor understand it today. Nor do they wonder too deeply at their role in it. This includes those who participated on behalf of the state.

One must also speculate that for many participants, especially the rank opportunists, the rupture of conscience had taken place much earlier, in the course of previous campaigns. Victims describe some of their attackers as people without conscience, who used the Cultural Revolution for their own advancement, attacking the innocent to get ahead. There is no reason to doubt that, in the basic level units where victims and persecutors continue to live and work side-by-side, those who seized the opportunity then would do so again without great pangs of conscience.

The fundamental question of guilt remains. Within China, the party itself has raised the question of blame and found responsibility to lie with a few high-ranking leaders, especially the Gang of Four. Mao Zedong has been found guilty only of "making mistakes," and the thought of Mao Zedong remains enshrined as one of the "four cardinal principles" to which all Chinese must subscribe. The Maoist concept of class struggle which motivated the Cultural Revolution has been muted but hardly rejected. Contrary to desultory promises that the guilty will be brought to justice, persecuted and persecutors continue to live and work side-by-side.

Certainly the Gang of Four was guilty of egregious wrongdoing. But to burden them with exclusive blame denies the fundamental circumstances of the Cultural Revolution. The crimes were not an exclusive preserve of a few, nor did they take place secretly, behind closed doors. The persecutions were public, and the citizens of China were asked not merely to stand as silent witness but to participate actively. And they did.

But the current leadership of China has good reason to refuse further investigation and to continue its insistence that the Cultural Revolution is "a thing of the past." For the party to delve further into the circumstances of the Cultural Revolution would risk further undermining its already severely eroded legitimacy. To focus too closely on Mao's role would bring public opprobrium onto the Lenin and Stalin of China, calling into doubt the legitimacy of the revolution itself. To question the function of Maoist ideology during the Cultural Revolution would call that ideology into question, challenging the very right of the party to rule. To investigate too carefully who persecuted whom would risk unleashing a spiral of revenge, with the victims of the Cultural Revolution rising as new oppressors. Such an investigation, in short, could not avoid questioning the order imposed by the Communist Party, its very right and ability to govern.

Avoiding such an investigation, on the other hand, leaves the country morally adrift. Recently, and most notably in the "River Elegy" television series, some of China's intellectuals have tentatively and obliquely broached the question. Their answers, too, are unsatisfying, blaming most of the country's ills on Chinese culture. No outside, impartial court has undertaken a review of moral responsibility for the Cultural Revolution. Western governments have chosen to remain silent in an era stressing China's economic development and an opening to the West.

The Cultural Revolution demonstrates how difficult the issues of individual judgment have become in modern authoritarian states. At the most fundamental level, responsibility for the Cultural Revolution lies in a dictatorial system which provides no checks against the flagrant abuse of power and which rests on principles defining a certain portion of its population as "enemies." If the problem lies in the system itself, how can individuals within that system be held responsible? Is it just to assign guilt to individual members of a culture that has no tradition of human rights, has taken subservience to authority as a primary tenet, and has long been steeped in violence? If right and wrong are not innate but instilled, can the young be blamed for behavior based on the values society instilled in them? If the political system rewards those who struggle for power, can such people rightly be called to task? Can mindless, unthinking followers be blamed for participating in events they could not understand? If human behavior is so much the product of circumstance, can individuals be deemed guilty for failing to rise above their circumstances?

These questions are without easy answers. The tools of the social scientist and historian are lacking in means to respond to them. As the inability of putatively "value free" social science to handle such questions becomes increasingly apparent, we must search for the tools that will permit us to make reasoned moral judgments. Meanwhile, it is surely the responsibility of the social scientist and historian publicly to decry the social and political system that leads individuals to actions that must be regarded as immoral. Similarly, while understanding and even forgiving the criminal, we must nonetheless deplore the crime.

References

A Great Trial
  1986 *A Great Trial in Chinese History: The Trial of the Lin Biao and Jiang Qing Counterrevolutionary Cliques.* Beijing: New World Press.

Bernstein, Thomas P.
  1977 *Up to the Mountains and Down to the Villages: The Transfer of Youth from Urban to Rural China.* New Haven, Conn.: Yale University Press.

Dittmer, Lowell
  1978 *Liu Shao-ch'i and the Chinese Cultural Revolution.* Berkeley and Los Angeles: University of California Press.

Fu Lei
  1981 *Fu Lei Jiashu (Fu Lei's Letters from Home).* Beijing: Sanlian Bookstore.

Huxley, Aldous
  1952 *The Devils of Loudon.* New York: Harper and Row.

Karnow, Stanley
  1972 *Mao and China.* New York: Viking.

Kraus, Richard Curt
  1982 *Class Conflict in Chinese Socialism.* New York: Columbia University Press.

Lasswell, Harold
  1971 *Politics: Who Gets What, When, How.* New York and Cleveland: Meridian.

Ling, Ken
  1972 *Revenge of Heaven.* New York: Putnam.

Lu Xun
  1972 *Selected Stories.* Beijing: Foreign Languages Press.

Mao Zedong
  1967 "Report on an Investigation of the Peasant Movement in Hunan," in *Selected Works of Mao Tse-tung,* 23-59. Beijing: Foreign Languages Press.

Milgram, Stanley
    1974 *Obedience to Authority*. New York: Harper and Row.

Rice, Edward E.
    1972 *Mao's Way*. Berkeley and Los Angeles: University of California Press.

Thurston, Anne F.
    1987 *Enemies of the People: The Ordeal of the Intellectuals in China's Great Cultural Revolution*. New York: Knopf.

Chapter 7

The Politics of Revenge in Rural China During the Cultural Revolution

Richard Madsen

Round and round
Spin the wheel,
The devil take
The commonweal.

Thus go the opening and closing stanzas of a poem that William Hinton says was written by a Chinese journalist to Mao Zedong during the Cultural Revolution (Hinton 1984:675-76). In *Shenfan*, his vivid account of the history of Long Bow village in the 1950s and 1960s, Hinton cites this poem to express his own anger and despair in the face of the seeming senselessness of the Cultural Revolution. In Hinton's account, one of the profoundest of the horrors of the Cultural Revolution was indeed its meaninglessness:

> Factionalism, the unprincipled struggle for power between individuals, cliques, bands and mass organizations, once launched at the center, soon burgeoned beyond control, expanded exponentially according to laws of its own, swept everything before it and swamped the country. I had no theory to explain it, no grasp of its magnitude, no true perception of the disaster it threatened. What I did see wherever I looked was irrational confrontation and, in society as a whole, frustration and the widespread stagnation of production (Hinton 1984:756).

As he describes the battles between "rebel" and "loyalist" factions in Long Bow Village and throughout Shanxi Province, he can discern no real purpose to the fighting except the raw struggle for power:

I use the terms *rebel* and *loyalist* with some hesitation and place them in quotes for good reason. No one should assume any important ideological or political differences between the two groups. . . . It was a case of the "outs" expressing dissatisfaction with the performance of the "ins," in part because that performance was flawed, but mainly because this expression gave the "outs" a chance to get in.

This distinction must be stressed because there is a notion widespread in the West that Mao urged political radicals to rise up, then betrayed and suppressed them. It would be unfortunate if the terms *rebel* and *loyalist* give credence to this myth. I use these terms for convenience only, to describe two sets of activists, with essentially the same politics, who quarreled over power (Hinton 1984:521).

In Hinton's account, contending factions seek power purely as an end in itself, certainly not to impose a distinctive vision of social order on China and not even to gain personal wealth or status. The ceaseless pursuit of power is self-defeating because it creates a world where power can never be enjoyed, because victories in the struggle for power engender counterattacks that leave powerholders constantly vulnerable.

What could engender such a senseless circle of violence? Although Hinton calls it *irrational*, he nonetheless sees it as expanding "according to laws of its own," although he has "no theory to explain it" (Hinton 1984:675-76). In this chapter, I suggest the beginnings of a theory to account for the "laws of its own" that drove the cycle of violence. My theory is a moral theory, designed to account for pervasive immorality. Its key elements are the themes of "collective memory" and "moral reciprocity," and my argument will analyze the circumstances under which these two important aspects of Chinese community life could lead to an unrestrained quest for revenge.

The theory I suggest is even more tragic than the Hobbesian theory that might seem the most obvious place for a Western social scientist to begin reflecting on the Cultural Revolution. In Hobbes's vision, the Cultural Revolution's horrors might be understandable as an outcome of the basic state of human nature, for human beings are radically selfish, and the "general inclination of mankind" is "a perpetual and restless desire of power after power, that ceaseth only in death" (Hobbes 1968:161). In my view, those aspects of the

Cultural Revolution described by Hinton call for a theory even more tragic, for they represent the perversion of a more hopeful dimension of human nature than that envisioned by Hobbes, the social-bondedness of human nature, through which individual identity and hence true individual self-interest is rooted in moral commitments to communities.

Hobbes's state of nature is a condition in which radically self-interested individuals seek to maximize their advantages, if necessary and if possible at the expense of other individuals. But the chaos which the pursuit of self-interest can potentially create can be held in check by appeals to rational self-interest. Calculating the degree of horrible insecurity that would be the cost of unrestrained pursuit of their basic inclinations to seek power after power, most individuals will conclude that it is in their fundamental self-interest to cede authority to a state that can impose limits on such action.

As portrayed in Hinton's *Shenfan*, however, the warring people of Long Bow showed no inclination to demand an imposition of state authority to deliver them from the cycle of violence that engulfed them during the Cultural Revolution. Central government authorities did indeed eventually conclude that it was in their interests that the violence stop, and they sent in the army to impose it. But from the point of view of the warring activists of Long Bow, the army's intervention was unwelcome. Both factions seemed to want to continue fighting, even when this, in Hinton's account, was causing them much more harm than good. This would suggest that Hobbes was too optimistic. The "desire of power after power" may be so overwhelming under certain circumstances that individuals may prefer that it lead to death rather than accept the order-bringing sovereignty of a political Leviathan.

Maybe this only means that people at the grass roots in China had for very rational reasons become so distrustful of the Communist state that they no longer wished to accept the authority of that particular Leviathan, although rejecting it meant a life of continuous insecurity. But the logic of a Hobbesian argument would suggest that rational individuals might find it in their self-interest to seek cooperation rather than contention among their peers even while rejecting the imposition of an external sovereign authority.

Modern social scientists use "game theories" to show how it can be in the rational self-interest of warring political entities in the international arena to cooperate with each other, even though they would not accept the sovereignty of any kind of international government. Assuming a world of interest-maximizing actors involved in ongoing interdependent relationships, Robert Axelrod and his associates have demonstrated that actors can most rationally maximize their self-interests by following a "Tit for Tat" strategy. That is, they must consistently reciprocate cooperation with cooperation and conflict with conflict (Axelrod 1984).

Individuals can get out of a situation where conflict may be mutually destructive by extending a modest offer of cooperation to an opponent. The most rational course of action for an opponent over the long run will be to reciprocate such a gesture with cooperation, which can then be rationally responded to with further reciprocation in kind, and so on. If any party to the relationship reciprocates an offer of cooperation with conflict, then the most rational course of action will be retaliation. But this formula for forging cooperation among contending parties devoted to the rational pursuit of self-interest did not seem to work in Long Bow. In the sections of *Shenfan* dealing with the Cultural Revolution, Hinton chronicled a downward spiral of retaliation so powerful that no one could ever expect that opponents would reciprocate cooperation with cooperation.

His account of the battles that enveloped Long Bow thereby suggests a human condition that can sustain episodes of violence so virulent that they will persist even when the individuals caught up in the violence would rationally calculate that it is not in their self-interests. And it suggests that this capacity for "irrational" violence is made possible by the capacity of individuals to find their truest interests in community loyalties that may demand self-sacrifice for the good of the whole.

Hinton's account suggests further that the Chinese, as with indeed any other people, are not in the last analysis self-seeking individuals who enter into social relationships only insofar as they perceive this to be in their individual self-interest. Rather, they are persons who are radically social, whose identities and whose very conceptions of what is in their self-interests are constituted by the cultural traditions of their society. Such traditions define a moral context in which loyalty to one's community—and not just to community members who are presently alive but also to those who are dead—comes prior to individual self-interest and ultimately constitutes one's ideas about what is in one's profoundest self-interest.

Such a view of the human condition can not only better account for moral heroism than can Hobbes's philosophy; it can also better account for the viciousness that comes from the desire for revenge. As Hinton portrays it, the Cultural Revolution's downward spiral of violence seems driven in large part by the imperatives of revenge. Unlike *retaliation, revenge* is a moral concept. Retaliation is a means to achieve one's self-interests, either through defense or offense, after having been harmed by an opponent. Revenge is not a means, but an end in itself. It is a way of honoring the commitments that constitute one's social identity. It is something one ought to do, given certain commitments, in order to rectify harm done to those to whom one is loyal. In a certain kind of moral tradition, revenge can be something that one must seek even at the expense of one's own concern for one's own well-being.

Certain aspects of the Chinese cultural tradition encouraged this way of thinking about revenge, even as other aspects provided moral resources for constraining the quest for revenge in the name of public order. After exploring these strands of the tradition, I use the story of Long Bow to show how the ideology and practices of the Maoist regime amplified those strands of the tradition that encourage revenge, while destroying those strands that could hold its destructive energies in check.

Revenge in Chinese culture

According to Alasdair MacIntyre, "all morality is always to some degree tied to the socially local and particular and . . . the aspiration of the morality of modernity to a universality freed from all particularity is an illusion" (MacIntyre 1981:119). This connection with the local and particular is due to the radically social nature of human identity. The human self is fundamentally constituted by its ties to communities—concrete communities with particular histories and particular limits, which set them off from other communities. As a result, in MacIntyre's words, "there is no way to possess the virtues except as part of a tradition in which we inherit them and our understanding of them from a series of predecessors . . . ." (MacIntyre 1981:119). To understand the strengths and weaknesses of Chinese political culture, then, we must specify the forms of community that constitute its context and the heritage of tradition that gives it its substance.

The boundaries of primary communities in rural China have, of course, long been defined by family relationships and by residence in particular localities. The historical traditions which constitute the identities of these communities in the present by rooting them in the past are collective memories of particular families in particular places. The traditional importance of the Chinese household as a primary unit of agricultural production and the relative lack of geographical mobility of members of rural communities have created a context in which collective memories can be carried on in a particularly vivid way.

Some of these memories are good memories, memories of glorious achievements rendered even more brilliant than they originally were through the mythologizing process of imaginative retelling. Other memories are dangerous memories, of suffering shared and perhaps even of evils inflicted. What responsibilities do sufferings endured by a community in the past impose upon its memories in the present? According to the Chinese ethic of reciprocity, one important responsibility can be the enaction of revenge. As Yang Lien-sheng put it:

> The Chinese believe that reciprocity *(bao)* of actions [favor and hatred, reward and punishment] between man and man, and indeed between men and supernatural beings, should be as certain as a cause-and-effect relationship, and, therefore, when a Chinese acts, he normally anticipates a response or return . . . . Of course, acceptance of the principle of reciprocity is required in practically every society. Nevertheless, in China the principle is marked by its long history, the high degree of consciousness of its existence, and its wide application and tremendous influence in social institutions (1957:291).

The principle of reciprocity not only requires the faithful repayment of favors with favors—according to Yang, "In extreme cases a poor scholar may decline all invitations to dinner simply because it is beyond his means to make the appropriate responses" (1957:292)—but also demands the redress of injuries. Although the classics of the Chinese cultural tradition do place a value on forgiveness for minor injuries, they give little support for forgiving serious injuries.

The classics are in some disagreement, however, whether the principle of reciprocity requires the direct repayment of injury with further injury. In the *Book of Rites*, Confucius said that it did; but he elsewhere said that injury should be recompensed not with injury but with "justice" *(zhi)* (Yang 1957:293-94). Most later Confucianists, however, modified the master's teaching to allow only the recompense of injury with justice. According to Yang Liensheng, the arguments advanced for this interpretation were as often realistic as idealistic: "If injury is recompensed with injury, when will mutual retaliation come to an end?" Justice was to be determined and administered by legal authorities subject to the emperor. The principle of recompensating injury with justice envisaged the control of local feuds by an order-providing state (Yang 1957:293).

The administrative institutions of the Imperial Chinese state were, of course, so arranged that its ministers owed primary loyalty to the emperor rather than to social groups within the territories they administered. And the scholar-officials who were ministers of the state were supposed to be "gentlemen," aspiring to a higher standard of morality than common people, a standard that encapsulated the demand for strict reciprocity with the requirements of "righteousness" *(yi)*. The gentleman "requires much from himself and little from others." The gentleman helps others without seeking reward; and he is willing to overlook minor wrongs or injuries. If someone acts unreasonably toward a gentleman, the gentleman does not immediately retaliate, but first examines himself to see if he may have unconsciously done something to provoke the unreasonable action. Even if, on self-examination, he finds himself blameless, he finds it beneath his station to fight against the unreasonable person, who is like a "mere brute."

Most people, unable to afford the education that made one into a gentleman, could not be expected to live up to such standards, however. The normal standard for "small men" was reciprocity, the straightforward requiting of good with good and injury with injury. It would be wrong to think of this "small man's" ethic as fundamentally unheroic, however. It could, in fact, claim to sustain a more vigorous kind of heroism than the ethic of the Confucians. The Confucian model of character was that of a person who stood so aloof from the conflicts of common people and was so committed to achieving social harmony that he could be called a "weakling" (*ru*, the original meaning of the word for "Confucian") (Yang 1957:306).

The character ideal that captured the imagination of ordinary people was that of the "knight-errant" *(xia)*, an ideal carried on through the centuries in popular literature. According to Yang, knights-errant

> were first recognized as a group during the period of the Warring States. At that time, the old feudal order had disintegrated, and many hereditary warriors had lost their positions and titles. As brave and upright individuals, and joined by strong sons of lower origin, they scattered throughout the country and made a living by offering their services (and even their lives) to anyone who could afford to employ them. The knights-errant were distinguished by their absolute reliability, which was their professional virtue. As described by Ssu-ma Ch'ien [Sima Qian] in his *Historical Memoirs*: "Their words were always sincere and trustworthy, and their actions always quick and decisive. They were always true to what they had promised, and without regard to their own persons, they would rush into dangers threatening others." This is the way they responded to friends who really appreciated their worth. Always seeking to right wrongs, the knights-errant proved most helpful to people who desired to secure revenge (1957:294-95).

The ethic of the knight-errant values "quick and decisive" retribution for injuries, even when he will not reap the benefit of such retribution, indeed even when such retribution puts him at the risk of his own life. This ethic also values retribution not only for injuries endured oneself but also for those endured by others to whom one owes loyalty. Primary among these bonds of loyalty are those defined by family membership. According to the principle of "sharing of fate" *(chengfu)*, rewards and punishments for good and bad deeds are shared among family members to the extent that present generations can be given honor or be made to suffer for the misdeeds of previous generations, and whole families or even a lineage can be punished for the misdeeds of a few members. Loyalty can also be owed, though, as a response to favors bestowed by nonfamily members (Yang 1957:299).

The knight-errant ideal of quick and decisive response to injuries received by members of the groups to which one is loyal often threatened to disintegrate local social life into violently feuding fragments (Lamley, this volume). Such disintegrative tendencies were held in fragile check at the cultural level—when they were held in check at all—by Confucian ideals of requiting injury with justice and the commitment of "gentlemen" to modify the principle of strict reciprocity with that of righteousness.[1] The knight-errant ethic not only survived the course of the Chinese revolution but was even enhanced by the ideology and organization of that revolution. The Confucian ethical solutions to holding that popular ethic in check did not survive the revolution, however. And under Mao, the Chinese Communist Party and state did not provide an ethic that could adequately take its place.

The politics of revenge in Long Bow

In *Shenfan*, William Hinton gives us vivid examples of the social and moral destruction wrought in Long Bow when China's ancient "knight-errant ethic" became unleashed from all countervailing moral restraints during the Cultural Revolution, and the "quick and decisive" quest for revenge became the dominant motive behind local political action. Long Bow was drawn reluctantly into the Cultural Revolution—the struggles against literary "poisonous weeds," the debates over education, and the attacks on high party officials who had "taken the capitalist road" at first seemed to have little relevance to the lives of ordinary peasants.

But Long Bow was no longer a relatively isolated rural community; by the mid-1960s, it was a suburb of an industrial city, which had a middle school that quickly began to boil over with contention among rival students' factions. It also had factories, which exploded into conflict among rival factions of workers. The battles among the central city middle school factions spilled over into the suburban middle school—the Luan Middle School—located in the heart of Long Bow Village. Even then, however, the Cultural Revolution seemed remote from the affairs of ordinary villagers:

> At the start the fractured student movement did not seem like a very serious matter to the peasants of Long Bow. Throughout 1966 and into 1967, the Cultural Revolution meant to them primarily a ringside seat for observing the activities and antics of the student movement at Luan Middle School . . . . The Cultural Revolution, they concluded, was for people with culture, so why not carry it on in a cultured manner and leave peasants, who had no culture, in peace (Hinton 1984:509).

But the villagers inevitably were drawn "from ringside to arena." A Central Committee Directive of December 15, 1966, called for the Cultural Revolution to be taken to the countryside. Long Bow's leaders implemented the directive by forming a Cultural Revolution Committee, which they hoped would carry out a relatively orderly investigation and punishment of politically disloyal members of the community. As Red Guards and revolutionary rebels seized power during early 1967 in major cities throughout China, local hopes for an orderly Cultural Revolution broke down. The atmosphere of the time gave licence for any group with a grievance to attack people who held power. Seven mass organizations materialized in Long Bow Village, each one formed by a different production team and each one set up to attack a different leading cadre in the village. Eventually the seven groups merged into two competing "headquarters"—the rebels and the loyalists, between which Hinton could discern no significant ideological or political differences (1984:509-21).

If Hinton is correct, then the ensuing events defy the kind of analysis in terms of interest group conflict that is standard among political scientists who study social movements. In such analyses, interest groups are defined as aggregates of individuals whose members share common interests in acquiring wealth or gaining power under circumstances in which the costs of collective action to achieve these ends do not outweigh the potential benefits to be achieved. As described by Hinton, however, the economic resources enjoyed by members of the opposed factions were roughly equal. The rebel faction, it is true, did consist mostly of people who did not hold major political offices in the village and who obviously hoped to gain such offices through rebelling.

Yet the economic rewards to be gained through such office holding did not seem significant, and in any case the travails the rebels endured trying to seize power seemed to overshadow by far the possible satisfactions that could be expected from holding power. The exploits of these opposing factions thus make sense if they are thought of not as economic or political, but as moral interest groups, whose members believed that they had opposing duties to fulfill the demands imposed upon them by common loyalties animated by common traditions of collective memory.

Those loyalties were first of all familistic. As Hinton writes:

> The truth of the matter was that Long Bow, though not clan-ridden like many traditional Chinese communities, had long been divided north and south on old clan lines. The division had created two competing temples. The Lu clan dominated the northern and larger section of the village, where the old North Temple, built by the Chi family, stood until *fanshened* peasants knocked it down in the 1950s. The Shen family played a major role in the southern section, where the old South Temple had disappeared much earlier but left behind persistent remnants of sectional pride. The Lu family, since Liberation at least, and possibly for a long time prior to that, had played an increasingly dominant role in village government. People in the know had long called Long Bow the "Lu Family Kingdom." To the ruling Lus an uprising based on the Fourth Team in the south and the Sidelines Team led by Little Shen meant that southerners, instigated by the Shens, were on the rampage and meant to take over. Obviously, self-respecting Lus had to stop them. They could not allow upstarts to get away with any such thing (1984:527).

These family ties were channels through which flowed the substance of different reservoirs of resentful memories. Some of these memories were recent. Fast Chin, the militiaman who was "the Lu family's closest ally" and a leader of the loyalist faction, bitterly resented Little Shen, the leader of the rebels, because Little Shen had married—in Chin's view, stolen—the woman Fast Chin had wanted to marry, in fact, the widow of Chin's brother. Fast Chin hungered to settle accounts for this, not only with Little Shen but also with those relatives and friends with whom his antagonist associated.

Even more potent collective memories involved injuries received twenty years previously, during Long Bow's violent land reform. A major source of conflict erupted around the remembered case of the middle peasant Wang Hsiao-nan, one of those who had been beaten to death during land reform. A prominent village cadre named Wang Wen-te had somehow been involved in that homicide, although he had at the time been officially exonerated of criminal responsibility for it. He had gone on to play an important role in the village's leadership. Little Shen's rebel faction now wanted to attack the loyalist Wang Wen-te—and all those he was associated with, including Fast Chin—for his "arrogance, high-handed methods, and rejection of criticism." To fortify themselves, they brought up the case of Wang Hsiao-nan.

This was, indeed, a dangerous memory to resurrect. Some villagers bitterly protested that it was out of order to raise the question of what had happened to Wang Hsiao-nan twenty years ago. The chain of events that followed illustrates how powerful collective memory is in rural China—and how destructive that memory can be when linked to an ethic of reciprocity under the kinds of conditions that prevailed during the Cultural Revolution (for a comparison with equally troubled times in late Qing and Republican China, see Lipman, this volume).

By recalling the memory of Wang Hsiao-nan's death, the members of the rebel faction helped to give one another reason to seek revenge against their rivals, the "loyalist" faction, whose leaders included a man who may have been responsible for that death. The loyalist faction countered by recalling memories of its own. The rebels, it alleged, were led by people descended from landlords, Japanese puppets, and local bullies in the old society. The sins of these progenitors surely tainted the characters of their descendants, rendering them unfit to challenge good people with pure backgrounds, such as the loyalists.

The memory of those past sins gave the loyalists reason to seek revenge against their rivals. Furthermore, it acted as a principle for interpreting the memories invoked by the rebels. Being morally tainted, the "rebels" had no right to bring up the memories of the killing of Wang Hsiao-nan. That case had been resolved by the Communist government; the killing deserved to be forgotten. Bringing it up was a symptom of the moral degeneracy which all knew characterized the members of the rebel faction, descended as they were from bad stock. All the more reason for the loyalists to attack the rebels violently.

Thus, the internecine struggles between Long Bow villagers, which to William Hinton seemed so irrational because they sought no new policies for the present and future—no changes in how collective agriculture was to be carried out or how political authority was to be wielded—gained a kind of rationality in the minds of the participants. They were captivated by the power of collective memory in rural China to define particular patterns of factional loyalty, rooted in a commitment to the past. They were also driven by the ethic of reciprocity to make the resolute quest for revenge the test of such loyalty. As the balance of power between the rival factions teetered back and forth, each faction accumulated injuries that demanded vengeful redress, deepening the spiral of violence. Unfortunately, by this time, Maoist ideology and practice had left the villagers without any moral resources to hold a cycle of revenge in check.

Because of the violence of so many phases of the Chinese revolution, the social landscape was littered with dangerous memories of arbitrary injuries endured and inflicted. The methods of mass mobilization used by the Maoists might have unintentionally deepened such memories. A major tool used in mass mobilization was systematic recall of injuries endured in the past. During land reform, peasants were urged to recollect in minute detail all of the evils inflicted on them by landlords, Guomindang agents, and collaborators with the Japanese. Those who could recollect the most vivid accounts of injuries gained important political advantages under the new regime.

In the campaigns to bring about collectivization in the 1950s, peasants were urged to remember the harm done to them by rich peasants. In the "remember the bitterness of the past and the sweetness of the present" campaigns of the early 1960s, they were supposed to remember systematically the evils done to them by all class enemies. In the Four Cleanups campaign, they were to dredge up memories of suffering inflicted by local cadres who, although objectively belonging to the "good classes," had become tainted with the mentality of the bad classes.

Even when mass mobilization campaigns were not being carried out, the importance of recalling the evils of the past was continually emphasized in the treatment of the infamous Four Bad types: landlords, rich peasants, counterrevolutionaries, and bad elements. Constantly harrassed, those who were unfortunate enough to be branded with one of these labels were held to be irrevocably contaminated with the sins of their past. Indeed, they supposedly passed that contamination on to their children and grandchildren. The memories officially evoked through these processes were, of course, very selective memories. All the harm the "bad classes" had done was recalled in the most lurid colors; and all the good that the Communist Party had done was recollected in the most glorious light. Yet, carrying on approved memories must have pulled along unofficial, unvoiced memories, dangerous memories that would never have been approved by the government.[2]

According to the principle of reciprocity, old memories of injuries received but not requited had to be redressed when the opportunity presented itself. Stalwart people who dared to redress these injuries deserved to be considered heroes, like the knights-errant of old. The Communist Party, under the leadership of Mao at any rate, encouraged this way of thinking without effectively providing any larger moral rationale for keeping the search for revenge in check. Whereas the moral traditions at the root of the Confucian state had stressed the need for order and unity under the aegis of the imperial government, the ideology of the Maoist state had stressed the need for continuing revolution. In terms of its legitimacy, the Confucian state had been an order state, which claimed to ensure that injuries inflicted by one group of its subjects upon another would be requited not by private revenge but by public justice. The Communist state in its Maoist variant was, in contrast, a vengeance state, which staked its legitimacy on the claim to ensure retribution for all injuries inflicted by the bad classes upon the good classes (see Thurston, this volume).

Thus as *Fanshen*, Hinton's first book on Long Bow Village, vividly illustrates, the Communisty Party justified expropriating landlords during the land reform campaign not simply because they had more property than they needed. Rather, the party claimed that they had constantly abused good—that is, poor—peasants for as long in the past as anyone could remember. The redistribution of land was not simply a means to build a better economy for China but a way for the poor classes to wreak vengeance on the rich classes (Hinton 1966:103-232). The Communist solution to the problem— that such vengeance-seeking could provoke retaliation from its victims—was to promise a "dictatorship of the proletariat" that would forcefully suppress any retaliation.

Fanshen illustrates how potent the appeal to class vengeance was as a motivating force behind mass mobilization. As *Fanshen* also illustrates, however, a major problem with this appeal to vengeance was that the bonds of loyalty and the reservoirs of collective memory that committed one group to seek revenge against another did not necessarily coincide with the class divisions that the Communists claimed were the central contradictions in Chinese society. This was exacerbated by the Communist leadership's tendency constantly to redefine the boundaries between antagonistic classes. Thus, at early stages of land reform in Long Bow Village, some people were literally beaten to death who, by later definitions of the boundaries between antagonistic classes, did not deserve their fate.

The need for poor peasants to seek vengeance for harm visited upon them in the past continued to be used as a major claim for the legitimacy of subsequent campaigns for collectivization and political rectification. But the boundaries between those who needed to seek revenge and those who deserved to receive it continued to be redrawn to match the goals set by Party Central for each campaign. This made it difficult to give any meaning to the idea that injury was not simply to be requited with other injury but with justice.

In the heat of the Cultural Revolution, as *Shenfan* vividly illustrates, the language of class struggle lost the last of its connections with substantive content. The warring factions in Long Bow each claimed that their opponents represented landlords and counterrevolutionary elements even though, as Hinton says, there was no factual warrant for either side to do so. What gave one license to define one's opponent as a class enemy was, purely and simply, raw power. When the rebels and loyalists were fairly evenly matched in Long Bow, each claimed that the other represented the bad classes, and each "felt justified in beating up members of the opposition." Later, however, the rebels began to lose ground, and the loyalist faction managed to link itself up with the provincewide United Faction, which got decisive support from the army.

> Then everybody began to denounce [the rebel faction] as a front for landlords, rich peasants, counterrevolutionaries, and bad elements, and to hold it up for contempt. When this happened, it became hard for [any member of the rebel faction] to hold up his or her head (Hinton 1984:664; see also Madsen 1984:72-80, 195-98, 261-62).

The Confucian tradition had little warrant for forgiving serious injury out of mercy, and the Communist Party continued this tradition. In the Confucian state, however, injury was supposed to be requited by justice. Although in the Communist state this was theoretically also the case—people were supposed to redress grievances according to principles of justice sanctioned by the party and state—in practice those principles shifted often enough and arbitrarily enough that requiting injury with justice meant little more than being utterly free to seek retribution, as long as present policy allowed you to get away with it.

When, for a while during the Cultural Revolution, the policy-making apparatus was in such disarray that people could think that they could get away with anything, there existed in the cultural landscape no plausible ideals that could be drawn upon to moderate the endless seeking of revenge. The party's policies thus legitimized the quest for vengeance and indeed incited it, without providing stable moral standards for keeping revenge-seeking in check. Peasants would be honored for harshly settling any old scores they wanted, as long as the objects of revenge happened, for the time being, to fall on the wrong side of a frequently redrawn class line.

In the Confucian tradition, the quest for revenge at the local level could also be moderated by the local influence of the scholar-gentry, who were supposed to aspire to a higher standard of morality than common people, a standard not dominated simply by the idea of strict reciprocity but by that of "righteousness." However, one result of the Communist revolution, like most other world revolutions, was a democratization of morality. No longer was there a special ethic for the superior man qualitatively different from that of the "small man." The values of the Communist Party cadre were now supposed to be those of the common person, the cadre being distinguished only by the vigor, reliability, and consistency with which he or she pursued those values.

In practice, the Maoist virtues were much closer to the traditional virtues of the valiant knight-errant than those of the Confucian gentleman. Never forgetting the class struggle, the cadre was to seek class revenge in a disciplined way under the guidance, such as it was, of the Communist Party. No wonder, then, that as the party ceased to provide any firm guidance and as the cycle of violence in Long Bow began, the local cadres turned out to be more part of the problem than of the solution.

The first reaction of Long Bow's leading cadres to being challenged by the rebel faction was to denounce the members of that faction with slanderous accusations about being landlords, rich peasants, and bad elements. As soon as the loyalist faction, through "persecutions and beatings," beat back the rebels' challenge and regained uncontested control over the village

> unchallenged power, coupled with the conviction that they had always been right, that they were revolutionaries who had steadfastly defended Mao Tse-tung Thought, went to [the "loyalists"] heads. They considered themselves heroes, and they began to think that the community owed them a debt of gratitude. Step by step they began to abuse their prestige and power . . . .

They used their power to engage in a wide variety of illicit sexual liaisons, indulged in blatant displays of high living at the village's expense—the village's official entertainment budget suddenly rose from fewer than 100 yuan to 800—and took advantage of their positions to engage in illegal profiteering.

In 1970, after order was firmly established in Shanxi Province by the army, and in anticipation of William Hinton's return to Long Bow to write a new book about it, a workteam was sent to the village to rectify mistakes that had been made there during the Cultural

Revolution. The leaders of this workteam could not be seen as impartial searchers after justice, however. Although the province-wide faction to which the loyalists in Long Bow claimed allegiance—the United Faction—had won control of the province, the members of the workteam had mostly been allied with the Red Faction, the opponents of the United Faction. The workteam deposed Fast Chin, Swift Li, and other loyalist supporters and used threats and pressure—including physical beatings—to compel loyalist supporters to provide damaging evidence against their leaders.

To carry out the beatings, they enlisted some bullies from the vanquished rebel faction, eager to take revenge on those who had oppressed them and their relatives. The beatings did not cause the loyalists to split apart, however. Solidarity with the relatives and friends with whom one had shared a common history was apparently more important to the "loyalists" than the advantage one might get through cooperation with the workteam. So the workteam did not initially effect an end to the cycle of revenge; it simply turned the cycle forward one more notch.

Finally, in 1971, after the demise of Lin Biao, but before news of his death had been made public, the workteam's approach to solving the problems of Long Bow softened. Fast Chin, Swift Li, and other loyalist leaders were declared to be not class enemies but simply "cadres who had made mistakes." Their jobs were reinstated. Little Shen, the leader of the rebel faction, who had been expelled from the party as a "class enemy" by the loyalists, was now also declared to have been unfairly persecuted. Hinton saw this as an "important victory that cleared the way for breaking down factionalism." Yet, as he privately interviewed the leaders of the two factions, he was disturbed at their refusal to recognize that they had made any serious mistakes or that their branding of their opponents as "class enemies" had been wrong. He left Long Bow burdened with "doubts about whether the road [to reconcile the factions], once cleared, would ever be travelled."

I do not wish to argue that a deficiency in moral culture was in itself sufficient to let loose the violent cycles of revenge characteristic of the Cultural Revolution. The spirals of vengeance would never have been started without a breakdown of the state's social control apparatus. The organizational failure is easy enough to see in Hinton's account. The purges of high-echelon officials carried out by Mao and his associates destroyed the ability of the party and state bureaucracies to sustain centralized control over the society. The way was then opened for ambitious political entrepreneurs at all levels of society to seek power with whatever resources they could muster.

In Shanxi Province, two rival regional leaders—Evergreen Liu and Zhang Erqing—eventually used a Byzantine array of power-brokering techniques to assemble coalitions of factions around themselves (the Red and United factions) and used these coalitions in a bitter battle for supremacy. At the level of Long Bow, the rival rebel and loyalist factions each sought the protection of different masters, and thus could each receive resources from regional networks of power to carry on their local programs of revenge (Hinton 1984:582-649). But even when political control apparatuses split apart, peasants would not have been swept into the vicious circle of violence if they could have drawn upon moral restraints embedded in their culture. My argument has focussed on the tragic fact that no such moral resources were to be found.

Because the ideology of the time did not contain resources that could plausibly be used to fashion a moral appeal for reconciliation, the wounds opened within Long Bow by the Cultural Revolution could only be staunched by force. The army intervened, as it did throughout China, to bring about order in Shanxi. But if the only thing that kept factions from forming and from seeking revenge against their enemies was external police force, what could guarantee the long-term stability of Chinese society?

Hinton's *Shenfan* is primarily concerned with telling the story of Long Bow down to about 1971, not with answering such questions. In the end, the answers will be provided only by the passage of Chinese history.[3] What direction has that history taken up to the present? Through the trial and imprisonment of the Gang of Four, the Deng Xiaoping regime attempted to settle accounts for the injuries suffered by millions of people during the Cultural Revolution by punishing a handful of its chief instigators. Accounts were further settled by purging from power all cadres who rose during the Cultural Revolution. But at the grass roots, in places such as Long Bow, no extensive effort to administer state-sponsored justice to those who caused injuries during that period appears to have been made. One reason was that so many people on both sides were involved in causing harm that punishment of them all would decimate local leadership.

For now, people have too much to gain economically and too much to lose politically to seek vengeance for injuries received. Currently, the political surface of rural China seems relatively calm, as peasants rush about frenetically, but apparently happily, trying to make as much money as they can for themselves and their families in the decollectivized agriculture of the post-Mao era. But in the enclosed social space of a village, consisting mostly of families that have lived in the community for generations, collective memories stay preserved for very long periods of time, and, instead of losing their power, easily ferment into potent legends in which the grievous wrongs endured as well as the glorious triumphs achieved become increasingly vivid with the passage of years. One thing that the story of Long Bow makes clear is that expecting peasants to forget who did what to whom during times like the Cultural Revolution is unrealistic. Instead of hoping that they will forget the past in their eagerness to get rich in the present, a wise political leadership might delicately seek to find ways gradually to help them to forgive.

Conclusion: Revenge and redemption
in modern politics

Viewing the conflicts within Long Bow Village as motivated, to a significant degree, by the felt duty to take revenge, allows a better account of the travails of that community during the Cultural Revolution than if the conflicts are viewed purely in terms of competition between opposing interest groups. From this point of view, the downward cycle of revenge was so self-defeating, so opposed to the self-interests of the parties to the conflict that Hinton was right to call it irrational.

However, if, applying the approaches of interpretive social science, we try to understand what this cycle of violence meant to the participants, the violence may indeed make sense from a variety of perspectives, which is not to say that it will become any less tragic. If we try to imagine what the cycle of violence might have looked like from the "inside," through the prism of the culturally patterned loyalties of the parties to the conflict, then perhaps the struggles do take on coherent logic and acquire moral meaning.

From the point of view of the vengeful parties to conflict, the pursuit of revenge had moral meaning as the fulfillment of obligations to carry out retribution against those who had harmed the members of one's community. From the "outside," however, from the point of view of one trying to see China as a whole, as a commonweal (or a potential commonweal) of interdependent citizens, the spiral of revenge could only appear to be a senseless destruction of the moral integuments that could bind China into something more than a "dish of loose sand" (Hinton 1984:675-81, 751-68).

And perhaps, during the Cultural Revolution in China, this was a case where both "inside" and "outside" perspectives were unfortunately correct. Loyalties to family and friends, as these were understood in traditional Chinese culture, demanded revenge, even when the welfare of the society as a whole could not tolerate it. Because the antagonists in the Cultural Revolution were simultaneously members of traditional communities and members of the larger society, perhaps these contradictory perspectives on the enactment of revenge even cut through their own consciousness, so that they saw themselves as acting sensibly on one level and absurdly on another.

By viewing the history of the Cultural Revolution through the thematic prism of revenge, we can look deeply into some of the central cultural dilemmas of China's recent history. The creation of an orderly, economically dynamic national society requires a strong state. To be truly strong, a state needs to be based on more than the coercive power of its military and police apparatuses. It must have some claim to legitimacy from the society upon which it is built.

Among other things, such a claim usually involves an effective commitment on the part of the state to enable its citizens to live meaningful lives in their domestic communities and to realize popular aspirations for justice. Yet herein lies a dilemma. If large numbers of citizens understand a "meaningful life" to entail loyalties to family and neighborhood communities sanctified through particular memory-myths of a distinctive shared history, and if they understand "justice" to mean retribution for injuries inflicted upon their communities over a long period, then popular aspirations to "community" and to "justice" can lead to vicious, pervasive social conflict. A state can only maintain order if it transforms such popular understandings of community and justice in such a way that citizens will see that their particular loyalties must be understood in light of general loyalties to the national community. They must also see that redress of injuries to one's particular community can only be properly carried out by agents of the state.

But if Alasdair MacIntyre, following Aristotle, is correct in saying that "all morality is always to some degree tied to the socially local and particular and . . . the aspiration of the morality of modernity to a universality freed from all particularity is an illusion," then transforming popular understandings of community and justice by denying their validity will not be possible. The most effective strategy of transformation encompasses popular understandings within an ideology that recognizes their partial validity yet plausibly asserts that their full meaning can be discerned only in light of a national whole.

The Maoist regime, clinging to the illusory aspirations of the morality of modernity, did not successfully do this. When it mobilized the masses, as in land reform, it exhibited great practical flexibility in identifying segments of local communities that had grievances against segments that stood in the way of the party's plans for national political domination and for economic collectivization. It gained the loyalty of such grievance-filled segments of the communities by giving them the wherewithal to seek revenge for the injuries that had caused their grievances. But the party under Mao never developed a convincing rationale for defining the limits to revenge-seeking in the name of the revolution.

The Maoist party-state claimed that its legitimacy was based on its commitment to allow the "good" social classes—workers and poor peasants—to seek redress of their historical grievance against the "bad" classes. But it kept changing its definitions of exactly who belonged to the good and bad classes so often that those definitions seemed arbitrary. All too frequently, the only thing required for one group to have license to seek revenge against another was that it happened to be defined as belonging to the good classes and its enemy as belonging to the bad classes. There was no moral vision to place local revenge-seeking into the context of national struggles. The only thing that kept the process of social mobilization relatively orderly was the coercive strength of the state apparatus that manipulated it. When that apparatus broke down, the way was paved for the vicious cycle of revenge.

The central cultural dilemmas of China's recent history are, in a sense, the dilemmas of all modern nations. All modern societies must find some way of reconciling popular aspirations for rooted-ness in particular communities defined by particular memories with loyalties to national political institutions. One way that the managers of modern societies—both capitalist and socialist—frequently try to resolve these dilemmas is by dissolving the loyalties that tie a citizenry to particular communities, whether in the name of personal "liberation" from traditional attachments or in the name of total devotion to the "general will" embodied in the state.

In our book *Habits of the Heart* (Bellah et al. 1985:152-62), my colleagues and I have followed MacIntyre in arguing that destruction of loyalties to concrete communities inevitably leads to meaninglessness and alienation rather than to a morally satisfying life, and we laid great stress on the need to preserve "communities of memory." In this chapter, I explored some of the dangers involved in preserving communities of memory, not to suggest that it is best not to preserve them, but rather to point toward ways in which those dangers might be overcome.

A moral context must be forged in which the bad memories of particular communities—the memories that cry out for revenge—must not be obliterated but must be assuaged by a commitment to justice for all members of society on the part of a legitimate governing authority. At the least, a good society needs a theory of the way injury should not be requited with injury but should, and under modern conditions realistically can, be requited with justice. And given the murderous resentments that arise from the night-marish memories that belong to so many particular communities in the turbulent history of this complicated modern world, a good social order could be greatly abetted by a moral vocabulary that could convincingly impart a sense of the redemptive qualities of mercy. As unrealistic as it may be to seek such a thing, it is perhaps less unrealistic than to hope for a just and peaceful world without it.

Notes

1. What ultimately holds antagonistic people in check is political power, not culture. But political rulers draw on culture for legitimation, and I assume that if the ideas needed to legitimize a certain style of rulership are no longer adequate to the task, exercising that style of rulership becomes more difficult.

2. See Chan et al. 1984 and Madsen 1984 for accounts that parallel Hinton's. In my view, the data from Chen Village could have sustained a similar analysis to the one I have made here of the politics of revenge in China. Because Hinton's account includes vivid eyewitness descriptions of political conflict all the way from the beginnings of land reform in the late 1940s to the end of the Cultural Revolution in the mid-1970s, it provides a better empirical basis for arguing about the importance of historical memories in rural political life.

3. Hinton promises a third volume in the Long Bow Village series that will recount the history of Long Bow Village to the late 1980s.

References

Axelrod, Robert
1984 *The Evolution of Cooperation.* New York: Basic Books.

Bellah, R. et al.
1985 *Habits of the Heart: Individualism and Commitment in American Life.* Berkeley and Los Angeles: University of California Press.

Chan, A., R. Madsen, and J. Unger
1984 *Chen Village: The Recent History of a Peasant Community in Mao's China.* Berkeley and Los Angeles: University of California Press.

Hinton, William
1966 *Fanshen: A Documentary of Revolution in a Chinese Village.* New York: Vintage Books.

1984 *Shenfan: The Continuing Revolution in a Chinese Village.* New York: Vintage Books.

Hobbes, Thomas
1968 *Leviathan* C.B. MacPherson, ed. Harmondsworth: Penguin. Original dated 1651.

MacIntyre, Alasdair
1981 *After Virtue.* South Bend, Ind.: University of Notre Dame Press.

Madsen, Richard
1984 *Morality and Power in a Chinese Village.* Berkeley and Los Angeles: University of California Press.

Yang Lien-sheng
1957 "The Concept of *Pao* as a Basis for Social Relations in China," in J. Fairbank, ed., *Chinese Thought and Institutions.* Chicago: University of Chicago Press.

Chapter 8

Violence Against Women in Contemporary China

Christina Gilmartin

When the Cultural Revolution ended in 1976, Chinese leaders proclaimed an end to all political movements, deeming them the cause of the ubiquitous turmoil and violence that had characterized the previous decade.[1] The new administration announced shortly after coming to power that its policies would usher in a period of stability and unity *(anding tuanjie)*. In so doing, it appealed to a deeply rooted traditional Chinese ideal that disdained violence as an embarrassing indicator of governmental mismanagement and championed harmony as critical to society's well-being.

In stark contrast to these official proclamations of the reestablishment of social order were an unprecedented number of reports in the Chinese press about violence against women—beatings, rapes, murders, and infanticides. Beginning in 1979, these accounts appeared in newspapers, legal journals, national and provincial women's magazines, and special collections of court cases. Although criminal aggression against women was by no means the only type of violence revealed in the press during those years, it constituted a significant portion of the reported crimes.[2] Unfortunately, the sketchy and editorialized nature of these published accounts precludes both a systematic examination of the legal intervention process and a statistical analysis of the frequency, most common occurrences, and geographical distribution of crimes against women. Nevertheless, these accounts are a valuable source for examining the social context of these crimes, their function in gender relations, and the role of the state in causing and controlling their occurrence.

At first glance, the bulk of the cases seemed reminiscent of the press accounts of gender violence in the early 1950s, such as daughters being beaten for refusing arranged marriages, wife-battering, and widows being killed for attempting to remarry. Yet, the government motivation for publicizing gender violence differed significantly in the early 1950s and the post-Mao era. Soon after establishing the People's Republic of China, the government unfolded a campaign against the "feudal" family, which was regarded as a critical agent of women's oppression (Meijer 1971:451). In the late 1970s, however, little official attention was given initially to the gender dimension of the crimes. In fact, the government objectives for publicizing these cases were not connected to any stated policies about the need to improve the social status of women or reform the family. Rather, the disclosures appeared to have been an inadvertent consequence of the new emphasis on legality following the promulgation of the Criminal Law in 1980, China's first comprehensive legal code since 1949.

The gender-related aspect of the rash of reported crimes first became apparent to me when I was invited, with a group of other foreigners living in Beijing, to attend a trial in order to witness the workings of the reformed legal system in 1979. As I listened to the case against a young factory worker named Wang Yongtai, charged with attempted murder, I was struck by the accused's extreme patriarchal views toward the female victim. He had bashed in the skull of a woman worker with a hammer, causing a serious fracture, because she had refused his request to be his girlfriend—in effect a proposal of marriage according to customary practice. Wang's violent response to this rejection by a woman whom he had barely known was motivated by his belief that a woman should auto-matically defer to a male initiative in courtship or face dire consequences.[3]

By the early 1980s, Chinese officials demonstrated their concern about the growing number of reports of violence against women. The All-China Women's Federation was particularly active in its role of social advocate for these victimized women and used its journals to draw greater attention to the problem, largely for didactic purposes. Specifically, the Women's Federation aimed to alert potential victims and warn would-be assailants that the state would adopt stern punitive measures when women's legal rights or persons had been violated. In addition, the Women's Federation established legal counseling services to advise women of their legal rights and to represent women in court (FBIS July 19, 1983:K 12; *Beijing Review* 1986:22-23). Many women's journals began featuring articles advising their readers of methods of handling difficult circumstances, such as how to fend off a rapist (Honig and Hershatter, 1988:281-82).

Clashes over marriage rights

A major focus of the published accounts of gender conflict concerned violations of women's marriage rights as stipulated in the Marriage Law of 1950 and revised in 1980. One publication that drew great attention to these issues was *One Hundred Legal Cases Involving Marriage*, which was published for public consumption in 1981 by the editors of a famous popular journal on law and society (Hunyin Anjian 1981; Chu 1985-1986). In the preface, and in the numerous newspaper and journal articles publicizing instances of violent conflicts over women's rights in marriage, tremendous explanatory power was attributed to the persistence of traditional attitudes (Chu 1984:16). In the official view, crimes involving intense domestic conflict over young women's rights to choose their own spouses demonstrated the vitality of the age-old attitude that marriage is a parental prerogative.

The case of one woman who attempted to withdraw from an arranged marriage revealed a particularly vitriolic demonstration of patriarchal power (Hunyin Anjian 1981:24-25). In early 1976, a young woman named Lu declared her intention to break off the engagement that her mother had arranged for her to the second son of the Ji family and to marry instead Wu, a teacher at the spare-time school in her village. When her mother failed to terminate the engagement, Lu took matters into her own hands, an unusual action for a young woman in contemporary China. On April 6, 1977, Lu went to the Ji home and offered to return the money and gifts the Jis had presented when the engagement had been contracted.

The father of the prospective groom rejected Lu's proposal. Moreover, he resorted to force as a way of challenging her bold assumption that she could take charge of her own affairs. The elder

Ji struck Lu a number of times in the face, then strove to humiliate her further by ripping off her jacket. With the help of his oldest son, a battalion commander in the local militia, he tied her up and announced his intention to detain her until he was well-compensated for the loss of his prospective daughter-in-law.

According to the testimony of witnesses in the subsequent court case, the father and oldest son traumatized Lu for the remainder of the day. They hurled a host of verbal abuses at her, threatened to cause irreparable damage to her looks, and refused her access to the toilet. Some of their worst threats, such as cutting off her hair and rubbing burning matches on her head, were reportedly prevented only by the intervention of neighbors. That evening, the two Jis widened their target of intimidation by collecting a group of friends and descending on the home of Lu's mother. They threatened to take her belongings as compensation for their loss of face and their financial expenses related to the engagement. More than 100 neighbors were said to have gathered at the Lu house to behold this spectacle.

It was not until the following day that the Jis agreed, after lengthy negotiations and the promise of a watch as further payment, to release Lu. She had endured degrading and humiliating detention, tied up, for more than twenty-four hours. Soon after returning home, she and Wu committed suicide.

Although this case was certainly one of the more brutal displays of patriarchal power reported, it contained characteristics that were representative of other published cases. First and foremost, it revealed the shortcomings in efforts to reform the institution of marriage that had been initiated at the beginning of the twentieth century and solidly endorsed by the Chinese Communist Party. Clearly, marriage was still considered by many Chinese to be a moral rather than a legal contract between families. And, despite the provision in the Marriage Law of 1950 that women had the right to choose their own spouses, family intervention and domination of the marriage decision was far from uncommon in the Chinese countryside.

The use of violence against Lu served to maintain the status quo, for it demonstrated the risks of challenging traditional norms of authority. The Jis' motivation for resorting to force was not to pressure Lu to change her mind and honor the marriage agreement but rather to humiliate her publicly. In so doing, the Jis sent an explicit message to women in the area about the inherent weakness of women's legal rights when they came into conflict with existing social mores. The failure of local authorities to come to Lu's aid while she was detained against her will and made into a public spectacle in the Ji courtyard only confirmed this message.

Lu's actions in this conflict were shaped by a mixture of modern and traditional influences. Of the many women depicted in these court cases for their efforts to resist arranged marriages, Lu represented the most daring of China's young women, willing to persist in their own interests in defiance of patriarchal power. Her decision to negotiate an abrogation of the engagement on her own behalf and not rely on family elders demonstrated the existence of a new sense of autonomy among rural women. Growing up in the first decades of the People's Republic, she and her peers were exposed to a plethora of ideas about the importance of women's equality and emancipation, values far removed from the social reality they observed. Lu thus belonged to a growing number of women seeking to break away from the social roles customarily assigned to women. Yet her sense of humiliation and degradation and her use of suicide as a weapon of revenge were traditional responses. If she had seen herself as a prisoner of war in the battle for women's autonomy, she probably would not have killed herself.

Lu's decision to opt for suicide rather than take her case to the courts conformed to the general pattern of female responses to gender conflict in the published reports. A number of women embroiled in marriage disputes exhibited little faith in the law as a champion of their rights, at least while they were alive. Rather, they acted on the belief that only suicide would effectively engage the legal system on their behalf and lead to the persecution of their attackers. Legal and social precedents deeply rooted in Chinese culture require authorities to regard any suicide as a potential case of premeditated murder and to launch a full investigation (*Renmin Ribao* February 2, 1984; Wolf 1975). Thus, in the Lu case, even though authorities failed to intervene during the period of her forceful detention, they were compelled by law and custom to investigate the Jis' complicity in her death once she had committed suicide.

Unlike Lu, some women left suicide notes recounting the mental and physical duress to which they were subjected in order to elicit court action. The wife of Xia, for instance, discovered in May 1977 that her husband was having an affair. When she raised his infidelity as an issue of discussion, he quarrelled bitterly with her and then began to beat her. Her mental anguish increased after she became pregnant in March 1979, and he insinuated that the child was not his. Finally, the defeated woman took her own life, but not before she had sent a 4,800-character letter to the courts, describing in great detail her husband's abusive actions. Xia was convicted of having caused her to commit suicide and sentenced to seven years in prison (Chu 1985-1986:78-79).

Because suicide is a common response women choose when confronted with seemingly unresolvable situations, some women have been tricked into suicide. The special law column in *Renmin Ribao* reported the case of a woman who attempted suicide at the suggestion of her boyfriend. He had convinced her that their lives would be ruined when it became known that she was pregnant out of wedlock. Their only recourse, he insisted, was to commit a double suicide. The two went to the side of a river, and she jumped first. By chance, she was fished out of the rushing waters downstream, only to discover that her boyfriend had not followed suit but rather had lured her into a suicide attempt as a way of disposing of her (*Renmin Ribao* February 2, 1984).

In order to encourage women to abandon this culturally sanctioned form of protest and use the legal system, the government began to publicize those cases in which women had turned to the courts with success. An example of such a case involved a woman named Yu, who was beaten by her father because she refused to back down from her decision to marry Jin, a man of her own choosing (Hunyin Anjian 1981:26). After her marriage to Jin in October 1977, her father continued to beat her violently, prompting the newlyweds to leave their home village and move to the neighboring province of Jiangsu. In August 1978, Yu quietly came back to her in-laws' home to give birth. Upon hearing of her return to the village, her father stormed into the Jin house, beat her, and broke windows and furniture. She was forced to flee for safety and gave birth in a relative's home.

One-half year later, Yu returned once again to her in-laws'

house to celebrate the Spring Festival, the most important holiday of the year, and again her father barged into the Jin home, this time badly injuring his daughter's left eye in the beating. Realizing that time was not going to soothe her father's feelings, Yu filed a suit against him for interfering in her marriage rights, and he was sentenced to prison.

Wife-beating: An enduring institution

Women not only showed a reluctance to involve authorities when their legal rights were violated, but also when they were physically threatened in a habitual manner. Although little official attention has been given to the subject of wife-beating, the picture that emerges from the published cases is that many women were battered in a fairly routine fashion. Usually such batterings did not cause the victims to seek legal recourse; instead, evidence of woman-battering surfaced almost incidentally in cases of a more serious nature. One such case involved an older woman named Yu Laopo, who was beaten habitually during her twenty-one-year marriage to Xi. One afternoon in April 1980, Xi fell asleep on his son's bed and did not wake for supper. After his wife had retired for the night, he arose and demanded a meal. When Yu Laopo refused because she was too tired, he beat her so savagely that she died of a brain hemorrhage (Hunyin Anjian 1981:63).

Press accounts depicted wives who were beaten not only for failure to please their husbands, but also for myriad other reasons as well, such as suspected affairs, failure to produce a son, refusing to exhibit a properly subservient attitude, or directly challenging a decision. As in other instances of gender conflict, officials portrayed these occurrences as a hangover from the past. Indeed, the sociological literature on China in the nineteenth and early twentieth centuries indicated that wife-beating was an institutionalized form of male domination. One commentator noted in the 1920s: "In China, up to recent times, it was considered good form for a man to beat his wife, and if the China man of humbler rank spared her a little, he did so only in order not to come under the necessity of buying a successor" (Wilkinson 1926:23). In fact, financial concerns were not the only constraints against the extreme maltreatment of a wife; certain social deterrents existed as well. Because marriage was in essence a joint affair of two families, a husband and his family were inhibited from wanton wife-batterings by the fear that the woman might commit suicide, and her kin group would then retaliate (Yang 1959:195; Lang 1946:47).

Perhaps because wife-beating was a common feature of the past, authorities in post-Mao China viewed it merely as a historical legacy and failed publicly to recognize the continuing function it played in Communist society. Clearly, these beatings served as a constant reminder of the stark reality of the terms of a woman's status in her family, namely that she held an inferior position. Such batterings constituted an almost ritualized display of male domination that ultimately inhibited women from asserting themselves or trying to claim their officially sanctioned rights to equality.

Another traditional practice thwarting women's efforts to gain a more equal status that persisted into the post-Mao period was the male prerogative to control property (Parish and Whyte 1978:195). Women attempting to assume their legal rights of remarriage or inheritance clashed with those family members, usually male, who believed a widow should remain loyal to her late husband's lineage and, in any case, had no claim to her husband's property. Thus, even though the inheritance rights of women were sanctioned by law, they did not win wide social acceptance. Widows continued to encounter stiff family resistance if they tried to claim their rights to the family property they had helped to accumulate.

The conflict often became violent when widows sought to take the property they had inherited into a new marriage. Opposition came both from relatives of their deceased husbands and from their sons. In one case, the widow was aware that her late husband's family was strongly opposed to her plan to remarry, so she tried to move out with her belongings in the middle of the night. To her chagrin, she and her new husband were discovered, whereupon her late husband's male relatives and friends tied up the new groom with a thick rope and hung him on a loquat tree for the remainder of the night. He died the next morning of a ruptured intestine (Chu 1985-1986:41-42). As in the Lu case, this widow should have been aided by the local authorities as soon as her late husband's relatives barred her departure. Instead, it was her former in-laws who received some community support that night, suggesting that most people in China today place more credence on traditional morality based on patriarchy than on modern concepts of legality (for a case involving a widow removing her sons from her late husband's family, see *Zhongguo Fazhi Bao* 1984:3).

Rape coming into full public view

Rape became a subject of public discussion in 1983 when, as part of a general crackdown on crime, the government named it as a serious criminal offense that was on the rise. In an effort to redress the situation, legal penalties for rape were stiffened, the death sentence was imposed in certain circumstances, and newspapers and journals carried stories of the harsh punishments meted out to the worst offenders. Official assertions, however, that the incidence of rape was increasing were not substantiated by the release of comprehensive statistics (for some official figures, see Scherer 1981, 1983, 1984, 1985). Rather, the government lumped the rape statistics together with those for murder, arson, and robbery and only provided partial figures or relative assessments on the occurrence of rape. It issued statements, for instance, that one-third of the thirty criminals executed in Beijing on August 23, 1983, had been convicted of rape (Scherer 1984:271), and that more rapes occurred in the first three months of 1986 than in the corresponding period of 1985 (FBIS May 21, 1986:K 9-10).

Such incomplete figures raise the distinct possibility that the reports of a rising number of rape cases actually reflected increased awareness and better reporting rather than an actual increase in incidence. However, an examination of the social context of post-Mao China provides evidence that lends support to the Chinese claim. The post-Mao economic reforms have both brought sweeping changes in political and economic structures and created new social problems and tensions. With the dismantling of the commune structures in rural areas, for instance, local control measures were disrupted, mobility was encouraged in order to stimulate the rural economy, more men held jobs outside the villages, and women no longer worked in the fields in large groups.

Also, for the first time since 1949, large numbers of young

people were unemployed in the cities for several years after graduation from high school. Chinese urban residents referred to the idle teenagers hanging around in the streets as hooligans *(liumang)* and viewed them as a source of social problems. In addition, those young people who decided to establish small businesses were quite mobile and largely unsupervised by the older generations. At the same time, the hold of the strict Confucian social mores and Communist puritanical codes of sexual morality, which had been weakened during the Cultural Revolution, was further loosened by the cultural opening of China to the outside world, the shift from a heavy emphasis on law through morality to a codified legal system, and the growing number of cadres' abuses of their official privileges. Such factors may well have spurred an increase in the incidence of rape.

According to the Criminal Law Code of 1980, rape was defined as "going against a woman's will, using violence, coercion, or other means to force a woman to have sexual relations" (Honig and Hershatter, 1988:277). Commentaries in legal journals and newspapers revealed that Chinese courts could interpret the rape statute quite broadly. Women who tacitly consented to having sexual relations after having been intoxicated were often considered rape victims. Such procedures represented a break with the Qing dynasty rape code, which stipulated that a woman had to resist an attack from beginning to end in order to qualify as a rape victim (Ng 1987:58).

At the other end of the spectrum, the definition of rape in China was not applied within the institution of marriage. Thus, women subjected to marital rape had no legal recourse, unless they had previously filed for divorce and the circumstances were extreme. In such cases, the courts might rule in favor of a female plaintiff, but not on the basis of the rape statutes. For instance, when one woman was physically forced back into her marriage after fleeing to her natal family and asking for a divorce, her husband was found guilty of forced cohabitation *(cuye qiangxing tongju)* (Hunyin Anjian 1981:32).

Questions about the applicability of the rape code also arose if women were found to have derived some tangible benefit from the sexual encounter. When a number of women yielded to the sexual advances of an official in charge of municipal housing because they desperately needed a place to live, some lawyers argued that he should be charged with a violation of the rape law. After lengthy deliberations, however, the court concluded that even though these women had not desired to enter into sexual relations with the official, ultimately they had not objected when he forced himself upon them, and in one case several sexual encounters had occurred. Convinced that he had committed a serious offense, however, the courts convicted him of hooliganism (Zhang 1984).

A great deal of public attention was focused on convicted rapists who were the sons of high-ranking cadres. To cite a few of the most infamous cases: In Hangzhou, two sons of a powerful army family were convicted of raping more than 100 women before they were apprehended in 1979; in Heilongjiang, thirty-six members of three hooligan gangs were convicted in late 1984 of rape, gang rape, and seduction (FBIS August 8, 1985:K 9); and in the spring of 1986, Hu Xiaoyang and Chen Xiaoming were executed for rape and indecent assault (FBIS March 10-17, 1986:K 8).

Despite government promises to deal sternly with such offenders, many women who were raped by high-ranking cadres or their children did not report the crimes. Some wanted to avoid the publicity; others doubted that authorities would actually prosecute powerful families. The published accounts of women who had succeeded in their court cases indicated the difficulties involved. For instance, a woman named Ding was subjected to beatings and other forms of cruel treatment by her husband, Zhao Guoxuan (*Renmin Ribao* March 10, 1984). Yet when she informed authorities, she was unable to elicit any legal intervention because Zhao's father was vice-secretary of the party in the city in which the couple resided. Later Zhao began to bring other women home, ply them with liquor, and rape them. In all, he raped six women, but none of them complained because of his father's power. Finally Ding was able to secure the assistance of the municipal Women's Bureau, where one strong-minded official successfully drew national attention to the case, forcing city authorities to grant Ding a divorce and prosecute Zhao. He was executed for raping six women, in accord with the Criminal Law Code, which allowed the use of capital punishment in extreme cases.

The press accounts of rape cases showed that Chinese women were raped both by strangers and acquaintances, and that older women are also vulnerable to attack. One man, for example, raped a fifty-two year old woman working alone in a field. His next victim was seventy-two (*Zhongguo Fazhibao* May 18, 1984). No statistical breakdown has been published on the percentage of women who knew their attackers. But regardless of whether women have been raped by strangers or acquaintances, it is not surprising that in China, as elsewhere, the threat of rape ultimately has driven women to seek male protectors, curtail their activities in the public sphere, and seek the safety of home life (Grossholtz 1983:60).

Despite increased public attention to rape, it is clear from the published cases that, for Chinese women, the social stigma attached to becoming a rape victim is enormous. In the early 1980s, Chinese women's journals were only just beginning to devote attention to the need to help women cope with the psychological and social repercussions of rape. The main message conveyed to women in the advice literature was that they could successfully repel an attacker if they resisted hard enough. The unstated assumption was that a woman who failed to ward off a rapist was a disgraced woman. This view tallied with the traditional morality code, which exhorted chaste women to commit suicide in the event of an attack. The gist of the chastity code was well-summarized in 1918 by Lu Xun:

> According to contemporary moralists, a chaste woman is one who does not remarry or run off with a lover after her husband's death .... In addition, there are two other types of chaste women: one kills herself when her husband or fiancé dies; the other manages to commit suicide when confronted by a ravisher, or meets her death while resisting . . . . In short, when a woman's husband dies she should remain single or die. If she meets a ravisher she should also die. When such women are praised, it shows that society is morally sound and there is still hope for China (1918:II, 14-15).

Infanticide

The resurgence of female infanticide in post-Mao China has received more publicity in the West than any other form of gender violence in China. The main cause for the rejuvenation of this old practice was the introduction of a stringent birth control policy in the late 1970s. Some farm families responded to the new policy by killing their newborn daughters in order to try again for a boy. They were motivated mainly by insecurity, for they believed that they would need a son to provide for them in their old age. In so doing, they were displaying a lack of faith in the government's ability to provide essential services to the elderly in rural communities in the next few decades. They were also demonstrating the endurance of patriarchal values and practices in Chinese culture, for sons are cherished more dearly than daughters because they carry on the family line.

The government's decision to adopt such a drastic population control policy was based on alarming demographic projections. With one-half of China's one billion people younger than age twenty, authorities predicted that even a modest population growth in the next few decades would create an inordinate burden on the economic and social resources of the society by the year 2000. Fearful that large-scale famines, similar in magnitude to the recent calamities in North Africa, could return once again to China, the current administration decided that strict population measures were needed.

The birth control policy designed by the government, however, was not sensitive to the concerns of rural families and did not include any measures that offset the cultural prejudices in favor of male offspring. For instance, the policy promised that children from single-child families would be given priority of admission to nurseries, schools, hospitals, and clinics, and that the fees for such services would be either waived or reduced. Yet, it contained no positive incentives for rural families raising one girl, such as giving these daughters priority in allocation of jobs in the state sector or dispensing retirement subsidies to their parents.

As a result, females bore a disproportionate share of the hardship resulting from this policy. Not only did female infants lose their lives, but mothers were verbally and physically abused by their husbands' families for giving birth to girls. In addition, birth control cadres focused much of their attention on women rather than on their families as the main violators of the birth control policy, subjecting them to continual monitoring, forced abortions, and involuntary sterilization. In short, the birth control policy institutionalized in yet another way the deep-seated patriarchal values that discriminate against women.

The magnitude of female infanticide was revealed not in the courts but rather by demographic studies. Chinese social scientists reported a 3-to-1 ratio and a 5-to-1 ratio of infant boys to girls in some outlying counties around Wuhan, for example. The Women's Federation in Anhui province reported a sharp increase in the number of newborn boys over the number of girls, indicating that female infanticide was becoming more common (FBIS April 8, 1983). Most suspected cases of female infanticide were not prosecuted because these babies were born at home, and state authorities lacked the resources to launch thorough investigations. Officials were much more willing to intervene in the sudden death of older female children, such as the case of a two-year-old Shandong girl who was drowned in the local well by her father.

Deeply imbedded in Chinese culture, this strong preference for boys has provoked both men and women to perpetrate the crime of infanticide. Even women who had not been pressured by their husbands or relatives to produce a son have been convicted of killing their infant daughters. One such case was studied by a Chinese social scientist, who concluded that the mother's actions had resulted from an overpowering sense of inadequacy for having produced a female child. These feelings had been fostered not only in her immediate family but also in the predominantly patriarchal culture. Furthermore, this social scientist argued that the Chinese cultural preference for males was not just a legacy of the past but was invigorated by the political and social structures created since 1949. He identified the recruitment system for employment and the university admissions system as critical perpetuators of patriarchal attitudes in present-day China because they discriminated against women (Mei 1983).

Role of the state

The Deng administration not only made little effort to combat the systemic discrimination against women, but many of its major policies stimulated rather than retarded the growth of patriarchal practices in post-Mao China. Most significant was the government's decision to return to family farming *(baochan daohu)* and replace the commune system with the contract responsibility system *(zerenzhi)*. Because this new agricultural system allowed heads of households to reassume great decision making power over their family's economic activities, such as the choice of crops to be planted in family fields, the deployment of the family's labor resources, and the purchase of fertilizer and agricultural implements, it effectively invigorated the traditional authority structures of the family (Robinson 1985). Moreover, family heads no longer were compelled to pay women for their farm work, whereas under the commune system women had been specifically credited with work points, thereby clearly recognizing and rewarding their contribution.

The revival of expensive marriages and the rise in bride prices in the late 1970s served as indicators of increased patriarchal controls and the sinking social status of women in rural communities. Eager to recoup the funds invested in the raising of their daughters, parents took advantage of the government call for rural families to become wealthy and raised the bride prices they demanded for their daughters. Even though a woman's reproductive value diminished greatly with the one-child birth control policy, grooms' families were willing to pay high prices for daughters-in-law because of the greater value derived from women's labor as a result of agricultural price increases. As reports of increased bride prices circulated in many areas, the atmosphere in urban centers was affected as well. In Shanghai, China's largest metropolis, one family set a bride price of 3,600 yuan, based on the calculation that it had cost 12 yuan per month to raise their daughter during her twenty-five years of life (FBIS September 18, 1980:L 22/25).

The rise in bride prices and the cost of weddings in rural areas had violent repercussions. For instance, the practice of kidnapping women for sale as new wives became more prevalent. In January 1982, five men were sentenced to prison for kidnapping and selling 115 women into forced marriages. The prices for these women ranged from $133 to $300 (Scherer 1983:465). Quite naturally, male family elders responded to this phenomenon by increasing vigilance and control over young women's public activities.

In such a social context, Chinese fears that gender violence has increased in post-Mao China seem plausible. As patriarchal controls have tightened, violent acts were one more expression of male domination over women (Brunes and Gorden 1983:506). Admittedly in some cases, women, especially older women, supported or instigated acts of violence against other women, usually because they perceived their vested interests as closely connected with the perpetuation of the existing power structure in their families. Female complicity in gender oppression was not a new phenomenon in Chinese society, but what may have been new was the heightened gender tensions in both the public and domestic domains resulting from social reforms of many kinds.

The gender tensions were further aggravated by the refusal of some women to accept passively certain forms of patriarchal control over their lives. Reared on the Communist idea of women's emancipation, transmitted through the schools and mass media, greater numbers of women asserted themselves when their interests collided with male authority figures in their families and communities. They not only resisted greater parental control over marriage choices, but also refused to surrender their economic rights. Some young women working in country towns or rural industries, for example, were unwilling to hand over all their pay to the head of the family, as traditional norms dictated (Fei 1983-1984:39). While such instances of strong self-assertiveness are far from common in China, they serve as important indicators of a changing female consciousness nurtured by Communist ideals. Significantly, women factory workers in the more modernized and industrialized society of Taiwan still hand over their wages to their parents (Kung 1983:203).

Another telling example of growing female assertiveness in contemporary China was presented in a penetrating film on women in a north China village. There, a group of young women took the unprecedented step of staging a walk-out from a village saw-blade factory because of unsatisfactory safety conditions (Hinton and Gordon 1984). Never before had women workers resorted to confrontational tactics as a means of forcing the male factory head, a powerful figure in village politics, to accede to their demands. The social tensions revealed in such nonviolent clashes provide insight into the entire social context of gender violence in post-Mao China. Moreover, if gender violence is on the rise in contemporary China, another reason for its growth may well be the heightened conflict between women who seek to assert their social and economic rights and staunch patriarchs whose power has been bolstered by recent state policies.

Concluding remarks

The general impression conveyed in these published accounts of gender violence is that considerable gender conflict has been occurring in post-Mao China, particularly in rural families. These accounts indicate that traditional beliefs and behaviors which discriminate against women have persisted. Clearly, the view that these traditional cultural patterns have endured in spite of government efforts to eradicate them is erroneous. Rather, state policies have reinforced the patriarchal order and systematized many discriminatory practices toward women. In so doing, they have contributed to the continuation of a social environment in which violence against women has served both to perpetuate patriarchal power and to retard social change. Indeed, recent economic and birth control policies may have stimulated an increase in gender violence.

It is uncertain how successful the government objective to use the new legal system as an instrument of social change will be. As the judiciary deepens its penetration of society, and the population becomes more knowledgeable about the uses of the law, women may in fact be able to exact greater justice. But until fundamental alterations are wrought in Chinese patriarchal culture, the occurrence of gender violence will serve as a continual reminder to Chinese women of their inferior social status.

Notes

1. An earlier draft of this article was presented at the Annual Meeting of the Association of Asian Studies, 1984. I would like to thank Gail Hershatter, Carma Hinton, and Emily Honig for their thoughtful and valuable comments.

2. Much press attention was also focused on robberies, embezzlement, and other so-called economic crimes. There were also cases reporting on domestic violence that victimized male members of families, such as sons injured or taking their own lives because of a conflict over an arranged marriage, and prospective grooms injured or killed for attempting to marry widows. Interestingly, however, certain types of domestic violence, such as child-beating or child molestation, receive little media attention, even though female child molestation is specifically listed as a crime in the new Criminal Law Code.

3. Interviews with a number of informants revealed that this case was far from unusual. Each person with whom I talked could recount similar cases, many resulting in the murder of the women involved.

References

Beijing Review
1986 "New Laws Uphold Women's Rights," *Beijing Review*, No. 11 (March 10), 22-23.

Brunes, W. and Gordon, L.
1983 "The New Scholarship on Family Violence," *Signs* 8(3).

Chu, David (trans.)
1984 "Editor's Introduction: Social Problems in Contemporary Chinese Society," *Chinese Sociology and Anthropology* (Winter).

1985-86 "One Hundred Marriage Cases," *Chinese Sociology and Anthropology* (Fall-Winter).

FBIS
various Foreign Broadcast Information Service reports. Hong Kong.

Fei Xiaotong
1983-84 "Lun Zhongguo jiating jiegou di biandong" ("On Changes in the Chinese Family Structure"), translated in *Chinese Sociology and Anthropology* (Winter).

Grossholtz, Jean
1983 "Battered Women's Shelters and the Political Economy of Sexual Violence." In Irene Diamond (ed.), *Families, Politics, and Public Policy*. New York: Longman.

Hinton, C. and Gordon, R.
1984 (film) *Small Happiness*. Long Bow Productions.

Honig, E. and Hershatter, G.
1988 *Personal Voices: Chinese Women in the 1980s*. Stanford, Calif.: Stanford University Press.

Hunyin Anjian
1981 *Hunyin anjian 100 li (One Hundred Court Cases on Marriage)*. Shanghai.

Kung, Lydia
1983 *Factory Women in Taiwan*. Ann Arbor: University of Michigan Research Press.

Lang, Olga
1946 *Chinese Family and Society*. Hampden, Conn.: Archon Books. (1963 reprint.)

Lu Xun
1918 "On Chastity," in *Selected Works of Lu Hsun*. Beijing: Foreign Languages Press. Vol. II:14-15.

Mei Hongjuan
1983 "Shasi qinshen Nüying shuomingle shenme" ("What is demonstrated by female infanticide?"), *Shehui (Society)* No. 1:28-30.

Meijer, M.J.
1971 *Marriage, Law and Policy in the Chinese People's Republic*. Hong Kong: Hong Kong University Press.

Ng, Vivien
1987 "Ideology and Sexuality: Rape Laws in Qing China," *Journal of Asian Studies* 46(1):57-70.

Parish, W. and Whyte, M.
1978 *Village and Family in Contemporary China*. Chicago: University of Chicago Press.

Renmin Ribao
1984a "Guyi sharen zui" ("The Crime of Premeditated Murder"), *Renmin Ribao (People's Daily)*, February 2, 1984.

1984b "Chujue fanzui fenzi Zhao Guoxian qianhou" ("Before and after the execution of Zhao Guoxian"), *Renmin Ribao (People's Daily)*, March 10, 1984.

Robinson, Jean
1985 "Of Women and Washing Machines: Employment, Housework, and the Reproduction of Motherhood in Socialist China," *China Quarterly*, No. 101:32-57.

Scherer, John (ed.)
1981 *China: Facts and Figures Annual* Vol. 4. Gulf Breeze, Fla.: Academic International Press.

1983 *China: Facts and Figures Annual* Vol. 6. Gulf Breeze, Fla.: Academic International Press.

1984 *China: Facts and Figures Annual* Vol. 7. Gulf Breeze, Fla.: Academic International Press.

1985 *China: Facts and Figures Annual* Vol. 8. Gulf Breeze, Fla.: Academic International Press.

Wilkinson, H.P.
1926 *The Family in Classical China.* Shanghai: Kelly and Walsh.

Wolf, Margery
1975 "Women and Suicide in China," in Margery Wolf and Roxane Witke (eds.), *Women in Chinese Society.* Stanford, Calif.: Stanford University Press.

Yang, C.K.
1959 *The Chinese Family in the Communist Revolution.* Cambridge, Mass.: Technology Press.

Zhang Li
1984 "Dui Zhumou liyong zhiguan jianwu funü di xingwei ying ruhe dingzui" ("How shall we charge and convict Zhu for using his official position to rape women?"), *Zhongguo Fazhi Bao (China Legal Report),* April 9, 1984.

Zhongguo Fazhi Bao
1984 "Liu Huannu fu wang zai hun shou baohu" ("The protection of Liu Huannu's right to remarry after the death of her husband"), *Zhongguo Fazhi Bao (China Legal Report),* May 23, 1984.

Glossary

This glossary contains Chinese proper names and terms used in the essays. Geographical names and Chinese words cited only in English translation are not included. Personal names are given in the Chinese order, surname first. Numbers in parentheses indicate the page on which the term first appears.

Agui (71) 阿桂

anding tuanjie (203) 安定團結

Ba Jin (154) 巴金

Baigu Jing (140) 白骨精

Bailian Hui (95) 白蓮會

Bailian Jiao (96) 白蓮教

Bailian Zong (95) 白蓮宗

Banjie (126) 半偈

Bang Hu (95) 棒胡

bao (43) 包

bao (180) 報

baochan daohu (217) 包產到戶

baojia (42) 保甲

baojuan (97) 寶卷

biao ming (100) 標名

Faqing (94)　法慶

Faquan (92)　法權

Fang La (104)　方臘

fangsheng (116)　放生

fangsheng chi (116)　放生池

fangsheng hui (116)　放生會

fengshui (60)　風水

Gedimu (75)　格迪目

gongou (31)　共毆

gua hao (100)　掛號

Guanyin (133)　觀音

Guo Pusa (95)　郭菩薩

hai (50)　海

Han (4)　漢

Han Er (70)　韓二

Han Hui yishi tongren (77)　漢回一視同仁

Han Lin'er (96)　韓林兒

Han Shantong (95)　韓山童

Han Yu (126)　韓愈

haosheng quan (132)　好生圈

haoyong doulang (35)　好勇鬥狠

Heifeng Guai (140) 黑風怪

Heishui He Guai (141) 黑水河怪

Hong Hai'er (141) 紅孩兒

Hou Xiyou Ji (117) 後西遊記

Huang Yubian (105) 黃育楩

Huangmei Laofo (141) 黃眉老佛

Huangpao Guai (141) 黃袍怪

huangtai zi (100) 皇胎子

Hui (4) 回

Huian (139) 惠岸

huixiang (50) 會鄉

huizu (50) 會族

Hunshi Mo (139) 混世魔

Jiang Qing (157) 江青

Jietuo Dawang (134) 解脫大王

Jin Ping Mei (121) 金瓶梅

Jinjiao Dawang (134) 金角大王

jitian (43) 祭田

Jiuling Yuansheng (141) 九靈元聖

jiuzhong (31) 糾眾

Junzi dong kou;
  xiaoren dong shou (8) 君子動口小人動手

Kou Qianzhi (92) 寇謙之

Lao Jun Yin Song Jie Jing (92) 老君音誦誡經

Laozi (92) 老子

Li Hong (92) 李弘

lianqian (31) 斂錢

liexie gedou (31) 列械格鬥

Lin Biao (192) 林彪

Linggan Dawang (141) 靈感大王

Liu Jinghui (92) 劉景暉

Liu Shaoqi (154) 劉少奇

Longhua Jing (100) 龍華經

Lü Kun (106) 呂坤

Lu Xun (156) 魯迅

Luocha Nü (141) 羅剎女

Ma Hualong (72) 馬化隆

Ma Laichi (69) 馬來遲

Ma Mingxin (69) 馬明心

Ma Tingxian (73) 馬廷賢

Ma Zhan'ao (72) 馬占鰲

Mao Zedong (149) 毛澤東

menhuan (76) 門宦

Min Fuying (81) 閔伏英

mingluo liexie (45) 鳴鑼列械

minzu tuanjie (83) 民族團結

mo fa (90) 末法

mouou (31) 謀毆

Muzi Gongkou (92) 木子弓口

niaoqiang (48) 鳥槍

Niu Mo Wang (141) 牛魔王

Nü Guai (141) 女怪

Nuocha (139) 哪吒

Pudu (95) 普度

Puxian Pusa Shuo
  Zhengming Jing (100) 普賢菩薩說證明經

qi (43) 齊

qiangshou (49) 槍手

qihui (50) 旗會

Qin Gui (117) 秦檜

qing (140) 情

Qing Yu (123) 鯖魚

quanbang jiaoshi (41) 拳棒教師

renao (156) 熱鬧

renming (30) 人命

ru (182) 儒

san jie (90) 三階

san zai (102) 三災

Sange Motou (141) 三個魔頭

sanshi yinguo (119) 三世因果

Sha Mi (126) 沙彌

Sha Wujing (126) 沙悟淨

shankou (38) 山寇

Shewei Guo Gongzhu (141) 舍衛國公主

shijia (41) 世家

shizhu pusa (104) 十住菩薩

Shouluo Biqiu Jing (92) 首羅比丘經

si (44) 私

sidou (30) 私鬥

Sihai zhi nei jie xiongdi ye (68) 四海之內皆兄弟也

Song Binbin (149) 宋彬彬

Song Yaowu (149) 宋要武

Song Zixian (94) 宋子賢

songshi (40) 訟師

Su Sishisan (70) 蘇四十三

wushu (78) 武術

wuxia xiaoshuo (16) 武俠小説

xia (182) 俠

xiang fa (90) 像法

Xiang Haiming (94) 向海明

xiangdou (50) 鄉鬥

xiedou (10) 械鬥

xingdou (50) 姓鬥

Xingshi Yinyuan Zhuan (121) 醒世姻緣傳

Xiyou Bu (116) 西遊補

Xiyou Ji (16) 西遊記

Xuan Zang (116) 玄奘

Yang Yao (105) 楊么

yi (181) 義

Yinjiao Dawang (134) 銀角大王

yixing (50) 異姓

yizhu pusa (104) 一住菩薩

yong (45) 勇

youshou haoxian (35) 游手好閒

youyuan ren (100) 有緣人

Yueguang tongzi (92) 月光童子

yueqi (31) 約期

yuncheng (100) 雲城

Zaohua Xiao'er (132) 造化小兒

zeren zhi (217) 責任制

Zhang Jue (91) 張角

Zheng Chenggong (38) 鄭成功

zheng fa (90) 正法

zhenkong jiaxiang (97) 真空家鄉

zhi (181) 直

Zhong Xiang (105) 鍾相

zhongmin (99) 種民

Zhu Shouzhuo (126) 豬守拙

Zhu Wuneng (126) 豬悟能

Zhu Yuanzhang (97) 朱元璋

Zhuan Lun Sheng Wang (93) 轉輪聖王

zhuchong (48) 竹銃

zongzu (38) 宗族

Zuo Zongtang (71) 左宗棠

zuzheng (42) 族正

CONTRIBUTORS

Frederick P. Brandauer is Associate Professor of Asian Languages and Literatures at the University of Washington.

Christina Gilmartin is Assistant Professor of History at Northeastern University.

Stevan Harrell is Professor of Anthropology at the University of Washington.

Harry J. Lamley is Professor of History at the University of Hawaii.

Jonathan N. Lipman is Associate Professor of History at Mount Holyoke College.

Richard Madsen is Professor of Sociology at the University of California, San Diego.

Richard Shek is Professor of Humanities at California State University, Sacramento.

Anne F. Thurston (Ph.D., political science) works in China and the U.S. for Academic Travel, and is the author of *Enemies of the People: the Ordeal of the Intellectuals in China's Great Cultural Revolution*.

INDEX

Abortion, forced, 215
Adoption: of cannon fodder, 45
Aeons, 90
Agui, 71
Ahern, Emily (Emily Martin), 4
Allegory: in *Xiyou* novels, 121, 134, 142-43nn.35, 37
Alliances: of fueding lineages, 43, 44, 50; of fueding localities, 50-51
Amnesty International, 7
Apocalypse, 88-89, 96, 97-98, 99; 102-6, 107
Aristotle, 196
Atwell, William S., 38
Authority, subservience to, 150-53
Axelrod, Robert, 178

Ba Jin, 154
Baker, Hugh D.R., 59n.3, 60n.5
Bang Hu, 95
Bao (alliance), 43
Baojia: ineffectiveness of, 42
Baojuan, 97, 103
Bauer, Wolfgang, 89
Beattie, J., 59n.1
Bellah, Robert, 197
Bernstein, Thomas P., 166
Birth control, 214-15
Black-Michaud, Jacob, 30, 33, 47, 58
Boehm, Christopher, 58
Boxing, 16; in Fujian and Guangdong, 41, 56
Boys, preference for, 215-16
Brandauer, Frederick P., 16
Brideprice: and male dominance, 217

Brigands, 13; in Guangdong/Fujian, 38
Brunes, W., 218
Buddhism: and cosmic cycles, 89-90; election in, 100; and idealism, 117-18; and imagination, 118-121; influence on Chinese literature, 118-19; Mahayana, 116; Maitreyan, 92-98; as non-violent, 115; in *Xiyou* novels, 118-27

Cadres: abuses by, 212-13; corruption of, 191; rape by, 212-213; role in rural revenge, 191
Campaigns, political, 154-55; and collective memory, 187-88; antirightist of 1957, 155; and ruptures of conscience, 166, 169
Campany, Robert F., 134
Candraprabhakumara, 92
Cannibalism, 104
Capital punishment, 7; for rape, 213
Cataclysms, *see* apocalypse
Chaozhou prefecture, Guangdong, 42-43, 51
Chen, Kenneth, 93
Chen Shengshao, 44, 46, 48, 53, 57
Chen Yuan, 90
Cheng Hanzhang, 42
chengfu (transmitting and bearing the burden), 89, 182-83
Chu, David, 205, 210
Chiang Siang-tseh, 5, 13
Chixie xiangge (armed confrontation), 38